3/8/16

W9-APA-985

For Gina

BLACK WALL STREET

FROM RIOT TO RENAISSANCE IN TULSA'S HISTORIC GREENWOOD DISTRICT

Hannibal B. Johnson

EAKIN PRESS ◆ Fort Worth, Texas
www.EakinPress.com

Copyright © 1998
By Hannibal Johnson
Published By Eakin Press
An Imprint of Wild Horse Media Group
P.O. Box 331779
Fort Worth, Texas 76163
1-817-344-7036
www.EakinPress.com
ALL RIGHTS RESERVED
1 2 3 4 5 6 7 8 9
ISBN-10: 1-57168-221-X
ISBN-13: 978-1-934645-38-3

Library of Congress Cataloging-in-Publication Data

Johnson, Hannibal B.
    Black Wall Street : from riot to renaissance in Tulsa's historic Greenwood District /
Hannibal B. Johnson.
        p.   cm.
    Includes bibliographical references and index.
    ISBN 1-57168-221-X
    1. Afro-Americans—Oklahoma—Tulsa—History. 2. Tulsa (Okla.)—Race relations.
3. Riots—Oklahoma—Tulsa—History—20th century. 4. Afro-Americans—Oklahoma—
Tulsa—Economic conditions.   I. Title.
    F704.T92J64   1998
    976.6'86—dc21   97-51180
                                                                                    CIP

CONTENTS

COVER ART BY
CLAY PORTIS

Clay Portis is a San Francisco Bay Area artist specializing in pen & ink, watercolor, and acrylic media. His work has been shown in the San Francisco Bay Area and in Tulsa, Oklahoma. Clay studied at the San Francisco School of Arts on a full scholarship. His work ranges from sketches to comic book characters. Clay's publications include *Kane*, an original comic book featuring an African-American superhero of the same name. For prints of the **Black Wall Street** cover, contact: Clay Portis, 1568 Vervais, Vallejo, California 94591; (707) 552-3951.

ACKNOWLEDGMENTS

I join a host of others in commending Oklahoma State Senator Maxine Horner and Oklahoma State Representative Don Ross for their heroic contributions toward restoring Tulsa's historic Greenwood District to at least a fraction of its original splendor. Their leadership and vision shaped the current renaissance.

Thanks to the following individuals and institutions for providing many of the archives and historical insights upon which this work is based: Dr. John Sibley Butler, Bettie Downing, Scott Ellsworth, Eddie Faye Gates, Jeanne B. Goodwin, James O. Goodwin, Esq., Jerry Goodwin, Jewell Hines, Millard House, Marian Jones, William D. LaFortune, Esq., Marcene Mackey, Judi Eason-McIntyre, Dr. Jilda Motley, Carmen Pettie, Robert Powers, Kavin Ross, George E. Schaefer, Shari Horner-Tisdale, and Josie Vann; the Business and Industrial Development Corporation, First Baptist Church of North Tulsa, the Greenwood Cultural Center, Mt. Zion Baptist Church, the North Tulsa Heritage Foundation, Inc., the Oklahoma Historical Society, the Oklahoma Jazz Hall of Fame, the Tulsa Historical Society, the University of Tulsa McFarlin Library, and Vernon Chapel A.M.E.

Turner Goodrum's technical skills and keen sense of place

and image produced stunning, evocative photographs. His discernment assisted greatly with the selection of the vintage photographs included in the book.

My immensely talented nephew, Clay Portis, designed the cover art for the book. His ability to conceptualize and translate experiences into compelling imagery never ceases to amaze.

Dr. Vivian Clark, Sarah Theobald-Hall, Lt. Lynn Jones, Kenneth J. Levit, Esq., Gary Pilgrim, Esq., Brenda Johnson Portis, and Adam Seaman provided thoughtful, constructive feedback on various drafts of this work. For those additional eyes I am enormously grateful.

Special thanks to: David L. Boren, president of the University of Oklahoma; Sanford Cloud, Jr., president & CEO of the National Conference for Community and Justice (formerly the National Conference of Christians and Jews); Dr. John Hope Franklin, James B. Duke Professor of History Emeritus, Duke University; Frank Keating, governor of the state of Oklahoma; Wilma Mankiller, former chief of the Cherokee Nation; M. Susan Savage, mayor of the city of Tulsa; and Rabbi Charles P. Sherman, Temple Israel, Tulsa. These individuals reviewed the book and provided comments.

Steve Walker's assistance with data entry helped enormously.

Friends Cheryl Brown, Judith A. Colbert, Esq., Nancy Day, Pinkie Farver, Sharon Gallagher, Lawrence A. Hall, Esq., Marvin Love, Calvin Moore, Esq., Loretta Radford, Esq., Rosetta Ross, and Fred Yette, Esq., provided much-needed continuity throughout the course of this writing.

Thanks to my parents, Bernice and Frank Johnson, whose love, encouragement, and support have never waned.

I set out on this stroll through Tulsa's famed Greenwood District, past and present, on a mission: to discover for myself the remarkable history of a community and to share my findings with the world. I did not walk alone. I offer a special "thank you" to those African-American pioneers, living and dead, who journeyed with me and upon whose shoulders I now stand. May our stewardship of their legacy honor their lives and memories for generations to come.

PROLOGUE

We must accept finite disappointment,
but we must never lose infinite hope.[1]

DR. MARTIN LUTHER KING, JR.

The bittersweet story of Tulsa's historic Greenwood District, once considered "The Negro Wall Street," is a tale of tragedy and triumph, oppression and opportunity, despair and dignity. It is a real-life human drama, set in a city dubbed the "Oil Capital of the World," starring a cast of African-American heroes whose courage, ingenuity, and faith sustained them through life's highest peaks and lowest valleys. It is, above all, a testament to the power of hope and a tribute to the resilience of the human spirit. Just how these African-American pioneers managed to transform the undeveloped land just north of the Frisco Railroad tracks into a thriving Midwest mecca, revive it from the ruinous Tulsa Race Riot of 1921, and set in motion its current rebirth remains one of the best kept secrets in America. Most Americans, and many Tulsans, native and otherwise, remain oblivious to the lasting historical significance of the Greenwood District.

The history of the Greenwood District may be viewed in four phases: (1) The Roots; (2) The Riot; (3) The Regeneration; and (4) The Renaissance. Thus viewed, the rich past of the Greenwood District evokes virtually every human emotion—pain and pride, horror and hope, regret and remembrance.

The true spirit of the Greenwood District pioneers is illustrated by the following exchange of letters between Curtis, a man in Detroit, and Oliver, his friend in Tulsa, in the immediate wake of the Tulsa Race Riot of 1921.

Dear Oliver:

I am, by our local newspaper, fully advised of the whole terrible tragedy there. Now that they have destroyed your homes, wrecked your schools, churches and business places, and killed your people, I am sure that the Negroes will rapidly give up the town and move North. Enclosed, please find draft for $40.00 to purchase your ticket to Detroit.
Will be expecting you.

CURTIS.

Dear Curtis:

How kind of you to volunteer your sympathetic assistance. It is just like you to be helpful to others in time of stress like this.
True it is, we are facing a terrible situation. It is equally true that they have destroyed our homes; they have wrecked our schools; they have reduced our churches to ashes and they have murdered our people, Curtis; but they have not touched our spirit. And while I speak only for myself, let it be said that I came here and built my fortune with that SPIRIT, I shall reconstruct it here with that SPIRIT, and I expect to live on and die here with it.

OLIVER.[2]

The lessons of this fragment of American history are legion. Few are more compelling and relevant than the realization that the human spirit may bend, but it need not break. Under the most severe of life's tests, in our darkest hours, faith and hope and fortitude work minor miracles. Every Oklahoman—indeed, every American—should take the time to learn how Tulsa's Greenwood District developed into one of the most prosperous African-American communities in the country, survived the worst race riot in United States history, literally rebuilt itself from ruins, and is now enjoying a long overdue renaissance.

THE ROOTS

Roots: The close ties that one has with some place or people as through birth, upbringing, or long and sympathetic association.[1]

At the dawn of the twentieth century, Tulsa shone brightly. She radiated youth, vibrancy, affluence, and naiveté. Initially called "Tallasi,"[2] Tulsa began as a slumbering outpost on the Arkansas River settled by a band of Creek Indians. Beginning their epic journey in Alabama in 1834, the Creeks embarked on a two-year odyssey that would eventually lead them to a place they called "Tallasi." Tallasi became "Tulsey Town" in the late 1800s. Tulsey Town turned to "Tulsa," an incorporated municipality, on January 18, 1898, and became a sprawling city—one of the largest in the Southwest—by the 1920s. By then, local boosters fondly dubbed Tulsa the "Magic City."[3]

Oil explained the rapid transformation from dusty hamlet to gleaming, prosperous city. Walter White, an official with the National Association for the Advancement of Colored People (NAACP), described the caterpillar-to-butterfly metamorphosis of Tulsa in a 1921 article:

Tulsa is a thriving, bustling, enormously wealthy town of between 90,000 and 100,000. In 1910 it was the home of 18,182 souls, a dead and hopeless outlook ahead. Then oil was discovered. The town grew amazingly. On December 29, 1920, it had bank deposits totaling $65,449,985.90; almost $1,000 per capita when compared with the Federal Census figures of 1920, which gave Tulsa 72,075. The town lies in the center of

1

the oil region and many are the stories told of the making of fabulous fortunes by men who were operating on a shoe-string. Some of the stories rival those of the "forty-niners" in California. The town has a number of modern office buildings, many beautiful homes, miles of clean, well-paved streets, and aggressive and progressive business men who well exemplify Tulsa's motto of "The City with a Personality."[4]

Tulsa was well on her way to earning her title as the "Oil Capital of the World," so-called "Texas tea" having been discovered around the turn of the century. But it was a tale of two cities: one black, isolated, and insular; the other white, boundless, and bustling. Living "across the tracks" had both literal and figurative significance. The Frisco Railroad tracks served as a line of demarcation between two separate, yet hopelessly interdependent, worlds. An amicable understanding of race-specific roles and responsibilities seemed to prevail—amicable, that is, so long as the African-Americans knew and remained "in their place."

Oklahoma's first contingent of African-American settlers arrived during the 1830s and 1840s. They came as a result of the forced removal of the so-called "Five Civilized Tribes" from the southeastern United States to the Oklahoma Territory. These tribes—slaveholders all—brought with them both African-American slaves and freedmen over the legendary "Trail of Tears." African-Americans and Native Americans intermarried. Leaders of the five tribes

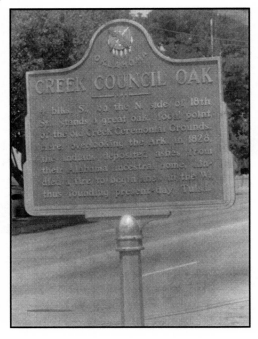

Marker for the Creek Council Oak, the site of the founding of the city of Tulsa. (Photo courtesy of Goodrum Photography, 1997)

(Chickasaws, Choctaws, Cherokees, Creeks, and Seminoles) met with federal officials in Fort Smith, Arkansas, after the Civil War and the ratification of the Thirteenth Amendment to the United States Constitution. Resultant treaties provided for the liberation of the slaves and the adoption of freedmen into the tribes with accompanying annuity and land rights. Most former slaves eventually received allotments of land ranging in mass from forty to 100 acres. The number of African-Americans in the Oklahoma Territory exceeded 6,000 by the year 1870.[5]

Like their white counterparts, African-Americans from the southern states saw the wide-open Oklahoma Territory as the California of its day.[6] The opening up of the Oklahoma Territory, one of the final frontiers in the continental United States, to "non-Native" settlement lasted almost twenty years.

Oklahoma became a state of national significance with the opening of the great oil fields like Glenn Pool in 1905, Cushing in 1912, and Healdton in 1913. Private fortunes were made. Boomtowns were born. From 1907 through 1928, a youthful Oklahoma boldly asserted itself, claiming its position as the number one oil-producing state in the entire country.[7]

Native American tribal conflicts, the influx of thousands of settlers in search of "free land" in Oklahoma, the absence of discernible economic markets, and unresolved cultural tensions combined to make Oklahoma, at least for some, anything but paradise.[8] Socialist newsman Oscar Ameringer painted a stark, albeit highly subjective, portrait of what he saw when he visited Oklahoma in 1907:

> I found toothless old women with sucking infants on their withered breasts. I found a hospitable old hostess, around thirty or less, her hands covered with rags and eczema, offering me a biscuit with those hands, apologizing that her biscuits were not as good as she used to make because with her sore hand she no longer could knead the dough as it ought to be. I saw youngsters emaciated by hookworms, malnutrition, and pellagra, who had lost their second teeth before they were twenty years old. I saw tottering old male wrecks with the infants of their fourteen-year-old wives on their laps. I saw a white man begging a Choctaw squaw man who owned the only remaining spring in that neighborhood to let him have credit

for a few buckets of water for his thirsty family. I saw humanity at its lowest possible level of degradation and decay. I saw smug, well-dressed, overly well fed hypocrites march to church on Sabbath day, Bibles under their arms, praying for God's kingdom on earth while fattening like latter-day cannibals on the share croppers. I saw wind-jamming, hot-air-spouting politicians geyesering Jeffersonian platitudes about equal rights to all and special privileges to none; about all men born equal with the rights to life, liberty and the pursuit of happiness without even knowing, much less caring, that they were addressing as wretched a set of abject slaves as ever walked the face of the earth, anywhere or at any time. The things I saw on that trip are the things you never forget.[9]

Despite the poverty and substandard living conditions in some parts of Oklahoma, they kept right on coming in search of something better. Wilhelmina Guess Howell talked of her family's escape from the South to a better land:

My relatives had come to Oklahoma to get away from racism, violence, and death. In fact, my grandfather Guess just barely made it out of Tennessee alive. The night before he left Memphis, the mob came for him. But he had gotten word that the mob would be coming for him and he had fled to a neighbor's house where he was hidden until he could get safely out of Tennessee. If it had not been for those kind, courageous neighbors, the mob would have lynched nine black men that night and I wouldn't be here today. We were always so proud of our ancestors. They had struggled so hard to take their families where they could be safe, get a good education, prosper, and serve the community.[10]

Oklahoma spelled opportunity. The Guess family and scores of families before and after them pulled up stakes and headed for the plains. Many of these African-Americans bought small parcels of land in the Oklahoma Territory from Native Americans. Others received land under then-prevailing federal government Indian allotment policy. Indeed, Oklahoma boasted more all-black towns and communities than any other state in the land. Remarkably, at one time there were some thirty African-American newspapers in Oklahoma.[11]

Langston University historian Currie Ballard attributes the

remarkable proliferation of all-black towns to treaties between
the United States and the Native American tribes that required
the Native Americans to free their slaves and allot them land.
African-Americans pooled their resources, and allotted lands
became communities. These communities opened their arms to
freed slaves from all across the country.[12]

Many African-Americans came to the Oklahoma Territory
in answer to the call of African-American Oklahoma "boosters."
These boosters viewed the Oklahoma Territory as an escape
from the racism, and sometimes barbarism, they faced in their
home states. Promotional literature touting free land, full citizenship rights, and an escape from race-based discrimination
proved irresistible for many.

The booster among boosters was Edwin P. McCabe, a
prominent African-American from Kansas. McCabe was a
Republican Party politician and the state auditor in Kansas
before coming to the Oklahoma Territory in 1889. He dreamed
of the day when the Oklahoma Territory would become an all-black state or, at a minimum, a state politically dominated by
African-Americans. McCabe purchased 320 acres near Guthrie
and coaxed long-suffering settlers to the site. This settlement
became the town of Langston, named for an African-American
Virginia congressman, John M. Langston. McCabe founded a
newspaper, the *Langston Herald*, and used it chiefly as a propaganda vehicle for his boosterism of the Oklahoma Territory.
McCabe appealed to African-Americans to abandon the back-breaking grind of Southern plantation living for the greener
pastures of the Oklahoma Territory: "What will you be if you
stay in the South? Slaves liable to be killed at any time, and
never treated right: but if you come to Oklahoma you have equal
chances with the white man, free and independent. Why do
southern whites always run down Oklahoma and try to keep the
Negroes from coming here? Because they want to keep them
there and live off their labor. White people are coming here
every day."[13]

Ultimately, McCabe's bold vision of an all-black state generated blind fear and dark suspicion among whites and Native
Americans. The mere prospect of losing significant power and
influence to African-Americans engendered a sense of dread

among Oklahoma's governing elites. Some feared the possibility that McCabe could become the territorial governor. Southern white politicians and plantation owners, fearful that the creation of an all-black state would wreak havoc on their primary source of cheap, unskilled labor, sought to persuade African-Americans that Oklahoma land was not suitable for farming. Even some African-Americans grew weary of McCabe's incessant boosterism. Black freedmen in Oklahoma came to resent new migrants from the South because of their submissive, servile behavior toward whites in the Oklahoma Territory.

Despite McCabe's efforts, African-American migration to the Oklahoma Territory slowed. Migration was costly and difficult economically, socially, and emotionally. Migrants, many from farming backgrounds, quite naturally feared the unknown. Agricultural prospects in the Oklahoma Territory, dubious at best, did little to quell the lingering doubts of these agrarian migrants.

McCabe's personal ambitions were likewise held in check. Although Republican Party leaders in Washington, D.C., nixed McCabe's bid for the governorship of the Oklahoma Territory, McCabe eventually became deputy auditor and held that position until Oklahoma became a state in 1907.

Undaunted, McCabe devoted his considerable talents to the development of all-black towns. Twenty-eight communities and one colony were founded prior to Oklahoma statehood: twenty-four all-black communities in Indian Territory and four all-black towns and one colony in Oklahoma Territory. The oldest of the towns, Tullahassee, was founded in 1859. But most were founded in the interim between the land run of 1889 and Oklahoma statehood in 1907. Lincoln City, organized in 1889, and Langston, organized in 1890, were the first two all-black towns in Oklahoma Territory. All-black towns in Indian Territory, many founded near Muskogee, included Taft, Boley, and Vernon.[14]

All-black towns emerged for several reasons. Some African-Americans found security in living "amongst their own" in this foreign land called Oklahoma. For others, all-black towns opened windows of opportunity for self-determination—in politics, in the economy, and in all other areas of society. Still others sought refuge from hate-mongers like the Ku Klux Klan. All-black towns, acting as escapist safe havens from the realities of race in America, proved attractive for African-Americans throughout the nation.[15]

Not all African-Americans lived in all-black towns. African-American landowners could be found in other communities as well. In the early years, some 500 African-Americans owned land in oil-rich Oklahoma Territory. For a fortunate few, "crude" bubbled beneath the surface. These African-Americans, despite repeated and persistent threats from whites, resisted all offers to part with their property at less than market value. While incremental increases in the price of oil produced more wealth for many of these landowners, bitterness and racial strife increased. Jealousy and envy gnawed at some prominent and vocal members of Oklahoma's white communities.

A 1907 article in *The Independent*, a national scholarly magazine, describes the brittle state of race relations in Oklahoma at the time:

> [T]he negro of Indian Territory is also a land-owner. The ex-slaves of the Five Tribes are protected in their holdings as are the Indians. And in the Oklahoma, or Western half of the new State, the negro was as free to homestead land as the whites. In the various "openings" we find considerable numbers of them obtaining claims. So in both divisions of the State there are probably a larger percentage of negroes who own their own homes and are in comfortable circumstances than elsewhere in the United States. So it will be seen that Oklahoma's negro population is hardly to be termed improvident.
>
> . . .
>
> An Oklahoman will give you . . . reasons for disliking the negro. [The Negro] is immoral, improvident, lazy and with all at times inclined to be impudent. After talking with many men, college graduates, professors and Northern men of education and station, I have yet to find the Oklahoman who does not admit a strong personal antipathy toward the blacks. That is, they much prefer not to come in personal contact with negroes, and regard the so-called "white towns" of the Territories as progressive, for the single reason that negroes are not allowed to reside there.

. . .

> [I]n Oklahoma the negro can hope for no political or
> social position that requires white encouragement.[16]

The culture of the day was decidedly racist. Despite this,
Oklahoma booster E. P. McCabe, himself African-American,
beckoned blacks to Oklahoma with an appealing promise of
equal opportunity. He simply could not deliver. Given the blatant prejudice, discrimination, and racism facing African-
Americans in early Oklahoma, it is remarkable that they
achieved so much so quickly. Tremendous accomplishments by
blacks, particularly in the entrepreneurial arena, were made,
especially in Tulsa. Attitudes in Tulsa, however, mirrored those
in other parts of the state and in the country generally.

In 1912 the *Tulsa Democrat* (which later became the *Tulsa
Tribune*) boldly proclaimed: "Tulsa appears now to be in danger
of losing its prestige as the whitest town in Oklahoma."[17] With
like venom, the paper declared: "Does Tulsa wish a double invasion of criminal Negro preachers, Negro shysters, crap shooters,
gamblers, bootleglegs [*sic*], prostitutes and smart elecs [*sic*] in
general?"[18] The *Tulsa Tribune* would later refer to the African-
American community in Tulsa—this city within a city—by the
alternate epithets "Little Africa" and "Niggertown."[19] Such utter
disdain and disrespect for a whole class of individuals would
shake any society to its very foundation. Just as surely as the
shifting and grating of the earth's plates produces earthquakes,
Tulsa's black-white friction would eventually provoke an equally
violent eruption.

Cast adrift in the crucible of a racist culture, Tulsa's African-
American pioneers nonetheless managed to create a remarkable
degree of prosperity. Landowners comprised just one segment
of the elite African-American population. The other significant
segment consisted of entrepreneurs.

African-Americans were welcome as servants in any part of
Tulsa. Indeed, it was common for African-American maids to
live in so-called "maid's quarters"—garage apartments adjacent
to the homes of their white employers. But the welcome mat so
graciously extended to them in their subservient roles disappeared
when they attempted to navigate the waters of the white world.

African-Americans could neither live among whites as equals nor patronize white businesses in Tulsa.[20]

Sound, *laissez faire* economics proved no match for the racism of the day. Racial politics dictated consumer markets. Segregation, for all its practical, moral, and philosophical deficiencies, forced the development of an insular African-American economy to cater to the needs of this walled-off community. With it, an affluent class of African-American entrepreneurs developed. In Tulsa, this increasingly prominent African-American entrepreneurial pool congregated primarily in a single business district, beginning at the intersection of Greenwood Avenue and Archer Street. Greenwood Avenue, likely named after Greenwood, Mississippi,[21] became known as "The Negro Wall Street."[22] Legend has it that famed African-American educator and author Booker T. Washington bestowed this moniker on Tulsa's vibrant black business district.[23]

Despite the success mounting on Greenwood Avenue, nearby side streets evidenced the elements of poverty and crime found in virtually any urban area. Shanties, houses made from packing crates, speakeasies, houses of ill repute, and "choc" joints were not uncommon. ("Choc" is short for Choctaw beer, a thick, milky-white intoxicant made from the Choctaw root, or Indian hemp.)[24]

Colorful "red light districts" like those found near Greenwood Avenue often give rise to socially acceptable cultural fare. James Haskins, an authority on black music in America, argues that jazz originated in towns along the Mississippi River, most notably New Orleans. First brothels, then speakeasies provided popular venues for the uniquely American musical artform and were integral to its widespread popularity.[25] Jazz would later become associated with the clubs and nightspots in the Greenwood District.

The legitimate enterprises in the Greenwood District had one thing in common with their less-desirable counterparts: black consumers doing business with black vendors. In segregated Tulsa, "buying black" became more a matter of survival and less a matter of choice for African-Americans. Consequently, providers of goods and services in the Greenwood District held captive an eager market and tapped into pent-up demand. Dollars circulated among the Greenwood District's inviting rooming houses, restaurants, billiard halls, hotels, smoke shops, shoemakers, barbers, hairdressers, shoe shiners, tailors, contractors, doctors, lawyers, dentists, and other professional and business establishments.

That African-Americans prospered in Tulsa is illustrated by home ownership in the Greenwood District. Tulsa's progressive African-American community boasted some of the city's more elegant homes. One such stately home belonged to Sam and Lucy Mackey. The Mackeys purchased the land for their spacious frame house, including three lots at 356 North Greenwood Avenue, from Marion and Eliza Martin in 1911. The Martins acquired the land from the Oklahoma-based Cherokee Nation.[26] The Mackeys fairly embodied the idyllic American dream. And Tulsa became, at least for a time, their dreamland. Through hard work and perseverance, the Mackeys prospered materially. The Mackey home reflected that fact, becoming both a monument to their prosperity and an inspiration to others in the community.

Segregation forced African-Americans to invest in their own community. Then, as now, such investment, whether coerced or voluntary, yields more than mere economic rewards. It promotes community self-sufficiency and self-determination as well. So it was in the Greenwood District of the early years. All African-American Tulsans benefited.

Mary Elizabeth Jones Parrish, an African-American woman from Rochester, New York, came to Tulsa in 1918. In her noteworthy book, *Events of the Tulsa Disaster*, she explained the magnetic allure that this Midwest metropolis had for African-Americans in the early 1900s:

> I had heard of this town since girlhood and of the many opportunities here to make money. But I came not to Tulsa as many came, lured by the dream of making money and bettering myself in the financial world, but because of the wonderful co-operation I observed among our people, and especially the harmony of spirit and action that existed between the business men and women. . . . On Greenwood one could find a variety of business places which would be a credit to any section of the town. In the residential section there were homes of beauty and splendor which would please the most critical eye. The schools and many churches were well attended.[27]

This magical, mystical, far-off place called "Tulsa" beckoned multiple souls in the early 1900s. Mary Elizabeth Jones Parrish was just one of the many pilgrims. These seekers, white and African-American alike, were old-fashioned American optimists. There was a better place somewhere out there, and they were determined to find it. Tulsa became their promised land. Most of the African-American seekers wound up in the Greenwood District.

The rich and varied history and culture of Tulsa's Greenwood District dates back at least to 1905. That year, African-Americans acquired a strip of land in the area.[28] At the time, a fair number of domestic workers "lived-in" with their white employers, and therefore lacked permanent residences in the African-American community. But residences slowly sprang up in the Greenwood District. As the Greenwood District grew, the need for educators and schools for the community's children became all too apparent.

Formal education in Tulsa for African-Americans also dates back to 1905. Jake Dillard, a constable and businessman, built Tulsa's first African-American school, housed in a small church at Archer and Kenosha streets, that year. The school moved to a location in another church between Cameron and Easton streets on Hartford Avenue in 1908. Rev. G. L. Prince and Lula Sims were the school's first teachers. By 1910, Dunbar School, a freestanding, two-story, eight-room brick school, had been completed for grades one through eight. J. W. Hughes was Dunbar's principal, and the staff consisted of Lula Sims, Marie Martin, S. D. McCree, Jane Johnson, Birdie Farmer, and Mrs. R. T. Bridgewater. To accommodate the eight students who had completed the lower grades, Dunbar School included the high school grades by 1912. J. W. Hughes and S. D. McCree taught the upper grades.

In 1913 Booker T. Washington High School, a four-room structure on Elgin Place and Easton Street, was erected. Ellis Walker ("E. W.") Woods, hired as principal in 1913, accompanied Lula Sims and Myrtle McKeever and fourteen students to the new facility. Its first seniors (two) graduated in 1916. By 1919, "Booker T." had grown into a two-story, sixteen-room brick building. Booker T. added its first sport, basketball, in

Booker T. Washington High School circa *1921. (Photo courtesy of the North Tulsa Heritage Foundation, Inc.)*

1921. Football, band, and the school tradition of crowning an annual football queen followed in 1922. E. W. Woods continued to lead this legendary high school[29] as principal in its initial decades of existence.[30]

A Mississippi native, E. W. Woods trekked to Oklahoma by foot from Memphis, Tennessee, in answer to a flyer proclaiming a desperate need for "colored" teachers in this area. Once in Tulsa, Woods landed a job, briefly, as principal of Dunbar School, then became principal of the new Booker T. Washington High School. Woods would occupy the latter post for thirty-five years, forever altering the lives of all who had the good fortune to know him. A champion of youth, Woods, with a bachelor's degree from Rust College (Holly Springs, Mississippi) and a master's degree from Kansas State (Pittsburg, Kansas), was considered by many to be the "quintessential Tulsan." A supreme motivator, he filled the minds of his charges with memorable exhortations, and often reminded Booker T. students of their self-worth and potential: "You're as good as 99 per cent of all the people and better than the rest."[31] Woods' words were meant not merely as preparation for life at Booker T., but for life in general.

A look back at the curriculum of Booker T. Washington High School in 1921, the year of the Riot, attests to Woods' unwavering commitment to excellence in education.

COURSE OF STUDY

FRESHMAN CLASS—Latin, English, Algebra, Drawing, Domestic Science and Art, Manual Training, Ancient History, Vocal Music.

SOPHOMORE CLASS—Latin, English, Geometry, Domestic Art, Drawing, Med. and Modern History, Economics, Music, Domestic Science, Manual Training.

JUNIOR CLASS—English, Algebra, Commercial Arithmatic [*sic*], Drawing, Manual Training, Business Spelling, Chemistry, English History, Civics, Domestic Art, Domestic Science, Vocal Music.

SENIOR CLASS—English, Physics, Geometry Solid, Typewriting, Vocal Music, Domestic Science, Manual Training, American History, Psychology, Trigonometry Plain, Book keeping [*sic*], Drawing, Domestic Art, Shorthand.

All classes are required to take part in some form of athletics.[32]

Woods, a true hero, died in 1948 at age sixty-three. Multitudes, both black and white, mourned his passing. His funeral, held in Tulsa's Convention Hall, befit his expansive, substantial life.[33]

In the business entrepreneurial arena, the Greenwood District debuted around 1905 with the construction of a grocery store on the corner of Archer Street and Greenwood Avenue by businessman O. W. Gurley. That, coupled with Gurley's addition of a one-story rooming house, spawned the growth of other businesses in the area. By 1921, the house that Gurley built had expanded to four floors and become known as the Gurley Building. (The rooming house had served as an early home to Tulsa's Vernon African Methodist Episcopal Church.) Like so many other community landmarks, the Gurley Building would not survive the events to come in 1921.

Other business pioneers in the Greenwood District included Thomas R. Gentry, Tulsa's first African-American real estate magnate; R. T. Bridgewater, Tulsa's first African-American physician; Dr. J. Littlejohn, Tulsa's first African-American dentist; and Rev. C. L. Netherland, a Baptist minister who owned a barber shop on Boston Avenue.[34] These trailblazers paved the way for scores of future entrepreneurs.

Many of the buildings in the Greenwood District were brick. It was no coincidence. Acme Brick Company, located two blocks north on Greenwood Avenue, provided a readily accessible source of bricks. Moreover, bricks were comparable in price, if not cheaper, than lumber. A number of knowledgeable African-American craftsmen lived in the Greenwood District, further facilitating the bricks and mortar construction boom.[35]

Gradually, brick by brick, the Greenwood District blossomed. In 1907, the same year Oklahoma became the forty-sixth state of the Union, two black physicians, a newspaper (the *Tulsa Weekly Planet*), three grocers, and several other business and professional establishments called Tulsa's African-American community home.[36] By 1910, Tulsa even boasted an African-American trade union, the Hod Carriers Local 199.[37] (A "hod carrier" is a worker who assists a bricklayer, plasterer, or mason by carrying bricks or mortar on a "hod"—a wooden trough with a long handle.) During this period, African-Americans comprised a full ten percent of Tulsa's total population.[38]

Businesses soon sprang up, including the landmark Williams Dreamland Theatre that premiered in 1914, the first African-American theater in Tulsa. The Williams Dreamland Theatre, occupying the first level of a two-story brick building on Greenwood Avenue, showed piano-accompanied silent movies and featured occasional live entertainment. Level two of the same building served as the Williams' rooming house. The Williams also owned a confectionery, a garage, and commercial rental property on Greenwood Avenue.[39]

Money flowed in the Greenwood District. It became fashionable for men to dangle twenty-dollar gold pieces from their watch chains. Joe Eaton, a shoeshiner at the Palace Building, sported three twenty-dollar gold pieces.[40]

Early on, Tulsa's police force was desegregated. Police Chief Sam Walker appointed Tulsa's first African-American police officer, Barney Cleaver. But the chance to be a "first" came with strings attached. Chief Walker gave Cleaver, a former deputy United States marshal in so-called "Choctaw Country," a specific charge: "[Your] hours of duty will begin in the evening and con-

A snowy day on Greenwood Avenue, 1917. (Photo courtesy of the North Tulsa Heritage Foundation, Inc.)

tinue through the night when things are most likely to happen there. [Your] duty is to enforce the laws in the colored section, and [you are] not to arrest any white man."[41] Despite this limitation, the appointment of Cleaver marked a significant moment in Tulsa history.

Opportunity abounded. The heart of the Greenwood District, "Deep Greenwood," grew into a veritable Monte Carlo.[42] Mabel B. Little describes the splendor she saw in the Greenwood District of 1913 when, at the tender age of seventeen, she arrived in Tulsa from Boley, Oklahoma, on a Frisco train with $1.25 in her pocket:

> Black businesses flourished. I remember Huff's Cafe on Cincinnati and Archer. It was a thriving meeting place in the black community. You could go there almost anytime, and just about everybody who was anybody would be there or on their way.
>
> There were also two popular barbeque spots, Tipton's and Uncle Steve's. J. D. Mann had a grocery store. His wife was a music teacher. We had two funeral parlors, owned by morticians Sam Jackson and Hardel Ragston.
>
> Down on what went by the name of "Deep Greenwood" was a clique of eateries, a panorama of lively dance halls, barber shops and theatres glittering in the night light, and a number of medical and dental offices.[43]

Simon Berry typifies the entrepreneurial spirit of the day. Few African-Americans owned cars, and most streets were unpaved, even Greenwood Avenue in the early years. The only taxi service in town enforced a "whites-only" ridership policy. For African-Americans, a rickety buggy for hire afforded the only available public transportation. Then Simon Berry started a jitney service using his topless Model-T Ford. A nickel would buy a ride all up and down Greenwood Avenue, and as many people could ride as dared hang on to the moving car.

Berry later started another line running down Lansing Street. That made it possible to go all the way downtown and back on one single nickel. He added a top to the Model-T, then built a jitney garage on Archer Street, where he trained African-American mechanics. Later, Berry brought in buses, and his mechanics became the operators. Having secured a franchise from the City of Tulsa, Berry eventually ran his buses downtown to accommodate those African-Americans who worked downtown or in South Tulsa. From downtown, riders could connect with privately owned buses going south. At the peak of his operations, Berry reportedly made as much as $500 a day—a phenomenal sum at the time.

Berry reinvested in the community that had been so good to him. In 1926 he acquired land and established a park on thirteen acres located on Madison Street between Virgin and Young streets, complete with a swimming pool, a dance hall, and picnic grounds. Berry extended his bus service to provide transportation to his park. Years later, the City of Tulsa acquired Berry Park.

Berry ran this thriving enterprise for some twenty-five years. Then, the City of Tulsa purchased the thriving, lucrative business in order to consolidate bus operations on a citywide basis. He sold only on condition that African-Americans be allowed to ride and that African-American drivers be allowed to operate the routes running in the Greenwood District.[44]

One of Oklahoma's first African-American aviators, Simon Berry owned his own airplane. He and partner James Lee Northington, Sr., a successful African-American building contractor, operated a popular airline charter service in Tulsa in the mid-1920s. Wealthy white businessmen patronized the business.[45]

Simon Berry possessed incredible business acumen. In addition to his pioneering initiatives in the ground and airline transportation industries, Berry owned and operated the Royal Hotel in the Greenwood District.[46] Unquestionably, Simon Berry ranks among Tulsa's blue chip entrepreneurs.

Prosperity in the Greenwood District, fueled by entrepreneurs like Simon Berry, drew an array of nationally prominent African-Americans to Tulsa. Entertainers, dignitaries, and notables from throughout the country visited frequently. Indeed, the family of James H. Goodwin hosted many of America's foremost African-American celebrities. At the time, so-called "Jim Crow" laws forced strict segregation of public accommodations. While on tour, even well-known African-American personalities often stayed in private homes rather than hotels. Among those visiting the Goodwins were educator Mary McCloud Bethune, scientist George Washington Carver, opera singer Marian Anderson, Teddy Horne (Lena Horne's husband), blues singer Dinah Washington, Yolanda Du Bois (daughter of W. E. B. Du Bois), and noted Chicago scientist Percy Julian. James Goodwin's son and daughter-in-law, E. L. and Jeanne Goodwin, continued the "host family" tradition in later years.[47]

The prosperousness emerging in Tulsa's early African-American community rested in part on the existence of segregated economic markets. African-Americans profited from Tulsa's rapid, oil-driven growth. As the city grew, so too did the need for laborers and service workers—in short, "Negro labor." In this segregated economy, African-Americans invested earnings from outside the Greenwood District in business enterprises within the Greenwood District.[48]

Dr. John Sibley Butler, a leading scholar on African-American entrepreneurship, contends that Durham, North Carolina, and Tulsa, Oklahoma, are prime early twentieth-century examples of a phenomenon called the "economic detour." Simply put, "economic detour" refers to the path a particular group takes (in this case, African-Americans) when something impedes or prevents its full and equal access to economic markets. Racism, segregation, and discrimination are the impediments that historically forced African-Americans to take an economic detour.

Early African-American business leaders in Tulsa patterned the development of Tulsa's thriving Greenwood District after the successful African-American enterpreneurial activity in Durham.[49] Durham and Tulsa differ, however, in terms of the response of the cities as a whole to the success of African-American entrepreneurs and professionals.

Durham represented one of the successful economic enterprises of early Afro-Americans. Operating under an economic detour, Afro-Americans were able to carve a mountain of economic stability out of an atmosphere of official racial oppression. Just as scholars today talk about the "Cuban Miracle" in Miami in the 1970s and 1980s, scholars around the turn of the century were excited about Durham, North Carolina. Just as the Japanese were able to develop economic success in California at the turn of the century, Afro-Americans were able to do the same. Like other groups, the Afro-

Americans of Durham developed a strong Afro-American middle class and began a tradition of economic security which con-
tinues to the present. Although other cities throughout the
country were not as strong as Durham, Afro-Americans in
other cities also developed a strong middle class which was
grounded in entrepreneurship and the professions. . . .

If Durham, North Carolina, stood as a show piece of successful entrepreneurship because of the solid application of
certain business principles and the presence of interracial support and cooperation, Tulsa, Oklahoma, represented the ana-
log of this success, which can be called the entrepreneurship
tragedy. Although this city was successful in the creation of
Afro-American entrepreneurs who attained a degree of economic security, it met with a fate which must be explained not
only by the theory of economic detour but also by certain
other specific theories of race and economics as well.[50]

The dilemma faced by African-American professionals illustrates the somewhat obvious hazards of reliance on a segregated,
albeit protected, market. While the "economic detour" in some
sense protected African-American entrepreneurs and professionals from competition with whites, it often hampered their
advancement. African-American doctors, denied the opportunity
to practice medicine using the modern equipment and facilities
that only white hospitals had, operated at a distinct disadvantage.
Although a few small African-American hospitals existed, those
institutions could not match the services, facilities, and equipment
offered by their larger, better-funded white counterparts.

African-American attorneys often faced prejudiced judges
and juries. Judges, wielding contempt power, exercised it in ways
designed to control African-American attorneys. Juries, faced
with an African-American attorney on one side or the other, dis-
counted otherwise legitimate legal claims on account of race.
African-American professionals, faced with blatant discrimination within their respective fields of expertise, established their
own professional associations of teachers, attorneys, doctors,
dentists, morticians, and the like.[51]

At the conclusion of World War I in 1918, economic competition between whites and African-Americans heightened. This
enhanced competition, coupled with charges of peonage (i.e., a

system of forced servitude to pay off indebtedness that left many African-American farmers in abject poverty),[52] further inflamed latent racial tensions in Tulsa. Simultaneously, African-American expectations rose. Buoyed up by the spirit of patriotism and emboldened by the American dream of better lives for themselves and their children, African-Americans became more vigilant in principle and assertive in action. Black soldiers, like their white counterparts, fought, bled, and died in the war. Upon return, they waged a civil war against injustice on the home front.

In many quarters, basic respect for these African-American patriots was all but nonexistent. So alarmed were a group of African-American Tulsans that they successfully implored J. J. McGraw, an Oklahoman and committeeman for the national Republican Party, to bring their concerns before the national Republican committee. In making the case to McGraw, the Tulsans illustrated the extent of the problem by recounting an incident that took place in Mississippi. There, a black officer in the United States Army was attacked by a white mob simply for wearing his officer's uniform—a privilege he had earned. The mob forced the officer to remove the uniform and gave him an ultimatum: leave town (and with it, home and family) that night or die. That this officer stood ready to sacrifice his life in battle for his country—for the very men who put him to the cruel choice he then faced—seemed the ultimate bitter irony.[53]

African-Americans across the country became increasingly incensed about widespread notions of white supremacy and its stark manifestations, most notably lynchings. A nationwide campaign spearheaded by the NAACP declared war on "Judge Lynch," the lynching of African-Americans by the Ku Klux Klan (the "Klan") and lawless white mobs.[54] The NAACP, founded in 1909, is a direct response to lynchings. It emerged in the wake of the Springfield, Illinois, riot of 1908. White men in Springfield lynched two African-Americans and drove many others African-Americans from their homes, then destroyed their property. Only after Illinois' governor called in thousands of troops was the riot contained.[55]

The Klan, notorious for terrorizing African-Americans, Jews, and Catholics, and for its particular brand of "justice," proved no stranger to Oklahoma. Klan activity in Tulsa during this era mushroomed. Indeed, Klan rosters from the era reveal a startling embrace of the organization at all levels of Tulsa society. Doctors, lawyers, judges, ministers, sheriffs, investment advisors, city employees, mail carriers, oil field workers, school teachers, school principals, policemen, firemen, police commissioners, bricklayers, barbers, plumbers, florists, and janitors—all were represented in the Tulsa Klan.[56]

Klan organizers, called "Kleagles," came to a receptive Oklahoma in 1920. Some original Klansmen had lived in the state since as early as 1870. George Kimbro, Jr., and George C. McCarron kicked off Klan activity in Oklahoma with a meeting of local fraternal orders in Oklahoma City in 1920. They brought letters of introduction from fraternal officials in Texas with them to this initial gathering. Kimbro, calling himself the Klan's "Grand Goblin," claimed to represent territory that encompassed sixteen states, including Oklahoma. Houston, Texas, was Kimbro's headquarters. McCarron, also from Houston, claimed the title "King Kleagle of Oklahoma," and set up his headquarters in room 503 of the Baltimore Building in downtown Oklahoma City.

Not long thereafter, twelve Kleagles or recruiters sold memberships to Oklahoma City residents from McCarron's office. They soon began to recruit statewide, focusing on fraternal orders like the Masons and on prominent members of the wartime councils of defense in Oklahoma County. The Oklahoma City Klan meetings were held in the Congregational Church, in the old Epworth University building, in the Huckins Hotel, and in the chambers of Judge George W. Clark, an early inductee into the Oklahoma City Klan. In a matter of mere months, Klan membership in Oklahoma City numbered more than 1,000. By September of 1921, the Klan's Oklahoma City membership roster alone surpassed 2,500.[57]

The activities of the Klan in Oklahoma in general and in Tulsa in particular became so notorious as to pose an imminent threat to social stability. Documented Klan violence in Tulsa exceeded that of any other city in Oklahoma during the 1921-1924 period.[58] Indeed, lawlessness and mob rule spurred Governor Jack Walton to place Tulsa County under martial law in 1923.

During the 1920s the Ku Klux Klan carried out attacks against a number of Oklahoma citizens. Most of this violence was directed against whites, but blacks felt the lash of the Klan's whip, and its intolerance menaced the lives of many decent citizens. The black press, especially the Black Dispatch and the Muskogee Cimeter warned the Klan that the black community would not bow to intimidation by cowards who paraded under sheets. Klan lawlessness was greatest in the Tulsa area. When conditions worsened in that county and elsewhere in the state in 1923, Governor Jack Walton sent troops to restore law and order. He pledged to stamp out mob rule and violence in Oklahoma if he had to place every county under military law. Walton's eagerness to smash the Klan, which had become a political force in the state, led him to extremes, and even some of the governor's supporters turned against him. He became engaged in a serious fight with the legislature, which Walton viewed as Klan controlled, that proved his undoing. The legislature impeached him. Klan violence soon decreased, and the organization never again became a significant political factor in the Sooner State. It returned during the civil rights movement of the sixties, but more as a small social irritant than anything else. The efforts of citizens' groups and law enforcement officials, and the cooperative endeavors of blacks and whites helped to effectively reduce racial tensions in the state.[59]

A look at the organic document of the Klan, the "Constitution and Laws of the Knights of the Ku Klux Klan," reveals an organization believing itself divinely inspired to promote white supremacy. The "Klan Kreed," the organization's expression of professed philosophical beliefs, states in part:

> I believe in God; Ineffable; Infinite; Eternal; Creator and Sole Ruler of the universe; and in Jesus Christ His Son our Savior, who is the Divine Word made manifest in flesh and demonstrated in life.
>
> I believe that God created races and nations, committing to each a special destiny and service; that the United States through its White, Protestant citizens holds a Divine commission for the furtherance of free government, the maintenance of white supremacy and the protection of religious freedom; that its Constitution and laws are expressive of this Divine purpose.[60]

The Klan's self-described "Objects and Purposes" reinforce white supremacy, the fundamental tenet of the Klan Kreed, while simultaneously professing morality, exemplary citizenship, and spirituality:

OBJECTS AND PURPOSES
ARTICLE II

Section I. The objects of this Order shall be to unite white male persons, native-born Gentile citizens of the United States of America, who have no allegiance of any nature or degree to any foreign government, nation, institution, sect, ruler, person or people; whose morals are good; whose reputations and vocations are respectable; whose habits are exemplary; who are of sound mind and sixteen years or more of age, under a common oath into a brotherhood of strict regulations; to cultivate and promote patriotism toward our civil government; to practice an honorable clannishness toward each other; to exemplify a practical benevolence; to shield the sanctity of the home and chastity of womanhood; to maintain forever white supremacy; to teach and faithfully inculcate a high spiritual philosophy through an exalted ritualism, and by a practical devotion to conserve, protect and maintain the distinctive institutions, rights, privileges, principles, traditions and ideals of a pure Americanism.

. . .

Section III. This Order is an institution of chivalry, humanity, justice and patriotism; embodying in its genius and principles all that is chivalric in conduct, noble in sentiment, generous in manhood and patriotic in purpose. Its peculiar objects are: First, to protect the weak, the innocent, and the defenseless from the indignities, wrongs and outrages of the lawless, the violent and the brutal; to relieve the injured and the oppressed; to succor the suffering and unfortunate, especially widows and orphans. Second, to protect and defend the Constitution of the United States of America, and all laws passed in conformity thereto, and to protect the states and the people thereof from all invasion of their rights from any source whatsoever. Third, to aid and assist in the execution of all constitutional laws, and to preserve the honor and dignity of the State by opposing tyranny, in any and every form or degree, from any and every source whatsoever, by a fearless and faithful administration of justice through due process of law; and to meet promptly and properly every behest of duty without fear and without reproach.[61]

Klan membership is rigidly restricted along racial, ethnic, gender, and religious lines. The Klan limits its membership to:

[A] White male Gentile person, a native-born citizen of the United States of America, who owes no allegiance of any nature or degree whatsoever to any foreign government, nation, institution, sect, ruler, prince, potentate, people or person; he must have attained the age of sixteen years, be of sound mind, good character, of commendable reputation and respectable vocation, a believer in the tenets of the Christian religion, and one whose allegiance, loyalty and devotion to the government of the United States of America in all things is unquestionable.[62]

Given its narrow definition of the "chosen" Americans, it is not surprising that the Klan found fertile field in Oklahoma, with its distinct Native American and African-American populations, for conflict. Despite references to chivalry, morality, godliness and other universally embraced character traits, Klansmen perpetrated horrendous acts of inhumanity, all the while cloaked in hooded white robes and shrouded under a cloud of secrecy. The historical record leaves little room for doubt: the legacy of the Klan is decidedly unchivalrous, immoral, and ungodly. Actions speak louder than words.

There were other ominous signs for Tulsa's African-Americans in 1921 that cannot be fully attributed to the Klan. Peonage punctuated the landscape. Mysteriously, unsigned warnings began to appear on the doors of homes and in an Okmulgee, Oklahoma (a community just outside Tulsa) newspaper. These warnings prophetically announced the dire consequences that would befall African-Americans who remained in Oklahoma after June 1, 1921. Some heeded the warnings. By so doing, they escaped the horrors of the Riot to come.

In the late spring of 1921, a group of eight African-

American refugees left Oklahoma and headed for New York City with little more than the shirts on their backs. Four of them, Lizzie Johnson, Stella Harris, Josie Gatlin, and Claude Harris, all from Okmulgee, arrived at the national office of the NAACP on June 2, 1921. They initially sought assistance from a group to which they belonged, the Universal Negro Improvement Association, led by back-to-Africa proponent Marcus Garvey. Denied help there, they turned to the NAACP. There they found solace and were provided with food, shelter, clothing, and financial assistance. The NAACP even started a relief fund for victims of the Riot.[63]

Law enforcement became conspicuous by virtue of its absence from the day-to-day lives of Tulsans, white and African-American alike. A vice ring tightened its already considerable grip on virtually every aspect of the city. By design or default, the community seemed to turn a blind eye on corruption and lawlessness. Tulsa gained a reputation, largely earned, as a wild and wanton Midwest town. When the Oklahoma legislature added two new district judges to the two existing district judges in Tulsa County in 1921, some 6,000 criminal cases awaited trial. Stated somewhat differently, about six out of every 100 Tulsans fell under some sort of criminal indictment, hopelessly clogging the justice system.[64] Despite these conditions, Tulsa's African-American community continued to prosper.

By 1921, Tulsa's African-American population numbered almost 11,000. The African-American community then included two schools, Paul Lawrence Dunbar and Booker T. Washington, one hospital, two newspapers, two theaters, a public library, twenty-three churches, and three fraternal lodges.[65] Building from its meager beginnings, the vastly expanded Greenwood District of 1921 exuded energy and excitement.

"Deep Greenwood," the first two blocks of Greenwood Avenue, just north of Archer Street, became the hub of Tulsa's African-American business community. Two- and three-story commercial buildings dotted the thoroughfare, housing Tulsa's unusually large number of African-American entrepreneurs and professionals.

The clothing stores, nightclubs, cafes, rooming houses, and other businesses lining the streets and avenues of the

Greenwood District provided ample opportunity for casual strolls, shopping sprees, and entertainment excursions. Greenwood offered a dab of this, a pinch of that—a little bit of everything.

The Greenwood District came especially alive on Thursday evening, the traditional "maids day off" for domestic servants living in the white community. (During this historical period relatively few African-American women could expect employment opportunities beyond domestic servitude.) The influx of these working women provided a rush of business and added luster to an already glittering community.

The Greenwood District in its prime rivaled the finest African-American business districts in America. Beautiful, bustling, and black, it held its own with Chicago's State Street and Memphis' Beale Street.[66] But few of its businesses employed more than a handful of workers. Economically, Tulsa's African-American community depended largely upon the wages paid to African-American workers by white employers. Despite its foreboding facade, the Greenwood District rested upon a rickety economic foundation, reflecting the ominous social realities of the time.

In addition to its legendary reputation as the nerve center of African-American social and economic activity, the Greenwood District later became one of the cradles of so-called "Kansas City jazz."[67] Nowhere were the hypnotic rhythms of African-American life in Oklahoma expressed more poignantly. Luminaries from the jazz pantheon graced Tulsa, often early-on in their careers. Guitar licks and saxophone wails filled the streets. Pulsating rhythms wafted through the air from open windows and doorways. The Greenwood District became synonymous with jazz.

Nightclubs like Clarence Love's Lounge gave birth to new forms of jazz. Many of the core members of the legendary Count Basie Band, including Earl Bostic and singer Jimmy Rushing, perfected their art in the Greenwood District. Innovators from Jay McShann, whose band included Charlie Parker, to jazz great Charlie Christian and lesser-known creative talents performed regularly in local nightspots. Electric and eclectic—that was Greenwood.

THE RIOT

*Riot: Wild or violent disorder, confusion, or distur-
bance; tumult; uproar.*[1]

The intersection of Greenwood Avenue and Archer Street
soon became the nucleus of African-American life in Tulsa. This
geographical location—a single corner—has had something of a
symbolic life of its own for much of the twentieth century. It
became an imaginary line of demarcation between the city's
black and white worlds. Constrained by law, racism, and social
custom, Tulsa's African-American community survived and
thrived for decades as a separate city, serving almost exclusively
the needs of its own residents. In so many ways, the story of the
Greenwood District parallels the triumphs and tragedies of
African-Americans in the United States.

For one remarkable moment in time, the music and merri-
ment so characteristic of the Greenwood District gave way to the
deafening silence of destruction and despair. In Tulsa, in
Oklahoma, and in America, race mattered. And it mattered a
great deal.

The events that transpired in Tulsa in the spring of 1921
are inextricably bound up in the look and feel of the America of
that era. For African-Americans, bitter ironies defined the period: opportunity in the face of oppression, race-pride in the face
of racism, patriotism in the face of paternalism. The years leading up to 1921 are noteworthy for their unprecedented violence.

In 1919 America witnessed sixty-one recorded lynchings of

27

African-Americans. The same year, dubbed "Red Summer" by James Weldon Johnson of the NAACP, marked a watershed moment for the country's African-Americans. More than twenty-five major race riots erupted throughout the country.

One of the worst of the Red Summer riots occurred in Chicago. Four young African-American boys attempted to cross the traditional dividing line between the segregated "white" and "black" beaches on Lake Michigan. An African-American swimmer was killed, touching off almost a week of nightmarish violence. By the time the militia quelled the chaos, thirty-eight African-Americans and whites lay dead and 537 individuals sustained injuries.[2]

In 1920 there were sixty-one reported lynchings of African-Americans. By then, the Ku Klux Klan operated in twenty-seven states and its membership rolls had inflated to more than 100,000—and growing.[3]

In 1921 there were fifty-seven recorded lynchings of African-Americans. Americans were well aware of the mounting carnage. Congressman L. C. Dyer of Missouri introduced a bill in the United States House of Representatives that would have made lynching a federal crime. Passed by the House, the bill charged federal officers whose responsibility it was to protect the lives of citizens attacked by mobs with the duty to make "reasonable efforts to prevent the killing." The dereliction of that duty by a federal officer could result in a fine or imprisonment for the offending officer under the proposed legislation. The bill also provided that a person who participated in a mob murder would be guilty of a felony. The county in which the murder occurred would be obliged to pay the victim's family $10,000. The bill died in the United States Senate, despite its introduction on three separate occasions.[4] The lynchings continued.

There have been forty-one recorded lynchings in the entire history of the state of Oklahoma. The number of "near misses" and unreported incidents remains a matter for pure speculation.[5]

Lynchings and civil unrest notwithstanding, other significant events in African-American history transpired in and around 1921. Harvard-educated Dr. W. E. B. Du Bois organized the Pan-African Congress in Paris, France. Sixteen countries and colonies participated in a three-day meeting designed to elevate

Africans to full participatory status in their governments. American civil rights leader William Monroe Trotter unsuccessfully argued at the Paris Peace Conference that the treaty ending World War I should outlaw racial discrimination.[6]

Within the nationwide context of lynchings and civil unrest and in the face of an international push for rights for persons of African descent, the Tulsa Race Riot of 1921 occurred. At that time the worst race riot in American history, the Riot abruptly halted the steady growth and momentum of the Greenwood District. In a matter of hours, ignorance, fear, and hate dimmed the bright lights of hope that had shone for years. Daylight turned to dusk—dusk to darkness. Under cover of that darkness all manner of unspeakable, unimaginable atrocities came to pass.

Fires raged. Dozens, scores, perhaps hundreds of lives were lost in the calamity. The unchecked, mob-driven lawlessness lasted less than twenty-four hours—less than a full day. But what a difference a day makes: more than 1,000 homes razed; scores of black-owned businesses ransacked and looted; African-American churches in a thirty-five-block area defiled, defaced, and destroyed. Property losses far exceeded the initial seven-figure estimates.[7]

Tulsa Race Riot—The burning Greenwood District is in the background. (Photo courtesy of the North Tulsa Heritage Foundation, Inc.)

In the loss of over 700 homes and 200 business houses the Negroes of Tulsa have sustained a loss of over four million dollars. Two of the finest hotels that the Negroes own in America went up in smoke. The Welcome Grocery Store carried as large a stock of groceries as did any retail white store in Tulsa. Mrs. Williams, who owned the Dreamland Theatres in Tulsa, Muskogee and Okmulgee, was perhaps one of the foremost Negro business women in the United States. She has one three-story brick on Greenwood, which housed her big confectionery and the other floors were used for offices for the professional men of the race. Farther down the street was her theatre, the pride of the Negroes of the city. The street had located on it three drug stores and two newspaper plants. The Tulsa Star had a plant worth fully $15,000. Fully 150 business houses lined this street alone, that required a Negro traffic officer to stand in the streets all day long, directing the busy activities.[8]

Some African-Americans experienced double-barreled devastation: the loss of a home and a business in the Riot. Among this number were O. W. Gurley and his wife, Emma. Theirs was the first business to locate on Greenwood Avenue. Disheartened by the loss of the home *and* business they had worked so hard for, the Gurleys did not rebuild.

Beyond its monumental physical devastation in terms of persons and property lost, the Riot also took a psychological toll too heavy to measure even with the grandest of scales. So much was lost so quickly, so senselessly, the pride of a tight-knit community savagely wrenched away.

At the time of the Riot, Tulsa was America's oil boomtown. In the preceding twenty years, its population ballooned from 13,090 to 72,000.[9] Crowded and bustling, the city seemed on the verge of bursting at the seams. But all was not well in Tulsa. All the ingredients for a major conflagration were already in the mix. Tulsans lacked confidence in the local police and the city administration. Just a few years prior, in 1915, Mayor Frank M. Wooden, Police Commissioner Thomas J. Quinn, and Police Chief Foster Nathaniel Burns had been ousted.[10]

Scant law enforcement, a police strike in 1919, and the resignations of several police officers in 1920 contributed to a general state of lawlessness and laxity.[11] Common vices poisoned the

The Greenwood District engulfed in smoke during the Riot. (Photo courtesy of the North Tulsa Heritage Foundation, Inc.)

"Little Africa On Fire"—The burning Greenwood District is in the background. (Photo courtesy of the North Tulsa Heritage Foundation, Inc.)

Mt. Zion Baptist Church on fire during the 1921 Tulsa Race Riot. (Photo courtesy of the North Tulsa Heritage Foundation, Inc.)

Mt. Zion Baptist Church on fire in the 1921 Tulsa Race Riot. (Photo courtesy of the North Tulsa Heritage Foundation, Inc.)

(Photo courtesy of George E. Schaefer)

Tulsa Race Riot of 1921.

(Photo courtesy of George E. Schaefer)

character of the community. Alcohol, gambling, and prostitution were widespread, open, and notorious.[12]

Hate groups perpetrated despicable acts of mob violence during Tulsa's early years. In 1917 mobs led by a motley crew of men known only as the "Knights of Liberty" assaulted unionists affiliated with the International Workers of the World (IWW).[13] The IWW became a target in part because of its Socialist Party leanings and in part because its philosophical message of racial equality did not square with the Knights of Liberty's racist ideology.

IWW members, all white, stood trial in Tulsa on trumped-up vagrancy charges. The perfunctory trial completed, a band of black-robed, black-hooded ruffians from the Knights of Liberty ambushed and seized the convicted unionists en route to the county jail. Helpless, and with no assistance from their armed police escorts, the IWW men were then tied to trees, whipped mercilessly, tarred, and feathered. Tulsa's establishment, including some of its leading citizens (the chief of police among them) either participated in, encouraged, or condoned this repulsive brand of home-grown vigilantism. Indeed, John Moran, deputy United States marshal, Tulsa office, remarked: "You would be surprised at the prominent men in town who were in this mob." After this stark display of brutality, signs sprang up across Tulsa warning: "NOTICE TO I.W.W.'S. DON'T LET THE SUN GO DOWN ON YOU IN TULSA."[14] The message was clear.

The Knights of Liberty was not the only secret society operating in and around Tulsa. The Ku Klux Klan fomented fear and hate in Tulsa as it did in so much of America.[15] Indeed, Tulsa became a hotbed of Klan activity and, later in the 1920s, distinguished itself with vibrant female and adolescent auxiliaries.[16] Typical of the Klan elsewhere, the Tulsa Klan counted among its members both the poor and the privileged, the known and the unknown, the powerful and the powerless.

The story of Tulsa's underbelly does not end with the Knights of Liberty or the Klan. Other events signaled a vengeful, ugly side to Tulsa's community personality profile. An eighteen-year-old white boy, Roy Belton, was hanged just nine months prior to the Riot for the killing of a twenty-five-year-old white taxi driver, Homer Nida.[17] As if it were just another party, thousands of ordinary Tulsans turned out for the public lynching of the teenager. Tulsans reported that local police officers directed traffic at the scene, affording spectators an equal chance to view the event.[18] Once the dirty deed was done, the leering crowd rushed eagerly to gather souvenirs off the flaccid corpse. The *Tulsa Daily World* described the gleeful, carnival-like atmosphere surrounding the death of young Roy Belton: "Hundreds rushed over the prostrate form to get bits of the clothing. The rope was cut into bits for souvenirs. His trousers and shoes were torn into bits and the mob fairly fought over gruesome souvenirs. . . . An ambulance was finally pushed through the jam of automobiles. The body was carried to the car, late arrivals still grabbing for bits of clothing on the now almost nude form."[19]

If even a white man could be publicly lynched, and if lynching were to be treated by the general public as mere sport, then the "Negro" had no hope of protection—no hope whatsoever. Of the three Tulsa newspapers, only the *Tulsa Star*, the African-American community newspaper, roundly condemned the Belton lynching.[20] That other media remained silent in the face of such brutality and mayhem spoke volumes about life in Tulsa.

Against this backdrop, the stage was set for a catastrophe of cataclysmic proportions. And the action would soon get under way. Tulsans seemed all too ready to accept instantaneous, mob-driven retribution in lieu of the slower, less predictable workings of the criminal justice system. The price paid for speed and certainty, however, is sometimes justice. And justice, once lost, can never be fully recaptured. The lynching of Roy Belton and the public spectacle accompanying it failed to teach Tulsans that important lesson. The pursuit of swift "justice" and the "string-him-up" mentality continued unabated.

The alleged Monday morning assault on a seventeen-year-old white girl, Sarah Page, by a nineteen-year-old African-American boy, Dick Rowland (also known as "Diamond Dick"),[21] destroyed the surface calm between the races. Smoldering racial tensions ignited into blazing racial hostilities. The resulting melee and inferno reduced the Negro Wall Street of America to ashes. There would be no warning. There would be no preparation. There would be no mercy.

Monday morning, May 30, 1921, began in the usual way for

Dick Rowland. Rowland, a five-dollar-a-week-plus-tips shoeshine boy in a Main Street parlor across from the downtown Tulsa Drexel Building,[22] boarded the elevator in the Drexel Building. The Booker T. Washington High School dropout was simply availing himself of an arrangement made by his boss. Rowland and his fellow "bootblacks" (i.e., shoeshiners) used the Drexel Building "facilities." There were none in their Main Street shoeshine parlor. Having caught the elevator, Roland headed for the upper-floor restroom as he had done on so many previous occasions. According to Rowland, the elevator lurched, causing him to lose his balance and fall against Sarah Page, a young white woman who operated the elevator in the Drexel Building.[23] She screamed. A clerk from the nearby Renberg's store, alarmed by Sarah's screams, ran to her aid. Fearful for his safety, Rowland fled. To some, Rowland's flight implied guilt. But to most African-Americans, well aware of the fate that had befallen other African-American men accused of sexual improprieties with white women, flight seemed reasonable and rational under the circumstances.

Sarah Page initially accused young Rowland of assault, but quickly retreated from that accusation.[24] The damage, however, had already been done. In this era in American history, white women were strictly taboo for African-American men. African-American men had been summarily executed for so much as looking at a white woman. And Rowland stood accused of—guilty of, in the minds of many—a far more serious affront.

Roy Wilkens, former executive director of the NAACP, put the Rowland/Page incident in historical context:

> The Tulsa riot illustrates the classic lie of criminal assault which was used for decades to justify lynchings and assaults upon Negroes in both the South and the North. Helen Boardman's study "Thirty Years of Lynching," made for the NAACP, was the first systematic effort to examine the crime. She found that in only 20 percent of the lynching was sex even mentioned; in less than 10 percent was any type of sexual relationship actually involved—not that the act itself always occurred, for in some of these it was not sexual intercourse, but such actions as passing notes or indicating a desire or intention.[25]

Dick Rowland was picked up by the police on Tuesday, May

31, 1921, booked into the city jail, and questioned. Summoned to the jail, Sarah Page provided a statement corroborating, in all material respects, Dick Rowland's account of the events of that fateful day. She admitted that her encounter with Dick Rowland had been inadvertent and innocent. She told officers that Rowland had come close to her on the elevator and that he had stepped on her foot. Of her own admission, she had panicked and overreacted. Page told officers that she slapped Rowland, at which time he grabbed her arm to prevent her from slapping him again. She screamed. He fled.[26]

Despite this less-than-sinister, straight-ahead "reinterpretation" of the Page-Rowland incident by Sarah Page herself, the original story meandered its way through Tulsa, gathering steam at every turn. The chance encounter between Sarah Page and Dick Rowland touched off an all-too-familiar pattern of race-tinged events, culminating in an unprecedented catastrophe. The match had been struck. The fuse had been lit. The inferno awaited.

In the immediate wake of the Rowland-Page elevator incident, Sarah Page and Dick Rowland became the talk of the town. News of the attempted rape of young Sarah Page spread like wildfire. But the "news" was mere fiction, even by Sarah's own account. The *Tulsa Tribune* hit the streets at about 3:15 P.M. on Tuesday, May 31, 1921, with word of the incident. An unknown man called the police at about 4:00 P.M. The word on the street, according to the caller, was that a white lynch mob planned to take the matter into its own hands. J. M. Adkison, Tulsa police and fire commissioner, called Sheriff Willard McCullough and told him of the lynch talk.[27] Indeed, so concerned was Sheriff McCullough that he reportedly telephoned the offices of the *Tulsa Star*, Tulsa's African-American newspaper. Sheriff McCullough warned that he expected an attack to be made on the jail that night, Tuesday, May 31, 1921. McCullough intimated that he might need the help of local African-American men to protect Dick Rowland from certain death at the hands of a lynch mob.[28]

Later, white men began to gather at the courthouse. By 9:00 P.M., some 400 white men had assembled.[29] Sheriff McCullough took pains to protect Rowland, rendering the jail elevator inoperable, ordering his jailers to barricade themselves on the top floor where Rowland was incarcerated, and ordering the assembled whites to cease and desist. (They did not.)[30]

The *Tulsa Tribune* contributed mightily to the talk of a lynching. Indeed, its largely fictitious account of the incident gives new meaning to the term "editorial license":[31]

NAB NEGRO FOR ATTACKING GIRL IN ELEVATOR

A negro delivery boy who gave his name to the public as "Diamond Dick" but who has been identified as Dick Rowland, was arrested on South [*sic*] Greenwood avenue this morning by Officers Carmichael and Pack, charged with attempting to assault the 17-year-old white elevator girl in the Drexel building early yesterday. He will be tried in municipal court this afternoon on a state charge. The girl said she noticed the negro a few minutes before the attempted assault looking up and down the hallway on the third floor of the Drexel building as if to see if there was anyone in sight but thought nothing of it at the time. A few minutes later he entered the elevator she claimed, and attacked her, scratching her hands and face and tearing her clothes. Her screams brought a clerk from Renberg's store to her assistance and the negro fled. He was captured and identified this morning both by the girl and the clerk, police say. Tenants of the Drexel building said the girl is an orphan who works as an elevator operator to pay her way through business college.

An editorial run in the *Tulsa Tribune* on the day of the incident (reportedly bearing the headline "To Lynch A Negro Tonight")[32] aroused, and perhaps incited, the Ku Klux Klan and other like-minded white supremacist groups and individuals to teach Dick Rowland a lesson. Mysteriously, copies of the offending issues of the *Tulsa Tribune* no longer exist. But accounts based on individual interviews after the Riot and scholars studying the event leave no doubt that the *Tulsa Tribune* fanned the winds of hysteria sweeping through Tulsa. Indeed, the adjutant general of Oklahoma, Charles F. Barrett, would later blame the Riot on "an imprudent negro, a hysterical girl, and a yellow journal."[33] Rowland was ultimately transferred to the county jail "for his own safety."

Just months before, white hoodlums took a young African-American man jailed for allegedly assaulting a white woman from his cell in Holdenville, Oklahoma, tied him to a telephone pole, and summarily executed him. He was shot to death, not lynched.[34] "Justice," Oklahoma style, was swift if it was anything.

The Tulsa National Guard, the local branch of Oklahoma's organized state militia, geared up after hearing rumors and receiving reports of the downtown unrest and looming crisis. A mob of white men attempted unsuccessfully to raid the National Guard armory in search of munitions for use in the all-but-certain racial conflict on the horizon. Maj. James A. Bell fended off the rowdy crowd of some 400 with a carefully calculated dose of bravado.[35]

At about 9:15 P.M., rumors of a planned downtown lynching reached the Greenwood District. Several African-American men decided to stand up and be counted. They would put their lives on the line to protect Dick Rowland from the lynch mob. Deputy Sheriff Barney Cleaver, a former Tulsa policeman (and Tulsa's first African-American to serve in that capacity), happened to be in the Greenwood District at the time. He tried in vain to dissuade local African-American men from going downtown.

Seventeen-year-old William Phillips witnessed the prelude to the Riot. Williams, years later, described to Ronald J. Trekell how things got woefully out of hand.[36] Williams' account closely mirrors the accounts of others who were there on those fateful days. All accounts paint a similarly grim picture of chaos fueled by racism and capped with rumor and innuendo.

Later on the night of May 31, 1921, at about 9:30 P.M., some thirty armed African-American men emerged from the Greenwood District. Concerned about Dick Rowland's safety, they trudged through the streets of Tulsa and into downtown en route to the courthouse. Undaunted and undeterred, the men reached the courthouse safely. They offered their assistance to Sheriff McCullough. Tulsa police officers quickly intervened, successfully persuading the men to return to the Greenwood District. The officers assured the group that there would be no lynching—that Rowland would indeed be safe.

Prompted by news of the growing white crowd at the courthouse, another group of some seventy-five armed African-

American men set out for the courthouse at about 10:30 P.M. The African-American men again offered to help protect prisoner Rowland. Sheriff McCullough declined the offer. Mollified for the moment, the African-American men began to retreat, bound for North Tulsa. (Tulsans refer to their historically African-American community as "North Tulsa"—a reference to its geographic location. The Greenwood District is part of North Tulsa.)

Contemporaneously, more white men began to gather. By some accounts, the retreating group of African-American men met with a larger group of men from the Greenwood District heading for the courthouse, and the combined group, now some 200 strong, returned to the courthouse.[37] Talk among the men was of forcibly removing Rowland from the jail. That, they figured, would be the only way to safeguard him from certain death at the hands of a growing, agitated white mob.

By this time, Barney Cleaver arrived at the courthouse and attempted to convince the assembled African-American men to return to the Greenwood District. Meanwhile, the white men now assembled, numbering up to 2,000 at the time,[38] grew increasingly restless. Sheriff McCullough did not order his deputies to conduct a general disarmament of the crowd, ostensibly (and ironically) fearing that such action would incite a riot. Neither Sheriff McCullough nor Police Chief Gustafson made a serious effort to disperse the white crowd. The full complement of Tulsa's police force was never summoned to the scene.[39] These acts of commission and omission on the part of local law enforcement would have disastrous consequences.

A uniformed white law officer invaded the ranks of the assembled African-Americans, who were by then in the process of leaving. As he meandered through the crowd, disarming men and making a pile of their weaponry, he approached a tough-looking African-American veteran. The black veteran held a 45-caliber pistol. According to some accounts, the following verbal exchange occurred:

White man: "Nigger, what are you doing with that pistol?"
Black man: "I'm going to use it if I need to."
White man: "No, give it to me."
Black man: "Like hell I will."

A struggled ensued. The weapon discharged skyward.

(Photo courtesy of George E. Schaefer)

Tulsa Race Riot of 1921.

(Photo courtesy of George E. Schaefer)

(Photo courtesy of George E. Schaefer

Tulsa Race Riot of 1921.

(Photo courtesy of George E. Schaefer

(Photo courtesy of George E. Schaefer)

Tulsa Race Riot of 1921.

(Photo courtesy of George E. Schaefer)

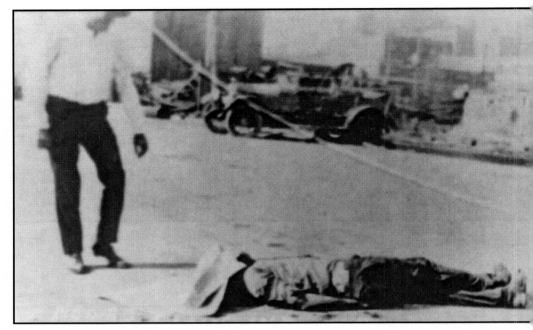

An unidentified black man killed in Riot. (Photo courtesy of the North Tulsa Heritage Foundation, Inc.)

Tulsa Race Riot of 1921. (Photo courtesy of George E. Schaefer)

"Charred Negro"—The burned body of an unidentified black man killed in the 1921 Tulsa Race Riot. (Photo courtesy of the North Tulsa Heritage Foundation, Inc.)

Within a matters of moments, gunfire erupted willy-nilly. Bullets felled some twelve individuals in this, the initial volley.[40] Utter chaos ensued. African-Americans fled east and north, toward the home turf, toward Greenwood Avenue. They tried in vain to protect and defend themselves, their families, and their community. Outnumbered and underarmed, they were at once valiant and vanquished.

Fearing the worst, the Tulsa National Guard mobilized at about 11:00 P.M. on the eve of destruction, Tuesday, May 31.[41] Meanwhile, the Tulsa police began deputizing white men—some of the very same men who had actively participated in the courthouse disturbance only hours earlier. Bands of white men in search of firearms and ammunition for the impending civil war looted hardware stores and pawnshops, seizing some $43,000 in guns and ammunition.[42]

Numerous accounts, including the affidavit of Van B. Hurley, a well-regarded Tulsa policeman at the time of the Riot, cite the use of airplanes not just as tools of reconnaissance, but as birds of prey—vehicles of death and destruction—in the raging onslaught on the Greenwood District. Hurley charged that airplanes swooped down from the northern sky, peppering homes and businesses with nitroglycerin, setting them quickly alight.[43] Others claim the airplanes dropped incendiary kerosene bombs.[44]

Fear filled the air. Tension loomed everywhere. Some African-Americans readied themselves for the unavoidable conflict on the home front. Others fled. Still others were left totally unaware and, as a consequence, singularly unprepared.[45] While there were options, there were no good options.

The first fire of what would ultimately be a scorching inferno started at about 1:00 A.M. on the morning of Wednesday, June 1, 1921, on the corner of Archer and Boston streets. Throughout the ordeal, white mobs prevented fire crews from extinguishing what would have otherwise been manageable fires.[46]

Most of the fierce fighting on the night of May 31-June 1 took place between Archer Street and the Frisco Railroad tracks. Among the many horrors amidst the confusion and chaos of the Riot, a car dragging the corpse of an African-American man paraded proudly through town for all the world to see. Tulsans reported seeing trucks loaded with corpses in downtown Tulsa and in some white neighborhoods.[47] By midnight, the beleaguered African-Americans retreated fully to the Greenwood District.

Whites began congregating along the railroad tracks north of First Street and east of Elgin Street. An unfounded rumor that a trainload of African-American men from Muskogee was on the way to reinforce their brothers in Tulsa caused Sheriff McCullough to block and turn back one train, fearing an ambush by an angry mob of armed whites.[48]

By dawn, some 15,000 whites had amassed, ready to strike at the heart of Tulsa's African-American community. And strike they did.

By 6:00 A.M., the African-American community had been invaded wholesale by frenzied, armed white men.[49] White boys as young as ten years old, armed and unduly disrespectful of both law and person, participated in all aspects of the brutality, mayhem, and horror that transpired.[50]

Incredibly, whites remained free to taunt and terrorize African-Americans, invading their homes and plundering their possessions at will. The long arm of the law did not extend to these acts. The fate of African-Americans, systematically disarmed, rounded up, and deprived of their liberty, depended upon the kindness of their captors. This law enforcement "strategy" of neutralizing African-Americans virtually assured the total decimation of the black community.[51] In practice, it left the Greenwood District defenseless and vulnerable, and extended an open invitation to the thieves, arsonists, and killers who ran roughshod through the streets of Tulsa.

At the height of the Riot, carloads of marauding white Tulsans streamed into the streets, firing indiscriminately at any African-American target in sight. Women and children proved no exception. An elderly African-American couple, kneeling in bedtime prayer in their Greenwood Avenue home, was startled by an invading mob. After murdering the couple execution style, the mob ransacked and pillaged the house before setting it ablaze.[52] The line between civilization and savagery had been crossed.

African-American homes became mere booty, the spoils of roving bandits set afoot in the Greenwood District with no purpose other than theft, destruction, and, too often, death. An African-American woman who lost her home in the Riot recalled:

> After they had the homes vacated one bunch of whites would come in and loot. Even women with shopping bags would come in, open drawers, take every kind of finery from clothing to silverware and jewelry. Men were carrying out the furniture, cursing as they did so, saying "These [damn] Negroes have better things than lots of white people." I stayed until my home was caught on fire, then I ran to the hill side where there were throngs of White people; women, men and children, even babies, watching and taking snap shots of the proceedings of the mob. Some remarked that "The city ought to be sued for selling [damn] niggers property so close to the city." One woman noticed the First Baptist Church [First Baptist Church of North Tulsa], which is a beautiful structure located near a White residence district. She said, "Yonder is a nigger church, why ain't they burning it?" The reply was, "It's in a White district."[53]

And then there were the horrific blazes, deliberately set, and the billowing, suffocating smoke they produced. The

American Red Cross reported: "Eye witnesses say that the methods used were, first, to pile bedding, furniture and other burnable materials together, then to apply matches. Eye witnesses also claim that many houses were set afire from aeroplanes."[54]

A joint telegram request from Sheriff Willard McCullough, Judge Valjean Biddison, and Police Chief John Gustafson to Oklahoma Governor James B. A. Robertson requested that military troops be sent to quell the Riot. By 3:00 A.M. on June 1, the mobilization of the National Guard in Oklahoma City was ordered. The dusk of Tuesday, May 31, 1921, bled into the dawn of Wednesday, June 1, 1921.

Troops arrived in Tulsa at about 9:15 A.M. on June 1. Governor Robertson declared martial law in Tulsa at 11:29 A.M. that day. Shortly thereafter, most of the violence ceased. The martial law declaration provided:

MARTIAL LAW DECLARED
Headquarters Oklahoma National Guard,
City Hall, Tulsa, Okla., June 1st, 1921

Following telegram from Governor J. B. A. Robertson received at these Headquarters at 11:29 A.M., places Tulsa and Tulsa County under Martial Law:

> Hon. CHAS. F. BARRETT,
> Adjutant General,
> Care City Hall,
> Tulsa, Oklahoma:

I have declared Martial Law throughout Tulsa County, and am holding you responsible for maintenance of order, safety of lives and protection of property. You will do all things necessary to attain these objects.
J. B. A. ROBERTSON, Governor.

THEREFORE, By authority of this order, I hereby declare the City of Tulsa and Tulsa County from and after the hour named in the telegram to be under Martial Law, which will be enforced with all the rigor necessary to accomplish the purpose of restoring peace and order within the boundaries of this City and County.

The people of Tulsa and Tulsa County will retire immediately to their homes and remain there, so far as possible until this order is modified or revoked.

All persons, except sworn officers of the law, found upon the public streets of Tulsa or in any locality in Tulsa County, will be promptly arrested and punished as a military court may direct.

All business houses in the city will close on or before 6:00 o'clock P.M. today and will not re-open until 8: [*sic*] a.m. June 2nd, and will observe these hours from day to day until further order, unless granted permission by the commanding officer of the Oklahoma National Guard.

Services of necessity, such as Grocery stores, Drug Stores, Dairies, Meat Markets and other agencies that contribute to the comfort of the people will be excepted from the provision requiring permission to render such service.

It is the hope of the commanding officer that a prompt compliance with this order will result in a speedy restoration of the public peace, and that the order can be so modified that there will be no interference with the ordinary process of business and commercial life in Tulsa or any surrounding city in Tulsa County.

Every good citizen should lend his or her best efforts to secure a prompt compliance with this order.

Automobiles, Trucks and other conveyances, except those used by Doctors, Officers of the Law, members of the Red Cross and other individuals or organizations contributing to the health and welfare of the people will not be allowed on the streets between the hours of 7:00 p.m. and 6:00 a.m.

Sufficient military forces are on hand to rigidly enforce this order, and it will be done.

Equal protection under this order is guaranteed to all persons, without regard to race or color. After the publication of this order, the man or woman, white or black, found with arms in their hands without permission from military authority or by virtue of proper commission under the civil law, will be considered as public enemies and treated accordingly.

Police officers and members of the sheriff's force will report through their chiefs to Brig-Gen. Charles F. Barrett for further orders.

By order of the Governor.

CHAS. F. BARRETT,
Brigadier General,
Commanding Oklahoma
National Guard.[55]

By the time the troops got settled and were deployed on the afternoon of Wednesday, June 1, 1921, precious little in the Greenwood District remained to be salvaged. Tulsa's thriving, prosperous African-American community lay in ruins, leveled and charred beyond recognition. Time stood still. Beneath the smoldering ashes lay the hopes and dreams—the lives and life-times—of an entire community.

The *Tulsa Tribune* trumpeted the destruction: "Acres of ashes lie smoldering in what but yesterday was 'Niggertown.'" Subsequent *Tulsa Tribune* headlines, not unpredictably, were equally insulting, inflammatory, and sensational: "PROPAGANDA OF NEGROES IS BLAMED"; "BLACK AGITATORS BLAMED FOR RIOT"; "PLOT BY NEGRO SOCIETY?"; "BLACKS HAD LEADERS"; "BLOOD SHED IN RACE WAR WILL CLEANSE TULSA"; "NEGRO SECTION ABOLISHED BY CITY'S ORDER."[56]

The Tulsa Ministerial Alliance boldly decreed that African-Americans were at the root of their own misfortune:

> The fair name of the city of Tulsa has been tarnished and blackened by a crime that ranks with the dastardly deeds of the Germans during the Great War, provoked by the bad element of the negroes, arming themselves and marching through the streets of the city. Block after block of our city had been swept by fire applied by the frenzied hand of the mob. Many of our people are dead, while thousands of innocent, peaceable, and law-abiding citizens have not only been rendered homeless, but they have been robbed and despoiled of all their earthly possessions. The pastors of Tulsa blush for shame at this outrage which renders our city odious and condemned before the world.[57]

One prominent local white minister publicly implied that outside black agitators were at the root of the Riot.[58] The *Tulsa Daily World* reported:

> That the visit of Doctor Dubois, editor of a magazine for negroes, "The Crisis" to Tulsa some time ago may have had a bearing upon the trouble of the past week was intimated by Bishop E. D. Mouzon in his sermon last night at the Boston Avenue Methodist church on the subject, "The Tulsa Race Riot

and the Teachings of Jesus Christ." The magazine was termed
by the Bishop "dangerous," and Dubois himself characterized
as the most vicious negro man in the country.[59]

The label "vicious Negro" hardly befits a man of Dr. Du
Bois' stature. This "vicious Negro," Dr. W. E. B. Du Bois, was the
first African-American to receive a Ph.D. from Harvard University, helped found the NAACP, and was known worldwide as
an intellectual, scholar, writer, and African-American activist.

Dr. Du Bois, who edited *The Crisis* (the NAACP magazine)
from 1910 until 1934, became what must have seemed at the time
like a lone voice in a vast wilderness against lynchings, Jim Crow
laws, and the political disenfranchisement of African-Americans.
In the 1920s, Dr. Du Bois helped organize several international
conferences on Pan-Africanism. He later championed the struggles for independence by African nations in the post-World War II
era and resisted "Cold War" foreign policy and McCarthyism. He
died in exile in Ghana, Africa, at age ninety-five in 1963.[60]

Dr. Du Bois himself cited black/white economic competition
as the underlying cause of the Riot:

> I have never seen a colored community so highly organized as
> that of Tulsa. There is complete separation of the races, so that
> a colored town is within the white town. I noticed a block of
> stores built by white men for negro business. They had long
> been empty, boycotted by the negroes. The colored people of
> Tulsa have accumulated property, have established stores and
> business organizations and have also made money in oil. They
> feel their independent position and have boasted that in their
> community there have been no cases of lynching. With such a
> state of affairs, it took only a spark to start a dangerous fire.[61]

These are the observations of an intelligent student of the
human condition, not the ravings of a "vicious Negro."

While some blamed outside "Negro agitators" like Dr. Du
Bois for the Riot, more objective voices laid blame squarely at the
feet of the locals. Maurice Willows and his American Red Cross
contingent, having come to Tulsa from St. Louis, concluded after
a thorough consideration that lack of law enforcement was the
cause-in-chief of "the short-lived civil war which turned Tulsa,

Oklahoma, into a bedlam on the morning of June 1, 1921."[62] Tulsa's "short-lived civil war" left a trail of causalities.

Like the rampant physical destruction, the human devastation was palpable. Mary Elizabeth Jones Parrish, a youthful Young Men's Christian Association (YMCA) typing instructor at the time, witnessed the Riot firsthand. Ms. Parrish recorded her own observations and those of her contemporaries in a self-published volume entitled *Events of the Tulsa Disaster*. Parrish paints a vivid, distressing picture of the wounded and suffering: "I can never erase the sights of my first visit to the hospital. There were men wounded in every conceivable way, like soldiers after a big battle. Some with amputated limbs, burned faces, others minus an eye or with heads bandaged. There were women who were nervous wrecks, and some confinement cases. Was I in a hospital in France? No, in Tulsa."[63]

Parrish's volume on the Riot became a "rare book" shortly after its initial printing. Some local whites bought up copies of the book in an apparent attempt to squelch the true story—in all its horror—of the Riot. According to some sources, fewer than a dozen copies of Parrish's original work are known to exist today.

Some African-Americans fled Tulsa immediately, never to return. No one knows precisely how many. Others—the casualties and fatalities of the battle—had no choice. Too frail to flee, or waiting to be buried, the Riot virtually insured that Tulsa would be their final resting place. Still others largely escaped physical harm and chose to stay put—to finish what they had started in the Greenwood District.

A dense gray pall loomed over the once picturesque northern horizon. Hordes of exhausted, perspiration-soaked, ashen-colored African-American men, women, and children trudged disconsolately through the oppressive June heat down Tulsa's Main Street. They were the main attraction in a twisted sideshow, on public display. Curious spectators leered. Nervous national guardsmen stood sentry.

Some white citizens, victors in battle, watched smugly as the vanquished paraded by. Sad, ironic, and bizarre—it was all of these. Beyond the point of exodus lay ruin and rubble. By June 2, 1921, Tulsa's racial warfare had come eerily to an end.

It was a sorry sight indeed: Black Tulsans, young and old,

rich and poor, educated and uneducated, streaming out of the ruins of their community—a community known nationwide as a model of and center for African-American industry, commerce, and collaboration. They marched involuntarily, heads bowed low, not in humility but in humiliation. They marched involuntarily, hands held high, not in salutation but in surrender. Among the "Negro" masses, class no longer existed. Black was black—doctor, lawyer, laborer, or thief—it simply no longer mattered:

> Some of our group who have been blest [*sic*] with educational or financial advantage are oftimes inclined to forget ourselves to the extent that they feel their superiority over those less fortunate, but when a supreme test, like the Tulsa disaster comes, it serves to remind us that we are all of one race; that human fiends, like those who had full sway on June 1st, have no respect of person. Every Negro was accorded the same treatment, regardless of his education or other advantages. A Negro was a Negro on that day and was forced to march with his hands up for blocks.[64]

There were no "special" blacks. Indeed, rioters often targeted "elite" African-Americans. Mobs took particular pleasure in meting out "justice"—through looting, ransacking, and burning—to "uppity" Negroes. Like thieves at a fire, these invaders knew no shame. Dr. R. T. Bridgewater, assistant county physician, recalled:

> On reaching the house I saw my piano and all of my elegant furniture piled in the street. My safe had been broken open, all of the money stolen, also my silverware, cut glass, all of the family clothing, and every thing of value had been removed, even my family Bible. My electric light fixtures were broken, all the window lights and glass in the doors were broken, the dishes that were not stolen were broken, the floors were covered (literally speaking) with glass, even the phone was torn from the wall. In the basement we gathered two tubs of broken glass from off the floor. My car was stolen and most of my large rugs were taken. I lost seventeen houses that paid me an average of over $425.00 per month.[65]

Dr. Arthur C. Jackson, a nationally renowned surgeon and

former president of the State Medical Association, was a prominent, well-respected African-American physician in Tulsa. The
Mayo brothers (of Mayo Clinic fame) called Dr. Jackson "the
most able Negro surgeon in America."[66] He counted among his
patients several white Tulsans—remarkable in the Tulsa of 1921.
Despite his renown, in the context of the Riot, Dr. Jackson was
"just another Negro." He was, in a word, expendable.

A teenage white boy murdered Dr. Jackson in cold blood as
he rushed unarmed from the flaming inferno he once called
home, hands held high in the air, during the peak of the Riot.
Dr. Jackson, grievously wounded by two bullets fired from the
gun of the young hoodlum, was loaded into a truck and deposit-
ed at Convention Hall. Suffering and given no medical attention, Dr. Jackson bled to death.[67]

Police Chief John Gustafson, in a post-Riot report to
Governor Robertson, listed the official death toll as nine white
men and boys and sixty-eight African-Americans, including
men, women, and children.[68] Other accounts of Riot fatalities
vary wildly, some being as high as 300.[69] For at least two reasons,
a precise count of the dead could not easily be taken. First, witnesses reported seeing black corpses hauled to the banks of the
Arkansas River and dumped like so much waste in a public
sewer.[70] These accounts can neither be confirmed nor denied.
Second, Chief Gustafson's report to the governor did not—
indeed, could not—account for the mortally wounded who may
have fled Tulsa and died elsewhere. Cities as far north as Kansas
City provided refuge for Tulsa's walking wounded.[71] Records of
Riot casualties, unlike fatality figures, are somewhat more defin-
itive. The American Red Cross listed 2,480 families or 8,624
persons in need of assistance, in excess of 1,000 homes and businesses destroyed, and the delivery of several stillborn infants.[72]

The Red Cross began its humanitarian relief efforts in Tulsa
on June 1. Initially located downtown, the Red Cross soon relocated its offices and an emergency hospital, central first aid station, and dispensary to Booker T. Washington High School.[73] By
all accounts, the Red Cross performed superbly, providing all
manner of assistance to Riot victims. The Red Cross also served
as a de facto liaison between black and white Tulsa.

Ironically, the seniors at "Booker T."—this high school-

turned-Red Cross nerve center—had been preparing for their
May 31, 1921, prom when the Riot broke out.

> It was supposed to have been the night of the senior
> prom. But, Ed Goodwin and the other members of the Booker
> T. Washington High School Class of 1921 found their prepa-
> ration for the gala interrupted by an escalating race war which
> would lay much of their parents' community in ruin.
> Ed and his sister Anna, later a prominent Tulsa social
> worker, were taken with their brother and sister to the new
> brick home James Henri and Carlie Goodwin were building
> for their family on Brickyard Hill for safety and Ed, always a
> practical thinker, headed for refuge in the bath tub. "If they
> shot through the house, they probably wouldn't hit me in the
> tub," he recalled thinking in later years.
> But his security collapsed, he would chuckle in recalling,
> when the elderly mother of a family friend found him, pulled
> him from the tub, and claimed the place of safety for herself.[74]

While the Booker T. seniors were deprived of their prom,
others were deprived of something far more significant: liberty.
Hastily arranged internment camps sprang up in various locations throughout Tulsa, including Convention Hall (located at
105 West Brady, now the Brady Theatre), McNulty Baseball Park
(then located at 10th and Elgin streets, the current site of,
among other businesses, Lyon's Indian Store), and the Tulsa
Fairgrounds (then, as now, located at 21st Street and Yale
Avenue). Like cattle, African-Americans arrested during and
after the Riot were corralled and "branded" with "green cards,"
paid for by the Tulsa City Commission and the Tulsa Chamber
of Commerce. Green cards, to be valid, required the signature of
the bearer's white employer.[75]

All relief to able-bodied African-American men came in the
form of work. The men received a wage of twenty-five cents per
hour, and were paid at the close of each day. The arithmetic is
simple: An eight-hour day yielded $2 for each worker. Meals
were available for twenty cents each.[76]

The shortage of African-American labor caused by the
internment brought Tulsa to a virtual standstill. Hotels and other
establishments dependent upon unskilled African-American

labor ground to a halt. To avoid certain economic paralysis, white employers readily countersigned the green cards of their African-American charges, freeing them up to return to work.

United States citizenship notwithstanding, African-American refugees faced certain arrest if discovered on the streets without proper documentation. Freedom and liberty could be denied at the whim of authorities or by the absence, failure, or refusal of a white employer to validate the identity of his employee. Schoolteacher J. W. Hughes told the American Red Cross:

> We were carried to the City Jail, the men were placed in the corridor down stairs, the women were carried up stairs. After so many were crowded into the corridor, we were carried to Convention Hall. Many people cheered and clapped their hands as we were marched four abreast with our hands above our head. A man was shot at the door of the Convention Hall while both hands were above his head. Many men who were shot out in the city were brought in the hall and we heard their cries and groans. Namely: Dr. Jackson, Johnson and Stovall. We looked out of the windows, saw our homes go up in smoke. At noon, we were fed sandwiches and coffee. . . . In the late afternoon, we were allowed to leave the Convention Hall only when some white person we had worked for would come and vouch for us. Mr. Oberholtzer, City Superintendent of Public Schools, came and called for all colored teachers, and we were taken to the Old City High School, where I met my wife again. All the lady teachers were taken to the homes of the city principals and cared for nicely. We were allowed to stay in the old High School all night. The next morning, I saw my wife much improved as to her dress. Miss Kimble of the Domestic Science Department of the white High School gave us our breakfast.[77]

The "green card" edict would not be lifted until July 7, 1921, and then only with respect to so-called "bona fide" Tulsa Negroes, not out-of-towners.[78]

Almost one-half of Tulsa's African-American citizens found themselves held captive, and under armed guard.[79] They were the defeated prisoners of a civil war, the enemy by virtue of skin color.

By Thursday, June 2, 1921, the Riot had captured the attention of the nation: "Washington, June 1—The Tulsa race riot was the principal topic of conversation at the White House, in senate and house cloak rooms and executive departments today. . . . President Harding received bulletins on it at the White House. . . ."[80] The fact that the uppermost echelons of American government took notice of the Riot attests to its importance beyond the geographic bounds of Tulsa.

In America, as in Tulsa, the unspoken question on many minds was: "What do we do about our 'Negro problem'?" Those who would blame Tulsa's African-Americans for the Riot almost certainly saw the assertiveness of the men who marched to the downtown courthouse for the purpose of shielding Dick Rowland from a reported lynch mob as evidence of the "uppity Negro" syndrome. These men acted upon Frederick Douglass' observation: "Power concedes nothing without demand." Standing up for themselves and their community would not guarantee justice. Not doing so would guarantee injustice. African-Americans were supposed to know and maintain their place rather than know and defend their rights according to the prevailing power structure. The Riot simply reinforced that point.

The Klan in Tulsa capitalized on the fear and anger among some white Tulsans in the wake of the Riot. Though the Klan cannot alone be credited with instigating the Riot, its presence undoubtedly sowed the seeds of discord that made the Riot possible.[81] Some local law enforcement officers were known to be Klansmen.[82] Others were likely Klan sympathizers. Law enforcement officers were among those who, by design or default, facilitated assault on the Greenwood District.[83]

Post-Riot Klan propaganda in Tulsa resulted in astounding recruiting success. Soon the Tulsa Klan was 2,000 members strong. Taking full advantage of the "goodwill" generated for it by the Riot, the Klan purchased the Centenary Methodist Church building for $60,000 and built one of its largest meeting halls in the Southwest on that site. William Shelley Rogers was the Tulsa Klan's "Chief Cyclops," and his membership roster read like a "Who's Who" of prominent Tulsans. It was said at the time that in Tulsa all district judges, the court clerk, the county sheriff, and all jury commissioners were members of the Klan.[84]

Just as the Klan's role in the Riot cannot be accurately gauged, mere words cannot sufficiently capture the magnitude of the Riot's physical and emotional devastation. Despite the inherent inadequacy of words, two Riot survivors, LaVerne Cooksey Davis and Alice Andrews, described what they experienced during those awful days in the spring of 1921.

LaVerne Cooksey Davis recalled the horrors of the Riot with chilling clarity:

> In Tulsa, the only job that I could find was being a maid for a white doctor in South Tulsa. After the Tulsa Race Riot of 1921, I left Tulsa. I just couldn't face the prospects of spending my life being a maid. . . . Oh, that riot was such a terrible thing. It left its mark on me; I just can't ever forget it. When the riot started, it was in the wee hours of the morning. I had gone to bed and after midnight, I got a telephone call from the doctor who was still downtown. I wondered why he was calling me at that late hour. He told me not to go into Little Africa. That is what people called North Tulsa in those days. I thought that was strange for him to tell me that. I wouldn't have been going into North Tulsa at that late hour anyway. Well, later on the doctor called me again, and this time he was more urgent in telling me not to go into Little Africa. He said, "Hell has broken out in Little Africa. Don't go down there!". . . . I was safe in my maid's quarters in South Tulsa, but many of my friends in the Greenwood area had their homes burned to the ground. Before their homes were burned, some of the people were taken out of their beds. They went to detention centers in their pajamas and housecoats because the police wouldn't give them time to dress. I was so disturbed. I didn't know where my friends had been taken. Later, I found out that most of them had been taken to the Convention Center. Five or six days after the riot, blacks could get passes from the militia to go down into the Greenwood area to try to find friends and relatives. That riot was a tragic thing and it has stayed on my mind all these years. . . . Although I was safe in South Tulsa in my maid's quarters, I could see that red blaze, and since my boss had warned me, I knew that blazing fire was destroying the beloved Greenwood community. When I did get down to Greenwood after the riot, I was so hurt by what I saw. To wake up and see nothing but ashes and buildings burnt to the ground, I couldn't keep the tears from falling.[85]

Forever seared into the consciousness of Alice Andrews, the Riot was the worst of times:

> The worst thing that happened to black people in Tulsa's history was that awful race riot in 1921. I knew Dick Rowland well; I had known his daddy, who everyone called "Dad" Rowland before Dick was born. Dick was the boy who accidentally bumped into or stepped on the foot of a white girl in an elevator. . . . I was asleep the night of May 31st, but my mother witnessed the riot and the riot aftermath. She said she sat at her living room window all night watching those people running down the Sante Fe Railroad tracks, just running and running and trying to get away from the horrors of the riot. There were no paved roads in North Tulsa then. That is why the women and children were running down the railroad tracks, so they could keep out of the mud. The women were still in their nightgowns and they were holding their children's hands and just dragging them along. The children were crying. We later learned that the men had been rounded up and taken to the Convention Center, the Fairgrounds, the 11th Street and Skelly Drive area (now, The University of Tulsa stadium area), Booker Washington High School, churches, and other places for "safekeeping." What that actually did was to leave the Greenwood area defenseless. What made it even worse was that the first militia that was sent in sided with the whites. That is what allowed things to get out of hand so quick. Mobs just went on the rampage with no restrictions put on them by white authorities. They looted and burned straight down Greenwood, all the way to Pine. But they did not cross over to the Lansing side. Before they could do that, a second militia group came (the Oklahoma National Guard sent by the governor of Oklahoma). That group took control of the crowd, but not before mobs had completely destroyed Greenwood! The next morning when I woke up to go to work, my mother told me about the riot. I looked out the window and was startled. It looked like the world was on fire.[86]

The utter decimation of the Greenwood District brought the governor of Oklahoma to Tulsa for a firsthand assessment of the damage. Governor James B. A. Robertson, on a June 2, 1921, visit to Tulsa, ordered a formal investigation of the Riot.[87] At his urging, a grand jury was impaneled, chaired by District

The Greenwood District just after the 1921 Tulsa Race Riot. (Photo courtesy of the North Tulsa Heritage Foundation, Inc.)

Tulsa Race Riot of 1921. (Photo courtesy of George E. Schaefer)

Judge W. Valjean Biddison, and assisted in its investigative functions by Attorney General S. P. Freeling. The grand jury commenced its work almost immediately. Its twelve-day session resulted in the filing of twenty-seven cases and a total of more than eighty-five individual indictments.

The grand jury indicted the central figure in the Riot saga, Dick Rowland, on June 6, 1921. In *State of Oklahoma vs. Dick Rowland*, the indictment for the assault and attempted rape of Sarah Page, the grand jury concluded:

> [We] find that in said Tulsa County, and State of Oklahoma, on the 30th day of May in the year of our Lord One Thousand Nine Hundred and Twenty-one and prior to the finding of this indictment one Dick Rowland did then and there, unlawfully, wilfully, wrongfully, forcibly, violently, and feloniously, make an assault upon one Sarah Page, a female person over the age of eighteen years [the *Tulsa Tribune* reported Ms. Page's age as seventeen], and of previous chaste and virtuous character, and not the wife of him, the said Dick Rowland, and did, then and there, and thereby unlawfully, violently, forcibly, and feloniously, and against her will, attempt to ravish, rape, and carnally know her, the said Sarah Page, but was intercepted and failed in the perpetration thereof.[88]

The witnesses whose testimony supported the indictment were Sarah Page (the alleged "victim"), C. A. Poulton, F. E. Voohies, and Henry Carmichael, a Tulsa police officer.[89] A local prosecutor, W. F. Seaver, county attorney, filed the information in the case (i.e., the prosecutor's charges against Dick Rowland) on September 15, 1921, three months after the grand jury issued its indictment. Rowland's attorneys, Edward Crossland, who had been Tulsa County district attorney in 1914, and Washington Elias Hudson, whose name ironically appears on the roster of the Ku Klux Klan,[90] moved to dismiss the information, but Judge Redmond S. Cole overruled their motion on September 16, 1921.[91]

The grand jury issued its final report on June 25, 1921. Not surprisingly, the all-white grand jury blamed "colored men" for the Riot.

> We find that the recent race riot was the direct result of an effort
> on the part of a certain group of colored men who appeared at
> the courthouse on the night of May 31, 1921, for the purpose of
> protecting one Dick Rowland then and now in the custody of the
> sheriff of Tulsa county for an alleged assault upon a young white
> woman. We have not been able to find any evidence either from
> white or colored citizens that any organized attempt was made
> or planned to take from the sheriff's custody any prisoner, the
> crowd assembled about the courthouse being purely spectators
> and curiosity seekers resulting from rumors circulated about the
> city. There was no mob spirit among the whites, no talk of lynch-
> ing and no arms. The assembly was quiet until the arrival of the
> armed negroes, which precipitated and was the direct cause of
> the entire affair.[92]

Moreover, the grand jury, instead of appealing to interracial understanding and tolerance, recommended just the opposite. Among other things, the grand jury suggested that race mixing be prohibited and that existing laws be strictly enforced so as to maintain the "proper" relationship between the races.[93] Attorney General Freeling, who had conducted the investigation of the Riot for the grand jury, publicly repudiated the less-than-objective conclusions reached by the grand jury and contained in its report.[94]

The twenty-seven cases initiated by the grand jury against blacks and whites involved a variety of charges—rioting, grand larceny, arson, assault with intent to kill, unlawfully pointing a pistol, and, in the case of Dick Rowland, attempted rape. Some of the cases involved indictments against more than a single individual. None of the cases proceeded to conviction. All were dismissed or simply languished for failure to prosecute. Despite the utter devastation—the loss of life and property—in the Greenwood District, not a single white Tulsan was made to answer to the criminal justice system as a consequence. "Doing the crime," at least in the Tulsa of 1921, did not result in "doing the time."[95]

Given the prevailing sociopolitical climate and the makeup of the grand jury, it should come as no surprise that the first case targeted a group of African-Americans, some sixty-three in number. The bitterly ironic charge: rioting. *State of Oklahoma vs. Will Robinson, et al.* indicted several prominent African-American Tulsans, among them A. J. Smitherman, editor and publisher of the *Tulsa Star,* and J. B. Stradford, attorney, businessman, and proprietor of the sixty-five-room Stradford Hotel at 301 North Greenwood.[96]

A. J. Smitherman founded his newspaper in Muskogee, Oklahoma, as the *Muskogee Star*. Smitherman came to Tulsa in the spring of 1913. The *Tulsa Star* was printed weekly by Smitherman's Tulsa Star Publishing Co., located at 118 North Greenwood Avenue. A one-year subscription to the newspaper sold for $1.50.

A staunch and vocal advocate for African-American voting rights, Smitherman, a Democrat, convinced local authorities to create a precinct election board consisting exclusively of African-American men. He had tried unsuccessfully to get blacks placed on election boards alongside whites. Though that attempt failed, Tulsa was redistricted and Smitherman became the first African-American inspector of elections under the new regime.

Equally concerned about the civil rights of African-Americans, in 1917 Smitherman personally investigated and reported to Oklahoma Governor R. L. Williams on mob activity in Dewey, Oklahoma. A mob there torched the homes of some twenty African-American families. Smitherman's dogged investigation resulted in the arrests of thirty-six men, including the mayor of the city of Dewey.

In 1918 Smitherman was summoned by telegram to Bristow, Oklahoma. Then justice of the peace in Tulsa County, Smitherman, accompanied by three other African-American men, went to Bristow to protect a young African-American man from a lynch mob. The man, Edgar Bohanan, had been arrested and charged with robbing and shooting a white man. Smitherman sent a simply worded telegram to the governor urging his assistance prior to embarking on the journey: "Hon. R. L. Williams, Governor. Oklahoma City, Okla. I am reliably informed that a race riot is imminent at Bristow. Kindly act at once—A. J. Smitherman."

Two hundred armed African-American farmers assembled in Bristow to prevent an even larger white mob from lynching Edgar Bohanan. The Bristow chief of police warned the lynch mob that he and his deputies would shoot to kill any man who dared to molest Bohanan. By the time the courageous

Smitherman and his companions arrived, law officers had spirited Bohanan out of town on a northbound train. Bohanan arrived, safe and sound, at the county jail in Sapulpa.[97]

That same year, Smitherman and his brother rescued an elderly African-American woman from peonage. The woman, who had been brought from Louisiana by a prominent Tulsa family, was taken in and cared for by Smitherman. Relatives of the old woman eventually came to her rescue.

Smitherman had the distinction of being selected by the governor to be among the select few—and the only African-American—to greet President Woodrow Wilson on his visit to Oklahoma City in 1919. Yet this visible, respected black firebrand found his prominence of little consequence or comfort during the Riot. He lost everything—his home and his business. He, his wife, and his five children went into exile following the Riot. Many whites blamed Smitherman's paper, the *Tulsa Star*, for fomenting discord between whites and African-Americans in Tulsa and blamed Smitherman personally for organizing African-American men in an attempt to prevent Dick Rowland from being lynched.[98]

State of Oklahoma vs. Will Robinson, et al.—the case that indicted several African-American men for Riot activities—came full circle on October 18, 1996, seventy-five years after its initiation, thanks largely to the courage and tenacity of the family of J. B. Stradford. The Stradford clan sought successfully to clear the historical record on the family patriarch, J. B. Stradford.

Stradford, the son of a Kentucky slave, was born a slave in Versaille, Kentucky.[99] A Greenwood pioneer, he came to Tulsa in 1899 at age thirty-eight or thirty-nine. Stradford held degrees from Oberlin College in Ohio and Indiana Law School, and became a prominent Tulsa attorney and businessman. Stradford built the first library in Tulsa for African-Americans, ran a rooming house, and owned the sixty-five-unit Stradford Hotel on Greenwood Avenue. The Stradford Hotel burned to the ground during the Riot.

The charge against Stradford stemmed from his participation in an attempt to calm tensions in downtown Tulsa on May 31, 1921, the eve of the Riot. Stradford and other African-American men had gone to the downtown courthouse after hearing talk of a lynching. These men simply refused to allow the angry white mob assembled at the courthouse to string up Dick Rowland, who stood accused of assaulting young Sarah Page. They set out to protect him. Their valiant efforts earned them an indictment for "inciting a riot." Ultimately, Dick Rowland would be protected, but at no small cost to Stradford and to so many other African-Americans in Tulsa.

For his role in the whole affair, Stradford was charged in a June 15, 1921, grand jury indictment. He fled Tulsa and was arrested two days later in Independence, Kansas. That led to a rather public extradition controversy. The *Okmulgee Times* reported: "If Governor Allen of Kansas wants to help the authorities fix the blame for the rioting at Tulsa last week, he will not refuse to grant extradition papers for J. B. Stradford, the negro who is held in Independence. Stradford, a generally undesirable citizen, can probably tell as much as anyone about the real cause of the trouble in Tulsa."[100]

J. B. Stradford's son, C. Francis Stradford, a Chicago lawyer, secured his father's freedom from incarceration. Fearful of his fate at the hands of Tulsa's justice system in the wake of the Riot, Stradford refused to sit idly by and await a trial. He fled Tulsa, never to return, leaving behind considerable wealth, estimated at $125,000. This heretofore upstanding, well-respected patriarch became a fugitive. Stradford eventually surfaced in Chicago. Starting once again from scratch, he emerged as a successful lawyer and entrepreneur.

So wide were the scars and deep was the pain from J. B. Stradford's ordeal that no member of the Stradford family would again set foot in Tulsa until October 18, 1996. (Stradford died in 1935.)[101]

Remarkably, Tulsa and the State of Oklahoma removed a substantial blot on the state's historical ledger on October 18, 1996. Twenty-one descendants of J. B. Stradford assembled in Tulsa. Having seen and read national media accounts of the Riot and the dedication of a memorial to those lost in the Riot, the Stradford clan decided to act. Judge Cornelius E. Toole of the Circuit Court of Cook County in Chicago (Stradford's great-grandson) and Ambassador Jewel Lafontant-Mankarious, a former official in the administration of President Richard M. Nixon (and Stradford's granddaughter) contacted Oklahoma State Representative Don Ross for assistance in clearing Stradford's name. Judge Toole and Ambassador Lafontant-Mankarious succeeded.

On motion of Tulsa County District Attorney William D. LaFortune, the charges against J. B. Stradford (and, by implication, against A.J. Smitherman and the other defendants in *State of Oklahoma vs. Will Robinson, et al.*) were dropped by order of Tulsa County District Court Judge Jesse A. Harris, representing the City of Tulsa:

MOTION TO DISMISS
COMES NOW William D. LaFortune, the duly appointed and qualified District Attorney, District No. 14, Tulsa County, State of Oklahoma, and moves the Court to dismiss the above entitled cause for the following reason, to-wit: THE BEST INTERESTS OF JUSTICE, DEFENDANT IS NOW DECEASED. COSTS TO STATE. WARRANT RECALLED.

ORDER
Now on this 14th day of October, 1996, the above entitled cause, coming on to be heard upon motion to dismiss said cause, and the court being fully advised in the premises, finds that said motion should be sustained; and, it is therefore ORDERED, ADJUDGED and DECREED that said cause be, and same is hereby dismissed for the reasons as set forth in said motion, and that the warrant of arrest be recalled.[102]

Oklahoma Governor Frank Keating issued an executive pardon for J. B. Stradford, and proclaimed October 18, 1996, "J. B. Stradford Day." Fittingly, Stradford, a prominent and skillful lawyer when he left Tulsa, has been posthumously admitted to the bar of the State of Oklahoma. A seventy-five-year-old wrong had been righted—too late, unfortunately, for J. B. Stradford and his cohorts to bear witness.

Stradford's descendants, who perhaps would have been great Tulsans had it not been for the wrong visited upon J. B., nonetheless went on to become outstanding Americans. Among their numbers are professionals in all fields of endeavor, many of whom call Chicago home. The Stradfords attending the historic ceremony included Ambassador Jewel Lafontant-

Mankarious, granddaughter; John W. Rogers, Jr., grandson; Emma Toole Monroe, granddaughter; John Toole, grandson; Judge Cornelius E. Toole, great-grandson; and Dr. Theron C. Toole, great-grandson. J. B. Stradford would certainly be proud of his clan and, of course, pleased with the restoration of his good name so needlessly dishonored on June 15, 1921.[103]

Sarah Page ultimately refused to assist in the prosecution of her alleged assailant. Dick Rowland, in the absence of testimony from the "victim," was exonerated.[104] A free man, Dick Rowland quickly fled Tulsa.[105] According to Rowland's mother, Damie Rowland Ford, Sarah Page followed her son to Kansas City.[106] Rumors still persist that Rowland and Page had a relationship.

Police Chief John Gustafson was subsequently indicted for failing to take proper precautions to prevent the loss of life and liberty during the Riot and for conspiracy to free automobile thieves and collect rewards. Convicted on July 22, 1921, Gustafson was ousted from office on June 30, 1921.[107] Gustafson's assistant chief, George E. Blaine, became chief on July 24, 1921.[108]

Barney Cleaver, Tulsa's first African-American police officer, remained in Tulsa. Paradoxically, he publicly blamed African-Americans for the Riot. Having lost property valued at $20,000 in the Riot, Cleaver is reported to have said: "I am going to do everything I can to bring the negroes responsible for the outrage to the bars of justice. They caused me to lose everything I have been years in accumulating and I intend to get them."[109] Cleaver earned a reputation as a tough law enforcement officer and a peacemaker. Affectionately known as "Uncle Barney," he ultimately gained the admiration and respect of many Tulsans, white and black.[110]

Relatively few whites exhibited empathy and compassion for their defeated African-American brothers and sisters. There were, of course, notable exceptions. A Jewish family, the Zarrows, ran a store at 1427 East 6th Street at the time of the Riot. The Zarrows' son, Henry, a Tulsa philanthropist who made his fortune in the oilfield equipment business, recalls how his family shielded African-Americans during the Riot: "I remember we hid people in our basement. My mother hid some of the little kids under her skirts."[111]

Several organizations, including the National Guard, the American Legion, the American Red Cross,[112] the Salvation Army, and various churches and individuals assisted with post-disaster relief. The Riot precipitated the American Red Cross to lend its significant resources to a humanitarian effort involving a "man-made" disaster for the first time. Riot victims fondly referred to Red Cross workers as "Angels of Mercy." These "Angels of Mercy" are estimated to have expended some $100,000 on the Greenwood District relief effort.[113]

Remarkably, two commissions on interracial relations were formed in Tulsa within thirty days of the Riot—one black, the other white. The "separate but equal" mold would not be broken, even when the stated purpose of convening was to foster interracial cooperation.

According to one of its members, H. T. S. Johnson, Judge Mather Eakes, who chaired the Tulsa County Commission on Inter-Racial Co-operation (the white group), provided critical assistance at a crucial time in the history of Tulsa's African-American community. The Tulsa City Commission, just days after the Riot, moved to extend the fire limits of the city of Tulsa to the north and west. The area was made part of the official fire limits of the city, with the result that structures rebuilt in the Greenwood District had to be fireproof—constructed of concrete, brick, or steel—and had to be two stories high. Consequently, many cash-poor African-Americans who had been burned out would not be able to secure the financing necessary to rebuild in accordance with the expensive, newly-applicable specifications of the fire code. White speculators would then be free to buy up the scorched earth at, quite literally, "firesale" prices.[114]

Based on a legal challenge to the ordinance by African-American businessman Joe Lockard, represented ably by lawyers P. A. Chappelle, I. H. Spears, and B. C. Franklin, judges declared the ordinance passed by the Tulsa City Commission unconstitutional. In so doing, the judiciary helped save Tulsa's African-American community.[115]

Real estate speculators pitched a tent on the grounds of Booker T. Washington High School and offered to buy land in the Greenwood District for $75 a square foot. On June 15, 1921, the following ad appeared in the *Tulsa Daily World*:

Through the Reconstruction Committee appointed by the Mayor and the City Commissioners (June 14), Tulsa extends a welcoming hand to wholesale houses and industrial plants which are to be located on the trackage property in Little Africa swept by fire and which is now within the city fire limits restricted to the erection of fire-resisting buildings.

The Committee also expressed a sentiment in favor of using a part of the burned area for a union station whenever such a project is ready for consideration by the railroads entering Tulsa.[116]

After the notice appeared in the *Tulsa Daily World*, the Colored Citizens' Relief Committee, a group set up to coordinate post-Riot relief for needy African-American families, called an emergency meeting at First Baptist Church. O. W. Gurley chaired the group, which included J. H. Goodwin (vice-chair), E. F. Saddler, John W. Bush, S. D. Hooker, I. H. Spears, A. L. Phillips, W. H. Smith, and R. A. Whittaker. Dimple Bush, the wife of John W. Bush, served as secretary.

The Colored Citizens' Relief Committee sent a delegation to visit city officials and demand protection for vulnerable African-American property owners. The delegation persuaded the Tulsa City Commission to deem invalid any deeds transferred during the immediate post-Riot period. Simultaneously, the Colored Citizens' Relief Committee held mass meetings to urge African-American property owners not to sell—to stay the course. Ultimately, it became a matter of pride to refuse to sell one's property, no matter how great the temptation or substantial the payoff.[117]

By and large, the prevailing social custom preempted the possibility of gestures of simple human kindness across the great racial divide. Some 1,000 African-American Tulsans spent the winter of 1921-1922 living in tents.[118] Tulsa's official response, recorded prominently in the annals of the Tulsa City Commission meeting minutes just after the Riot, apportioned blame on and withheld both sympathy and empathy from the victims of the Riot.

In his June 14, 1921, address to the Tulsa City Commission, then Tulsa Mayor T. D. Evans laid blame squarely on the shoulders of the usual suspects—members of Tulsa's small but vibrant "Negro" community. Said Mayor Evans:

> Let the blame for this negro uprising lie right where it belongs—on those armed negroes and their followers who started this trouble and who instigated it and any persons who seek to put half the blame on the white people are wrong and should be told so in no uncertain terms. We are told that twice before we assumed power as city officials that armed mobs of negroes visited the white section of the city and made certain demands under threats of force. They have come only Once [*sic*] in this administration. We are not Prophets [*sic*], but we wager that trip number two will not take place soon.[119]

Incredibly, Mayor Evans went even further. He indicated clearly his scorn for the successful, bustling, affluent Greenwood District.

> It is the judgement [*sic*] of many wise heads in Tulsa, based upon observation of a number of years, that this uprising was inevitable. If that be true and this judgement [*sic*] had to come upon us then I say it was good generalship to let the destruction come to that section where the trouble was hatched up, put in motion and where it had its inception.
>
> All regret the wrongs that fell upon the innocent negroes and they should receive such help as we can give them if within our power. It, however, is true of any warfare that the fortunes of war fall upon the innocent along with the guilty. This is true of any conflict, invasion, or uprising. Think what would have happened had the Allies marched to Berlin.[120]

Equally telling are the comments of a white woman who witnessed the Riot and wrote of her reflections. Pondering the cause of the Riot and whether it could recur, she noted: "I never knew positively whether the revolt had been seething a long time and the incident in the elevator was the spark that caused the riot. I don't think anyone ever will know. . . . Could it happen again in Tulsa? We never know what thoughts are in a Negro's mind. Long years of servitude has [*sic*] caused the negro to conceal his real thoughts from the white man."[121]

African-Americans around the nation saw things differently. Walter F. White, an official with the NAACP who later became its executive director, visited Tulsa and interviewed Tulsans immediately following the Riot. White, a light-skinned African-American, was able to "pass" for a white man. His color afforded him entree into spheres in Tulsa that would not be accessible to darker-skinned African-Americans. White penned an article about the Riot for the Wall Street edition of the *New York Evening Post* on June 11, 1921. He zeroed in on the root causes of the Riot:

> The contributory and underlying causes of the riot conflict at Tulsa, which cost this city irreparable damage to its name, the lives of between 150 and 200 citizens, and a property loss of $1,500,000, are not so important in themselves were they not so typical of conditions in many other towns and cities of America, north and south. Corrupt and inefficient rule in municipal affairs, the total lack of understanding between white and colored citizens, and the growth of race prejudice, fostered and nurtured for economic gain—all these exist to a greater or less degree in many American cities. Because Tulsa failed to realize how serious a situation was being bred by these causes, she has had to pay the penalty.[122]

The NAACP expended upwards of $3,500 to the relief and legal needs of the Riot victims.[123]

Editorial writers from across the country took special note of the Riot, providing a national context for an otherwise local event. There had been far too many other civil disturbances, though none as costly or as deadly. A riot in East St. Louis on July 7, 1917, resulted in 125 deaths. In a July 19, 1919, riot in Washington, D. C., seven people lost their lives and scores were injured. A July 26, 1919, riot in Chicago resulted in thirty-eight deaths and some 500 injuries. On October 2, 1919, a riot in Elaine, Arkansas, resulted in thirty deaths and more than 100 injuries. A riot in Omaha, Nebraska, on October 5 of that year resulted in three deaths and several casualties. Omaha's mayor was hanged by the rioters but cut loose in time to save his life.

National editorialists by and large agreed that the causes of the riots were several: lynch laws, peonage, racial prejudice, black-white economic rivalry, radical propaganda, unemployment, corruption in politics, community leadership vacuums, and a new sense of African-American self-assertion. They pondered aloud about how the United States could credibly condemn so-called "uncivilized" acts abroad when the very same acts were being readily and regularly perpetrated within the boundaries of our American democracy. The conclusion to be drawn from the comments of the editorial writers of the day was a prophetic one: America had failed to address the troublesome, ever-present, just-beneath-the-surface issue of race.[124]

How best do we begin to heal the open, festering wounds born of bias, bigotry, and racism and burned into our collective consciousness by virtue of tragedies like the Riot? One answer bandied about with considerable frequency and worthy of serious consideration is the provision of reparations for victims of America's egregious racial injustices.

Some present-day African-American leaders in the Tulsa community, notably Oklahoma State Representative Don Ross, now call for reparations to be paid by the City of Tulsa and the State of Oklahoma to the surviving Riot victims and their heirs.[125] Ross' call for "righting" the historical wrongs of the Riot through reparations rests principally on three grounds: (1) that the City of Tulsa and the State of Oklahoma bear at least some responsibility for the Riot; (2) that the City of Tulsa breached its post-Riot promise to rebuild the Greenwood District; and (3) that the effects of the Riot linger to this day, and have substantially diminished African-Americans' opportunities for the accumulation of wealth generated by their Riot-era ancestors.[126]

The Oklahoma House of Representatives, at the urging of Oklahoma State Representative Ross and with the support of Oklahoma Senator Maxine Horner, passed a resolution in 1997 calling for the creation of a commission to study the Riot and develop a full and accurate historical record.[127] The resolution does not specifically endorse the concept of reparations for Riot survivors and their heirs. The findings of the nine-member commission, which could include a specific recommendation on issue of reparations, are to be presented in the form of a written report to the governor, members of the Oklahoma legislature, the mayor of Tulsa, and the Tulsa City Council on or before January 5, 1999.[128]

Senator Maxine Horner urged that the commission charged with studying the Riot not be mandated to conclude that reparations are in fact due: "To send this commission to work toward a predetermined conclusion would be as intellectually dishonest as the concerted coverup that's gone on for decades about the 1921 riot."[129] Oklahoma Governor Frank Keating supported the formation of the Riot commission, but reserved judgment on the issue of whether Riot survivors are entitled to reparations. According to Governor Keating: "To tell the truth is in our best interest." Describing the events of May 31 and June 1, Governor Keating continued: "It was not a race riot. It was an assault on the black community."[130]

Tulsa's leading African-American newspaper, *The Oklahoma Eagle*, endorsed the concept of reparations, if not Representative Ross' specific proposal, noting:

> The $6 million reparations to the families of those victimized by the infamous 1921 Tulsa Race Riot are the right thing to do and long overdue. If made, it will and should close the book on the worst days in Tulsa history. But interested parties should proceed with dignity and decorum. . . . It is a debt of character and justice. But it doesn't have to be made in cash. How else can anything be done to repay the debt? The amount is small in comparison to the loss of property and life. How do you put a monetary figure on the bloodiest day in the history of Tulsa? Mayor Susan Savage is keeping an open mind on the proposal, and that is encouraging. If people believe this is a good idea, they should talk to their city councilors—unless they have an alternative. Would it not be a better idea to set up a $6 million trust fund to stimulate economic development on the north side or to set up a scholarship program for students? Should this award go only to African-American families? There were White families who lost life and home during those terrible days in 1921. What about the families who fled Tulsa and never looked back? Will they be included and do they qualify? These are tough questions for a sticky issue. How do you right a great wrong?[131]

Dr. John Hope Franklin, noted historian, scholar, and native Tulsan, has embraced the concept of reparations for Riot victims. According to Dr. Franklin, the City of Tulsa and the State of Oklahoma should muster the courage to do something in the way of reparations. But reparations cannot bring full closure to the Riot saga. What is truly essential, urges Dr. Franklin, is that the City of Tulsa and the State of Oklahoma, and, indeed, the United States of America, live up to the promise of assuring equal opportunity for all, now and in the future.[132]

The call for reparations is in part a plea for accountability. Evidence suggests that the Riot could have been controlled, if not prevented outright, had the City of Tulsa taken a proactive law enforcement posture. The culpability of the State of Oklahoma is presumably in large measure derivative of the culpability of the City of Tulsa.

Representative Ross' second rationale for reparations—that Tulsa failed to honor its commitment to rebuild the ravaged Greenwood District following the Riot—is supported by the historical record. Following the Riot, on June 14, 1921, Tulsa Mayor T. D. Evans appointed an all-white "Reconstruction Committee" to address the property claims of both African-Americans and whites.[133] The Reconstruction Committee replaced the Public Welfare Board, a body that had already begun working with the Red Cross and was to have engineered a rehabilitation and housing program. Indeed, the Red Cross reported:

> When everything was running smoothly, like a thunderclap out of a clear sky the Mayor of the City, T. [D.] Evans, declared the Welfare Board out of commission, and in its place appointed a new committee of seven which he called "The Reconstruction Committee."
>
> Thus, the backbone of financial support had been broken, most abruptly. The original Public Welfare Board resigned office at a mass meeting and at the time of their resignation recommitted itself collective and individually to stand by the Red Cross Relief Committee if their services should be necessary.
>
> The Red Cross therefore was placed in a position of having to deal with a new Reconstruction Committee. It was understood, at first, that the new committee was to function as the agent of the city in the same manner as the old committee. Time, however, has proven that the new committee was politically constituted and was chiefly interested in maneuvering for the transfer of negro property and the establishment of a new negro district.[134]

As the Red Cross pointed out, the Reconstruction Committee attempted to facilitate the transfer of property in the devastated Greenwood District from black to white ownership and displace the black community farther north. The "Reconstruction" in "Reconstruction Committee" was a misnomer. Reconstruction was never really intended. The weight of the evidence suggests strongly that Tulsa's leaders actively discouraged the rehabilitation and redevelopment of the Greenwood District. Scott Ellsworth, author of the seminal book on the Riot, *Death in a Promised Land*, notes: "One myth that persists is that the white community created a generous relief effort and rebuilt black Tulsa. The City fathers tried to keep black Tulsans from rebuilding. They tried to swindle them out of their land. They refused donations from charitable organizations around the country, while telling people they were going to rebuild the black community."[135]

Indeed, Ellsworth contends that, while somewhat sympathetic to the African-American plight following the Riot, whites contributed to the relief and rebuilding effort only marginally.

> The fact is that, contrary to these announced intentions in the [Tulsa] World and elsewhere, white Tulsans did not rebuild black Tulsa. Indeed, as has been shown, the city government and other white groups tried to prevent it. Any role which local whites had in the rebuilding came through three indirect avenues. First, there were some local donations to the Red Cross. Second, some whites were property owners in black Tulsa, and these people rebuilt the destroyed structures on the land which they owned—in order to once again collect rent from black tenants. And lastly, some whites loaned money to black employees for rebuilding purposes.[136]

The "accumulation of wealth" rationale for reparations, while compelling, poses its own set of difficulties. It is impossible to predict with certainty how Tulsa's African-American community would look had the Riot not occurred. But it is a historical fact that the Riot caused millions of dollars in physical damage (not to mention unquantifiable psychological pain) and impelled many prominent African-Americans to flee, never to return.[137] The economic impact of the Riot itself, coupled with the losses attributable to those individuals who fled, unquestionably shaped Tulsa's present African-American community. The Riot drained much of the existing wealth in Tulsa's black community and dimmed prospects for the accumulation of wealth over generations. Imagine what might have been.

Reparations requests, while not common in cases of domestic civil unrest, are not without parallel. Reparations paid to World War II-era Japanese internees, authorized by Congress pursuant to a 1988 civil liberties act, provide precedent for Riot reparations.[138] Likewise, 1994 legislation passed in Florida provides for reparations in the form of scholarships to the descendants of the victims of the notorious January 1923 Rosewood, Florida, race riot.[139]

When Congress passed the Civil Liberties Act of 1988, that act provided $20,000 in restitution to each eligible person of Japanese ancestry who was interned during World War II. (Certain Pacific Islanders who suffered injustices while under United States control during World War II are also eligible for restitution under the Act.) The only justification for the internment of Americans of Japanese ancestry was a perceived, but wholly unfounded, loyalty on the part of these individuals to the enemy, the Japanese government. The Civil Liberties Act of 1988 has as its explicit purposes to: (1) acknowledge injustices; (2) apologize on behalf of the people of the United States; (3) provide public education so as to prevent the recurrence of similar injustices; (4) make restitution; (5) discourage similar injustices in the future; and (6) lend clarity and credibility to declarations of United States' concern for violations of human rights committed by other nations.[140]

In 1994 the Florida legislature created the "Rosewood Family Scholarship Program" for the descendants of the 1923 Rosewood race riot victims. Eligible descendants are entitled to scholarship assistance of up to $4,000. Then Florida enacted a statute that seeks to fulfill "an equitable obligation to redress the injuries sustained as a result of the destruction of Rosewood, Florida. . . ." Rosewood was an African-American community totally annihilated by neighboring whites during the week of January 1, 1923. The Florida legislature concluded that the State of Florida and the local government knew of the impending tragedy, but turned a blind eye. Moreover, those officials failed to investigate the riot, bring the perpetrators to justice, and make the area safe for the return of the displaced African-American riot victims.[141]

The rationales posited for making reparations to the Japanese internees and the Rosewood riot descendants apply equally well to the victims of the Tulsa Riot. Chief among such rationales is the documented complicity of governmental organs and officials, by commission or omission, in the perpetration of injustices on a group of American citizens who happen to belong to a particular, identifiable racial group and were powerless to defend themselves against superior physical or coercive force.

Interestingly, the president of the Metropolitan Tulsa Chamber of Commerce just after the Riot released a statement to the press that called for Tulsa "to formulate a plan of reparation in order that homes may be rebuilt and families as nearly as possible rehabilitated."[142] The call for reparations, then, began almost immediately after the Riot. That call has yet to be answered.

The appropriateness of reparations raises several compelling questions: (1) Will providing reparations in the case of the Riot "open the floodgates" to other groups who feel "entitled" to recompense for historical wrongs?; (2) Is it sound public policy to visit the "sins of the fathers" on their sons and daughters (i.e., to make current generations—taxpayers—pay for wrongs for which they are not directly responsible?); (3) Is it possible to identify accurately those who are entitled to reparations in the event that reparations are provided?; (4) Are reparations owing to whites who may have been Riot victims?; (5) Is it possible to come up with other than an arbitrary formula for calculating reparations if they are provided?; and (6) Might the establishment of a scholarship fund for descendants of Riot victims or the establishment of a business development fund for the enhancement of the Greenwood District better serve the community as a whole than would cash outlays to individual Riot victims and their heirs? In light of these complex questions, it remains to be seen how the issue of reparations will be dealt with by the City of Tulsa and the State of Oklahoma.

Time may not heal all wounds. But time, if used wisely,

affords an opportunity for sober reflection, introspection, and rededication. A May 26, 1996, *Tulsa World* editorial puts the Riot into perspective in terms of its significance to the Tulsa community. Entitled, quite appropriately, "Tulsa's Riot, Tulsa's Shame," the editorial reads, in part:

> May 31, 1921, and the days following are a shameful time in Tulsa's history, days when open race war raged. The number killed, black and white, still is disputed. . . . The Tulsa Daily World's reportage of the racial war is filled with details of a nightmare night of fighting, killing and burning. A newspaper of about 35,000 circulation in a city of about 75,000 at the time, the paper's editors put their full staff on what to this day still is the biggest story in Tulsa history. . . . On June 2, The World editorialized: "Tulsa comes before the bar of Christian civilization this day, and with head bowed, the mantle of shame on her cheek, and, we sincerely hope with deep regret in her heart, asks that she be pardoned of the great offense that some of her citizens committed. The entire race war was as unjustified as it was unnecessary." The World publisher, Eugene Lorton, started a fund for black relief. . . . The riot shocked Tulsans, at least its leaders. The culture of the day was racist. But while most white people held narrow and ignorant views of white superiority, most did not condone killing blacks and burning their homes and possessions. The collective conscience was jolted.

What might we learn from the Riot? How could things have gone so horribly wrong? The lessons are several.

The formula for hate is a mixture of ignorance and fear. Hate left unchecked leads inexorably to disastrous consequences. A tiny spark of misunderstanding, flung upon the smoldering embers of hate, stoked by the hand of a sensationalistic press, and ignored by irresponsible law enforcement ignited a level of civil unrest unparalleled in American history.[143]

Out of rubble and ruin, new life may spring. "The Negro Wall Street" rose like a phoenix from the ashes of its own destruction. Tulsa's Greenwood District would not be denied.

History teaches only to the extent that it is known. The Riot has significance for all Americans. Beneath the surface calm, race and racism continue to complicate our lives. Even a volcano is, more often than not, calm on the surface, masking the destructive forces seething within. By remembering the Riot and learning its lessons, we may be able to avoid a similar eruption. Our shared history "[c]annot be unlived, but if faced . . . [w]ith courage, need not be lived again."[144]

On June 1, 1996, Tulsans, black and white, commemorated the Riot with a series of special ceremonies, most notably, the dedication of the "1921 Black Wall Street Memorial" to the Riot victims, both individuals and businesses. Mt. Zion Baptist Church, central to the history of African-American Tulsa and itself a victim of the Riot, hosted the ceremonies. Among the luminaries on hand for this public expression of collective cultural memory were Benjamin Hooks, then director of the NAACP; David Boren, University of Oklahoma president, former United States senator, and former Oklahoma governor; Tulsa Mayor M. Susan Savage; Scott Ellsworth, author of *Death in a Promised Land*; and Riot survivors LaVerne Cooksey Davis, Robert Fairchild, George Monroe, and Julius Williams. The healing had finally begun in earnest.

THE REGENERATION

Regeneration: A being renewed, reformed, or reconstituted.[1]

The Riot, for all its horrors, triggered a regeneration—a phenomenal display of courage and character—among Tulsa's beleaguered African-American citizens. Typical of this spirit is the story of Mabel and Pressley Little. Out of a single three-room shotgun house, Mabel ran a beauty parlor and Pressley operated a shoeshine shop.

Business boomed so fast we were forced [to] go searching for a bigger place. We located one in the downtown business section of North Tulsa (as the black community was called), at 612 Archer Street. We were glad to be on a paved street.

[T]he Lord blessed me and Pressley. At the time I am reckoning, we had worked hard to better ourselves, for seven long hard years. At the end of our efforts, we had two rental houses, a new beauty salon, a comfortable home, with five rooms of brand-new furniture. We thought we were sitting pretty.

In a matter of four days in the early summer of 1921, all went up in the runaway flames and smoke in the horror now known as the Tulsa Race Riot. We lost everything. . . .

In the end, we didn't get hardly any help from the white community. We had to save our own, use what small means we had, and cooperate together. Our top wages then were $5 to $10 a week, and we couldn't even borrow money. We had to cooperate together; there was no other choice. Little by little, we built our businesses back up—beauty shops, our own drug stores, grocery stores, our own barbershops, tailor shops, you name it.[2]

Tulsa's African-American community knew what it meant to take care of business, literally and figuratively. Like Mabel and Pressley Little, others in the community banded together to regain a portion of the economic prosperity they lost in the Riot. Despite all the forces working against them, including the unavailability of loans and the lack of insurance,[3] they refused to give up.

Among the other forces working against the crushed African-American community was the local press. The *Tulsa Tribune*, the local daily that had so inflamed the community by sensationalizing the Rowland/Page incident, once again showed its true colors. On Saturday, June 4, 1921, the *Tulsa Tribune* ran an editorial disparaging the Greenwood District and beseeching the community not to let it be rebuilt:

IT MUST NOT BE AGAIN

Such a district as the old "Niggertown" must never be allowed in Tulsa again. It was a cesspool of iniquity and corruption. It was the cesspool which had been pointed out specifically to the Tulsa police and to Police Commissioner Adkison, and they could see nothing in it. Yet anybody could go down there and buy all the booze they wanted. Anybody could go into the most unspeakable dance halls and base joints of prostitution. All this had been called to the attention of the police department and all the police department could do under the Mayor of this city was to whitewash itself. The Mayor of Tulsa is a perfectly nice, honest man, we do not doubt, but he is guileless. He could have found out himself any time in one night what just one preacher found out.

In this old "Niggertown" were a lot of bad niggers and a bad nigger is about the lowest thing that walks on two feet. Give a bad nigger his booze and his dope and a gun and he thinks he can shoot up the world. And all these four things were found in "Niggertown"—booze, dope, bad niggers and guns.

The Tulsa Tribune makes no apology to the Police Commissioner or to the Mayor of this city for having plead with them to clean up the cesspools of this city.

Commissioner Adkison had said that he knew of the growing agitation down in "Niggertown" some time ago and that he and the Chief of Police went down and told the negroes that if anything started they would be responsible.

That is first class conversation but rather weak action.

Well, the bad niggers started it. The public would now like to know: why wasn't it prevented? Why were these niggers not made to feel the force of the law and made to respect the law? Why were not the violators of the law in "Niggertown" arrested? Why were they allowed to go on in many ways defying the law? Why? Mr. Adkison, why?

The columns of The Tulsa Tribune are open to Mr. Adkison for any explanation he may wish to make.

Those bad niggers must now be held, and, what is more, the dope selling and booze and gun collection must STOP. The police commissioner, who has not the ability or the willingness to find what a preacher can find and who WON'T stop it when told of it, but merely whitewashes himself and talks of "knocking chairwarmers" had better be asked to resign by an outraged city.[4]

In the face of open hostility engendered by the *Tulsa Tribune* and others, the Greenwood District arose from the ashes, not magically, but by the blood, sweat, and tears of the determined African-American pioneers who called it home.

One institution has consistently steeled African-Americans against the external forces of oppression and the internal pressures of self-doubt: the African-American church. For that reason, it occupies a special place in American history. For many African-Americans, the church did much more than attend to spiritual needs. In Tulsa, in the state of Oklahoma, and in all of America, African-American churches condemned white supremacy, and preached social equality and social justice. Ministers and parishioners often became social activists, challenging and chiding white Christians for their failure to address racial injustices.[5] This perhaps contributed to that fate that befell several of Tulsa's African-American churches during the Riot and their pivotal role in the regeneration of Tulsa's beloved

Greenwood District thereafter. In the Greenwood District, the sacred and the secular somehow managed peaceably to coexist.

The hallowed halls of Tulsa's African-American churches proved to be no sanctuary from the riotous mobs. Among the damaged or destroyed African-American houses of worship were the Methodist Episcopal Church, the Colored Methodist Episcopal Church, the Seventh Day Adventist Church, Paradise Baptist Church, Metropolitan Baptist Church, Union Baptist Church, Mt. Zion Baptist Church, and the African Methodist Episcopal Church (now Vernon Chapel A. M. E.). Notably, First Baptist Church of North Tulsa was spared—spared because it was mistaken for a white church. Each church has its story. But the stories of the latter three churches, Mt. Zion Baptist Church, Vernon Chapel A. M. E., and First Baptist Church of North Tulsa—the "mother churches" of the African-American community—fairly encapsulate the spirit of Tulsa's pioneer African-Americans in the face of monumental challenges.

Mt. Zion Baptist Church, Tulsa's largest African-American church in 1921 with some 1,000 members, was torched during the Riot.[6] But the rioters could not snuff out the faith of its members. The saga of the church before, during, and after the Riot is nothing if not inspirational.

In 1909 Mt. Zion Baptist Church was organized as "Second Baptist Church" in a one-room wood frame school building. Under the leadership of Rev. Sandy Lyons, services were held on the 300 block of North Hartford. The founders—Reverend Lyons, Aaron Ellis, Kate Bell Baldridge, Rev. Alexander Brown, Georgia Brown, Cornelia Dallas, Mary A. Grayson, Hannah Hale, Jim Hale, Ella Bell Johnson, Caroline Lollis, Ella Suggs, Ida Rector, Jeanette E. Webb, Nellie Brown Wharton—were, for the most part, largely former members of First Baptist Church who, after internal squabbling, broke off from that congregation. The founders quickly concluded that the "Second" in the name Second Baptist Church conveyed a sense of inferiority that was, at best, inappropriate. Second Baptist Church became Mt. Zion Baptist Church.

"Mt. Zion" symbolizes the beautiful city of God in Christian lore.[7] One stanza of gospel singer Mahalia Jackson's classic recording of "I Will Move On Up A Little Higher" captures the beauty and majesty that is Zion:

> Soon as my feet strike Zion,
> Gonna lay down my heavy burden.
> I'm gonna put on my robe in glory,
> I'm goin' home one day—tell my story.
> I've been climbing over hills and mountains,
> I'm gonna drink from the Christian fountain.
> You know all of God's sons and daughters that mornin',
> Will drink that old healing water.
> Meet me there early one mornin',
> Meet me there somewhere 'round the altar.
> Meet me there—
> Oh, when the angels shall call God's roll.[8]

Despite the grandeur of its namesake, Mt. Zion Baptist Church began modestly. The first $20 for operating the church came from Deacon Aaron Ellis. Reverend Lyons soon resigned, setting off a succession of leadership changes. Reverend Lyons passed the baton to Rev. T. L. Leonard, who in turn passed it to the next pastor, Rev. C. L. Netherland. In 1913 Rev. Frank White took the reins. Still growing, the church desperately needed additional space, and purchased property at 419 North Elgin. In ill health, Reverend White resigned in 1914 and was replaced by Rev. R. A. Whitaker.

Reverend Whitaker faced an immediate crisis. On three days' notice, Mt. Zion Baptist Church was forced to vacate the school in which it held services. The church moved into a dance hall on North Greenwood Avenue. C. Henry, a builder in the community, assisted the church in the construction of a frame structure simply known as the "Tabernacle," while construction of the actual church began on the adjacent lot on North Elgin.

Years of planning had gone into the new church. The congregation had accumulated some $42,000, but the cost of the new building approached a whopping $92,000. The church accepted the offer of an unsecured $50,000 loan from a Jewish contractor.

In 1916, with an initial investment of $750.15, builders laid the foundation for the new church. Five years later and $50,000 in hock, the $92,000 religious edifice was completed. An enthusiastic congregation held its first services on April 4, 1921. But the triumph of the moment masked a tragedy in the making.

Prior to the Riot, rumors circulated among whites that Mt. Zion Baptist Church housed a cache of weapons and served as the planning headquarters for the beleaguered and besieged African-American community. On the strength of these rumors, Mt. Zion (and some twenty-three other houses of worship) went up in smoke.

Afraid, shell-shocked, and shaken, Mt. Zion members gathered within the ruins for prayer and damage assessment. The church was a total loss. There was insurance, but the insurance policy contained an exclusion for damage occasioned by an "act of riot." A few members left the flock, but most took a vow of solidarity. Church members voted unanimously not to file for bankruptcy protection from creditors. The outstanding debt on a church building that no longer existed would nonetheless be repaid. Church members began the long and arduous task, on evenings and weekends, of clearing the debris and readying the site for rebuilding.

Charles Page, a wealthy oilman from Sand Springs, Oklahoma, heard about the plight of Mt. Zion. Page offered to donate the bricks for the rebuilding, but he died before the gift was made. No written record of his commitment existed. The bricks were never delivered.

For five years, Reverend Whitaker led his congregation along the path toward the liquidation of the debt. Before a new church could be built, the indebtedness had to be accounted for in full.

Sick, emotionally drained, and burdened by criticism from within, Reverend Whitaker resigned involuntarily. More members of Mt. Zion slipped away. The obvious difficulty of recruiting a new pastor amid the internal tumult and the impending financial crisis caused by the still-owed mortgage threatened the very survival of Mt. Zion.

A rapid succession of ministers followed: Reverends N. C. Randall, Jim Yates, Willie Drew, and A. L. Grant came and went. At times, Mt. Zion simply managed without a pastor. Facing imminent foreclosure, generous benefactors saved Mt. Zion from the throes of ruin. Mr. and Mrs. James H. Goodwin lifted the contested mortgage.

Rev. C. A. Hamilton arrived at Mt. Zion in 1926. Like a dark cloud, Mt. Zion's substantial debt loomed in the minds of its members, causing constant controversy. Reverend Hamilton felt that the $50,000 debt could be eliminated; after all, there was no formal "legal" obligation—the money owed came as the result of a "good faith" transaction. The deacons and trustees disagreed, citing a moral imperative to repay the debt. The church split virtually down the middle. Reverend Hamilton resigned in 1928 and established New Hope Baptist Church. He took droves of Mt. Zion members with him.

The weakened congregation and the ever-present debt led to the padlocking of the church. For a period, Mt. Zion members worshiped in the home of Mabel B. Little. Finally, the legal issues were settled in court, and the church reopened.

Rev. W. E. Bradford led the church from 1929 through 1934, longer than any of his predecessors. He united the church and shepherded the congregation through the depths of the Great Depression, then, because of failing health, resigned. He was succeeded by Rev. H. E. Owens, who served from 1935 through 1937. Ironically, Reverend Owens came from First Baptist Church, Mt. Zion's "birth mother." Reverend Owens' tenure witnessed the roofing of a dirt floor basement, the assembly of makeshift pews, and a substantial reduction in the church's debt. Mt. Zion pressed on, though the mortgage payments lagged further and further in arrears. Architects W. S. and J. C. Latimer, brothers, graduates of Tuskegee Institute, and members of Mt. Zion, drafted plans for the new, more expansive, and more expensive, Mt. Zion.

In 1937, six months after Rev. J. H. Dotson was installed as the new Mt. Zion pastor, sixty new members joined the church and $3,000 was raised. Reverend Dotson instituted a new fundraising initiative: the "White Elephants Drive." The whiteness of each of the elephants represented a debt of $1,500. Brown patches used to cover the white elephants cost $3.25 each. It took 104 patches to cover each elephant. When all of the white elephants were covered in brown, the debt would be retired.

The success of the White Elephants Drive led to yet another

initiative: the "Envelope System." Each member was given fifty-two envelopes for weekly donations throughout the year. In addition, the "Joash Chest" initiative also assisted in funding the building drive. The Joash Chest, still evident today at Mt. Zion, is a large rough box trimmed in tin bands. Members are asked to deposit at least a dollar a week in the box.

Church improvements continued and a new parsonage was built and dedicated. In fifteen months, $7,500 had been raised and 116 new members joined the rolls of the church. On November 23, 1942, the mortgage on the first structure was paid in full.

In 1945, *Time* magazine picked up on a story by long-time North Tulsa resident and *Tulsa World* reporter Merle Blakey:

> One spring night in 1921, flames completely destroyed the new $92,000 Mount Zion Baptist Church. It had taken the church's 600 members seven years to finance and build their first church. There was an out: the congregation could go into bankruptcy, default on the debt and start over. But they decided to pay. First, money was raised for a brick, dirt-floor, basement: it would be the foundation of a new church building. It took 21 years—until Nov. 23, 1942. The two hundred and thirty-six pound, pulpit-filling Reverend J. H. Dotson promptly started a building fund. He installed three small boxes near the door for contributions. The plan worked well. After that, bit by bit, still paying as they go, Mount Zion's members will complete their $150,000 building, a monument to patient perseverance—and a quietly Christian rebuke to racial intolerance.

Plans for the new structure were well under way. In ten years the abstract plans would become concrete reality. Meanwhile, the media attention paid to the inspiring Mt. Zion story precipitated contributions to Mt. Zion from all across the nation.

On Sunday, October 21, 1952, dedication services for the new building were held. The cost of the structure had by then risen to a whopping $300,000. Nearly a year later, Reverend Dotson's health began to fail. Many speculated that his hands-on supervision of every detail of the construction of the new church had taken its toll.

Mt. Zion Baptist Church. (Photo courtesy of Goodrum Photography, 1997)

On August 16, 1953, a young, educated minister from Kentucky accepted the assistant pastorship at Mt. Zion, providing some relief for Reverend Dotson. The young minister, Rev. G. Calvin McCutchen, took the reins when Reverend Dotson retired.

Reverend McCutchen preached his first sermon on October 20, 1957, and was installed as pastor on January 12, 1958. Under his leadership, Mt. Zion established a nursery, hired a secretary, embarked on new fund-raising projects, and made numerous enhancements, some substantial, to the Mt. Zion facilities.

Mt. Zion Baptist Church remains a living testament to the power of faith and hope and perseverance. It is a monument to the human spirit—a historical marker at the opposite end of the spectrum from the Riot.[9]

Vernon Chapel African Methodist Episcopal (A.M.E) Church. (Photo courtesy of Goodrum Photography, 1997)

Yet another "mother church" in the Greenwood District endured the Riot and thrives to this very day. In 1905 African-American pioneers brought African Methodism to Tulsa. Tulsa's first African Methodist Episcopal (A.M.E.) church operated out of a one-room house at 549 North Detroit. Charter members J. J. Byrd, William Walker, Emma Lofton Woods, Maggie Vaden, Carrie Peck, Marie Barksdale, Mary Ivory, and Laura Martin began the A.M.E. tradition in Tulsa.

In 1906 the church moved briefly to Gurley Hall, located at 114 North Greenwood Avenue, then to Barksdale Hall at Archer and Hartford streets. Membership increased, and the church counted seventy-one souls among its number by 1908. Members named the church "Burton Chapel." Shortly thereafter, church trustees made a down payment toward the purchase of the

Vernon Chapel A.M.E meeting. On front row, third and fourth from left, respectively, are Rev. Benjamin Harrison Hill and his wife, Fannie Hill. (September 13, 1961). (Photo courtesy of the North Tulsa Heritage Foundation, Inc.)

present church site at 309 North Greenwood Avenue. The name of the church was changed to "Vernon Chapel."

In 1914 the old church came tumbling down. In its stead, a brick basement was fully funded and built. Then came the Riot. The entire new Vernon Chapel structure lay in ruins. Seared by the loss but determined to press on, church members raised the $3,100 needed to rebuild the basement and adorned the structure with suitable furniture. Pastor P. W. Delyle and his family lived there. Membership continued to rise, and had reached 216 by 1922 and 400 by 1925. Church trustees and members laid out plans to raise enough money to complete the church building. Donations of cash, labor, and materials were secured, and the church obtained a mortgage. The new structure, adorned with freshly hewn wooden pews and pulpit furniture, played host to significant religious gatherings.

By 1940, membership rose to 800. By 1945, all indebtedness had been retired. And by the late 1950s, various clubs and organizations had been established within this community-minded church.

One of Vernon Chapel's most celebrated contributions to the Greenwood District and to Tulsa was its noted pastor through the 1960s, Rev. Ben H. Hill. Reverend Hill, an editor of *The Oklahoma Eagle*, the *A.M.E. Review*, and the *Vernon Digest*, was a leader of the first magnitude in the community, the city, and the state. Indeed, Reverend Hill became an Oklahoma state representative in 1968 and served in that capacity until his death in 1971.

By 1974, Vernon Chapel had purchased one block north and one block south of its building. The church initiated pulpit exchanges with other congregations (i.e., arrangements whereby ministers literally switched congregations on a given Sabbath). Additional improvements to the church were made in the following years. In 1994 a major renovation project began, led by the new minister, Rev. Isaac Nelson Hudson, Jr. The new facilities were dedicated in ceremonies on November 4, 1995. Vernon Chapel remains a pillar of the Greenwood District, steeped in history and courage and faith.[10]

First Baptist Church of North Tulsa is the third and final of the "mother churches" of the Greenwood District. Begun in 1899 by H. B. Lollis, Robert Grayson, and James Grayson, and

First Baptist Church of North Tulsa. (Photo courtesy of Goodrum Photography, 1997)

originally called Macedonia Baptist Church, it is the oldest African-American church in Tulsa. Rev. J. A. Duncan was its first minister, and George Terrill and Henry Clay its first deacons. The small congregation, in an ecumenical spirit, invited Methodists in the community to share the same worship facility. One of those joint worship services took place in a building on the corner of First Street and Boston Avenue in downtown Tulsa, now home to The Williams Center. After three-and-one-half years, Rev. James Smith succeeded Reverend Duncan. In 1907 Rev. Charles L. Netherland took the reins. During Reverend Netherland's tenure, the congregation changed its name from Macedonia Baptist Church to First Baptist Church. Membership grew and church facilities were enhanced.

Rev. Sandy Lyons succeeded Reverend Netherland. Dissension in the church grew, and eventually the congregation split. Part of the congregation left and founded Second Baptist Church, which later became Mt. Zion Baptist Church. Rev. G. L. Prince took over the pastorate of First Baptist Church for a brief period.

Dissension in the ranks once again set in. A succession of ministers followed. Eventually, under the pastorate of Rev. J. F. Kirsh, another church split occurred. Those who left formed Metropolitan Baptist Church.

Rev. J. H. Abernathy took over in 1917. Negotiations were begun to construct "The Church on the Hill" on Archer Street at a cost of $60,000. The old building was razed and work began on the new structure in April 1918.

First Baptist Church, the former "church home" of many of Mt. Zion's initial members, escaped the Riot unscathed. Mt. Zion lay gutted, as did Vernon Chapel and several other congregations. But rioters mistook First Baptist Church for a white church, as it bordered a white residential district. Nevertheless, members of the church were just as affected by the Riot as all other African-Americans in Tulsa. Stunned and saddened, they passed a poignant resolution commending the American Red Cross on its heroic efforts in the aftermath of the Riot:

> On the 31st night in May, 1921, the fiercest race war known
> in American history broke out, lasting until the next morning,

June 1st, 1921. As a result of the regrettable occurrence, many human lives were lost and millions of dollars worth of property was stolen and burned. Hundreds of innocent Negroes suffered as a result of this calamity—suffered in loss of lives, injury from gunshot wounds, and loss of property. Many of us were left helpless and almost hopeless. We sat among the wrack and ruin of our former homes and peered listlessly into space. It was at this time and under such conditions that the American Red Cross— that Angel of love and mercy—came to our assistance. This great organization found us bruised and bleeding, and like the good Samaritan, she washed our wounds, and administered unto us. Constantly, in season and out, since this regrettable occurrence, this great organization, headed by that high class Christian gentleman, Maurice Willows, has heard our every cry in this our dark hour and has extended to us practical sympathy, as best she could, with food and medication and shelter she has furnished us. And to this great Christian organization our heartfelt gratitude is extended.

Therefore be it resolved that we, representing the entire colored citizenship of the city of Tulsa, Oklahoma, take this means of extending to the American Red Cross, through Mr. Willows, our heartfelt thanks for the work it has done and is continuing to do for us in this our great hour of need.

Resolved further that a copy of these resolutions be sent to the American Red Cross Headquarters, a copy be mailed to Mr. Willows and co-workers.[11]

Reverend Abernathy departed in 1922, and after financial strain overwhelmed the church, returned shortly thereafter. He again departed in 1924. Rev. Hosea E. Owens succeeded him. Reverend Owens remained at First Baptist Church for ten years. When he departed in 1934, the church stood free and clear of indebtedness.

Rev. William P. Mitchell succeeded Reverend Owens, and continued along the course of putting the church on firm financial footing. He was succeeded by Rev. Calvin K. Stalnaker, who completed Reverend Mitchell's plans for a new church. On May 3, 1953, the new First Baptist Church on Greenwood Avenue was completed. The church held its mortgage burning celebration for the $305,000 facility in September of 1957. Reverend Stalnaker retired on December 31, 1961, and was replaced by

Rev. Leroy K. Jordan, unanimously confirmed as pastor on February 23, 1962.

Reverend Jordan became a Tulsa legend for his community leadership, compassion, and vision. When he retired in 1994, interim pastor Rev. Chester Wilson filled the void. In 1996 Dr. J. W. Johnson became pastor.

First Baptist Church of North Tulsa occupies three city blocks in the Greenwood District. In addition, the church owns and operates a complex of single and multi-family apartments for the elderly and the disabled.[12]

The three mother churches of the Greenwood District—Mt. Zion Baptist Church, Vernon Chapel A. M. E., and First Baptist Church of North Tulsa, share a common legacy of leadership in Tulsa's African-American community. Ironically, the Riot helped mold these solid-as-a-rock institutions into the pillars of the community they have become.

Like the African-American churches, individuals and institutions in the community stepped in to assist in the Greenwood District recovery effort. Notable among them was a group of courageous lawyers. Just after the Riot, the law firm of Spears, Franklin & Chappelle was formed. As a testament to the devastation of the Riot, the firm initially pitched a tent at 607 East Archer and called it a law office. This makeshift office hardly befit the brilliant young minds who occupied it. These three men spent countless hours tending not just to the legal needs of the Riot victims, but to some of their spiritual needs as well. Spears, Franklin & Chappelle lodged more than $4 million in claims against the City of Tulsa and various insurance companies for property damage arising out of the Riot. The firm counseled, consoled, and comforted literally thousands of dazed Riot victims, advised prominent African-American organizations throughout the country of the catastrophic devastation in Tulsa's Greenwood District, and made an urgent nationwide appeal for assistance.

In November of 1921, Spears, Franklin & Chappelle moved from its modest tent-office into a permanent office located at 107½ North Greenwood, on the second floor of the Howard Building. The three lawyers worked tirelessly, but they found time to enjoy themselves and to entertain others. They accepted

Attorney B. C. Franklin (right) and associates set up office in a tent after the 1921 Tulsa Race Riot. Franklin and associates successfully overturned a City of Tulsa fire ordinance that would have made rebuilding in the Greenwood District cost-prohibitive. (Photo courtesy of the North Tulsa Heritage Foundation, Inc.)

all comers, with one exception: there would be no tolerance for self-pity. For them, the misery all around them stopped at the office door. Their office became a safe haven, providing respite from the harsh reality all around.

On August 13, 1921, Spears, Franklin & Chappelle filed suit in district court to enjoin the enforcement of an ordinance passed by the Tulsa City Commission in June of that year. The ordinance made rebuilding in the Riot-scorched Greenwood District cost-prohibitive for most African-Americans. The district court case was *Joe Lockard vs. the City of Tulsa*. Joe Lockard sought legal authority to rebuild on his property and, more importantly, to enjoin the post-Riot City of Tulsa fire ordinance. The court declared that the ordinance constituted an invalid taking of property without due process of law.[13] The firm also assisted, free of charge, African-Americans arrested for and charged with violating other existing fire ordinances during this rebuilding phase in the Greenwood District.[14]

In addition to dedicated professionals such as the Spears, Franklin & Chappelle law firm, a determined group of African-American entrepreneurs vowed to fight hate with hope, destruction with dedication. Through their valiant efforts and clarity of vision, much of the Greenwood District underwent massive reconstruction in 1922. The rebuilding was a textbook lesson in self-help. Few in the greater Tulsa community bothered to offer assistance of any significance in the rebuilding effort.

The reconstruction of "The Negro Wall Street" after the Tulsa Race Riot of 1921, particularly that of Deep Greenwood, was nothing if not remarkable. Perhaps more than anything else, this rebuilding evidenced the determination of Tulsa's African-American pioneers to persevere, even in the face of seemingly insurmountable odds, in their struggle for freedom and economic independence.

Wilhelmina Guess Howell, an elementary schoolteacher in Tulsa for four decades and the niece of Dr. A. C. Jackson, the nationally renowned African-American surgeon killed in the Riot, recalled: "[My father] went off to Howard University in Washington, D. C. to become a lawyer. Then he returned to Tulsa to devote his life to helping his people. When the riot burned down his office, he rebuilt it and continued to practice law until his death in 1931."[15]

Another Riot survivor, Juanita Alexander Lewis Hopkins, also recalled the phoenix-like quality of the Greenwood District: "After the Riot, Tulsa rebuilt from the ashes. In fact, [the Greenwood District] after the riot was even more impressive than before the riot. . . .There are so many stories to be told about [the Greenwood District] and its determined people—about its struggles with racism, about its creativity, adaption, and survival."[16]

As a testament to the resilience and self-sufficiency of Tulsa's African-American community, the rebuilding began even as the ashes flickered. By 1922, the rebuilding of Deep Greenwood was well under way. More than half of the destroyed churches began to hold worship services again. More than eighty

Twenty-sixth annual meeting of the National Negro Business League, August 1925, Tulsa, Oklahoma. (Photo courtesy of Norman and Eddie Faye Gates)

businesses in the Greenwood District reopened. "The Negro Wall Street" (later referred to as the "Black Wall Street of America," reflecting the African-American community's changing sociopolitical identification) was well on its way to reclaiming its national reputation as an African-American business center par excellence. The burned-out shells of the pre-Riot structures were for the most part torn down. Many of the new buildings, however, assumed the forms of their predecessors. The 1922 Williams Building, for example, bore a great resemblance to its pre-1921 structure. The red bricks used in the reconstruction came from the local brickyard located on Standpipe Hill, two blocks north of Greenwood Avenue.

Few of the affected property owners had insurance. Those who did were notified that unless they could prove that either the city or the state was negligent in the protection of their property, the insurance policy would be void. Given the realities of race relations, this proved an impossible task. What is more, the insurance companies disclaimed liability for fires caused by rioting or civil insurrections.

Some whites, cognizant of the plight of African-American property owners and eager to take advantage, attempted to purchase the scorched real estate at far below market value. Adjutant General Charles F. Barrett, commander of the Oklahoma National Guard, halted the practice by ordering the county registrar of deeds to stop the registration of titles from the blighted area.[17]

The view of the Greenwood District from an outsider after the Riot and during the rebuilding phase was captured by George W. Buckner, special representative of the National Urban League, in the article "Second View of City of Ruins":

> "Wonderful" is the spontaneous acclaim of anyone who visits Tulsa today after seeing the burned area immediately following the disaster there June 1st of last year. The former business sections which consisted largely of Greenwood Avenue has been transformed from ragged, unsightly walls to modern structures where small, thriving businesses of every kind are meeting the needs of the people. The formed [sic] residential sections which resembled a camp of soldiers in war, having been covered with tents and improvised shacks, are now being

rapidly replaced by more substantial homes. But very few of the tents furnished by the Red Cross now remain. So much for a hasty material perspective. What about the spirit now mani-fested by the Negroes? Let if be said unreservedly that the spirit exhibited from the beginning by the Tulsa Negroes, on the whole, should be the pride of the whole race. Under the most cruel and soul-crushing conditions they have simply put their backs against the wall determined to die, if needs be, in Tulsa. One well-to-do man epitomized the general feeling when he said, "I told one of the commissioners the other day when he asked me what I was going to do, that I was going to start over right here in Tulsa where I started before." Most of the people who had acquired property at all had secured it there. It is but natural, therefore, that they felt bound to their home. With this feeling the Negroes have succeeded in squelching the agitation about taking their land for industrial purposes. They have succeeded in preventing the fire zone from being extended, and in winning to their cause many of the prominent white people.[18]

Tulsa's own "East End Relief Committee" expressed a simi-lar sentiment about the resilient African-American spirit in a let-ter to the American Red Cross:

The courage with which Tulsa Negroes withstood repeated attempts of the city administration to deliver the "burned area" over to certain land grafters is the subject of most favorable comment all over the country. The rapidity with which business buildings and residences are being rebuilt, in most instances, better than before is proof in wood and brick and in stone, of the black man's ability to make progress against the most cun-ningly planned and powerfully organized opposition.[19]

Sam and Lucy Mackey's white frame dream house was one of the more than 1,000 homes destroyed in the Riot. The Mackeys built the house in 1915 after mortgaging their house at 356 North Greenwood Avenue. In 1926, with the support of an employer, the couple mortgaged their property for $6,500 to the Oklahoma City Building and Loan Association. No Tulsa bank or lending institution would make loans in the Riot-marred Greenwood District. The Mackeys built a new, red brick, fireproof home. The builders used no wood framing in its construction. In 1930 the Mackeys paid off the mortgage on the house and borrowed $9,000 from C. A. Hereford to make home improvements. The house remained in the Mackey family until purchased by the Tulsa Urban Renewal Authority in the 1970s. Substantially restored, it is now the "Mabel B. Little Heritage House."

Many outstanding individuals and prominent establishments graced the Greenwood District through the years. For so long, the Greenwood District boomed. A stroll through the Greenwood District during its heyday—the 1920s through the 1950s—reveals a glimmer of the vast array of goods and services available to African-Americans in their own community.

In the blocks of Greenwood Avenue and Archer Street were the offices of Drs. Patrick, Payne, and Lythcott. Dr. Lythcott, an ear, nose, and throat specialist, doubled as a gynecologist/obstetrician. The Royal Hotel, owned by Simon Berry, sat across the street. As previously noted, Berry built Tulsa's first (and at the time the only) public park available to African-Americans and founded a jitney/bus service in the African-American community, later sold to the City of Tulsa. Two morticians and their wives, Sam and Eunice Jackson and Escoe and Bertha Jackson, owned the Jackson Funeral Home next door to the Royal Hotel. Down the street on Archer sat Williams Garage, owned by the Williams family.

Nearby were Clarence Love's Lounge, a popular night spot, the Small Hotel, Spinner Cafe, a grocery story, a Swedish bath house, and a bowling alley. Still farther down was Leona Corbett's dress shop, Neal's Jewelry, Spann's Pool Hall, Warren's Cafe, and the offices of Dr. A. G. Bacoats, attorney Amos T. Hall, and attorney Primus Wade. In the same vicinity were the offices of *The Oklahoma Eagle* newspaper, American Business College, L. H. Williams Drugstore, Caver's Cleaners, Swindall and Joe Bullock barber shops, the Dreamland Theatre (owned by Lulu Williams), the Owl Tavern, Roy Johnson's Pool Hall, Isaac Rebuilders, a U. S. Post Office substation, Sam McGowan Variety Store, Boulware Grocery Store, Walter Grayson Realty, and the E. L. Goodwin popcorn stand.

Across the street was Diggs barber shop, Neely & Vaden Pool Hall, Walter Tate Electric Shop & Recreation Parlor, the Calypso and Bonneville clubs, Art's Chili Parlor, the Flamingo nightclub, Smith's Grocery and Confectionery, Kyle's Drugstore, and

Archer Street at Greenwood Avenue looking north in 1938. (Photo courtesy of the North Tulsa Heritage Foundation, Inc.)

several beauty shops. The Sunset, Rainbow, Ritz, and Your Cab companies kept things moving along. Attorney Buck C. Franklin, father of world-renowned historian, author, and humanitarian Dr. John Hope Franklin, had an office just to the north.

Residents of the Greenwood District could meet their daily needs yet still patronize black-owned businesses in the community. There was Mrs. Weaver's Flower Shop, Holloway's grocery, Williams Drugstore, and the offices of Dr. E. L. Hairston, a dentist. Dr. Charles Bate occupied an office above Holloway's grocery.

Alexander's Barbeque and the Jarrett family neighborhood grocery were popular establishments. Earl Cissel owned a cleaning establishment. There were others, many others, who distinguished themselves in the Greenwood District. Though many are long gone, the memory of these Greenwood District entrepreneurs lives on.[20]

The Greenwood District prospered through the Great Depression of the early 1930s and through the latter part of that decade. In 1938 a group of concerned African-American men led by E. W. Clarke met for the express purpose of forming an organization dedicated to African-American participation in the areas of business, civic, and social activity. Joining Clarke were, among others, prominent Tulsans J. T. A. West, Amos T. Hall, F. Melvin Payne, E. L. Goodwin, M. M. Mann, J. Hughes, B. A. Waynes, Thomas R. Gentry, Robert Fairchild, and Rev. J. N. Wallace. These men had all borne witness to the Riot. Many of them had urged African-Americans to stay the course and remain in Tulsa after the devastation wrought by the Riot.

E. W. Clarke, elected president of the group by a unanimous vote, spoke eloquently of the role of the newly formed Greenwood Chamber of Commerce: "If the Chamber means anything at all it must stand out as a clearing house for civic betterment. Divorced of [p]olitical and [s]ectarian affiliation, the Greenwood Chamber of Commerce shall be limited only by its ultimate resources to serve the people of Tulsa." Today, the Greenwood Chamber remains committed to spurring economic development in the Greenwood District, as well as in other areas of Tulsa's African-American community.[21]

World War II and the precipitous upturn in demand for war-related goods generated so-called "war industries." That brought even more prosperity to Tulsa. An African-American business directory listed more than 400 businesses in the Greenwood

Ramsey Drug Store, 1202 North Greenwood Avenue, one of the many businesses in the Greenwood District, circa 1945. (Photo courtesy of Marian Jones)

District in the early 1940s. Riot survivor Juanita Alexander Lewis Hopkins recalled Greenwood's glory days with nostalgia:

> Oh what a history Tulsa has! When Greenwood was in its hey-day there were ten black hotels in the Archer/Greenwood area, numerous drug stores, grocery stores, cleaners, shoe shops, millinery and dress shops, tailor shops, pool halls, theaters funeral homes, doctors' and lawyers' offices, restaurants, and schools in the area. There were unskilled, semi-skilled, and professional people coexisting side by side—barbers and hair-dressers, businessmen and professionals, and black policemen, including my father C. J. Alexander who was one of Tulsa's first black policemen. There were mostly good people, but there were some "underworld" characters, too, mainly boot-leggers and numbers runners. There were cultivated, sophisti-cated black people, there were working class, salt-of-the-earth people, and there were a few eccentrics and "crazy" people.[22]

The end of World War II in 1945 closed some of the limit-ed windows of opportunity it had opened. Moreover, it marked another watershed moment for the Greenwood District—the beginning of a slow but steady downward spiral.

The participation of some 1.2 million African-Americans in World War II heightened expectations and aroused hope for a swift end to the unrelenting apartheid-like conditions African-Americans faced at home. But America remained as seg-regated as the military in which they had served during the war. Thwarted expectations and dashed hopes weighed heavily on the minds of these African-American patriots who returned home to face conditions no better, and perhaps in some ways worse, than when they left. Immigrant laborers competed with them for jobs. Some whites resented even the meager honors these repatriated warriors received. Famed author and essayist James Baldwin said it best:

> The treatment accorded the Negro during the Second World War marks, for me, a turning point in the Negro's relation to America. To put it briefly, and somewhat too simply, a certain hope died. . . . You must put yourself in the skin of a man who is wearing the uniform of his country, is a candidate for death in its defense, and who is called a "nigger" by his comrades-in-

arms and his officers; who is almost always given the hardest, ugliest, most menial work to do; who knows that the white G. I. has informed the European that he is subhuman . . . ; who does not dance at the U. S. O. the night white soldiers dance there, and does not drink in the same bars white soldiers drink in; and who watches German prisoners of war being treated by Americans with more human dignity than he has ever received at their hands. And who, at the same time, as a human being, is far freer in a strange land than he has ever been at home. Home! The very word begins to have a despairing and diabolical ring. You must consider what happens to this citizen, after all he has endured, when he returns—home: search, in his shoes, for a job, for a place to live; ride, in his skin, on segregated buses; see, with his eyes, the signs saying "White" and "Colored," and especially the signs that say "White Ladies" and "Colored Women"; look into the eyes of his wife; look into the eyes of his son; listen, with his ears, to political speeches, North and South; imagine yourself being told "wait." And all this happening in the richest and freest country in world, and in the middle of the twentieth century. The subtle and deadly change of heart that might occur in you would be involved with the realization that a civilization is not destroyed by the wicked people; it is not necessary that people be wicked but only that they be spineless.[23]

Baldwin eloquently expressed the sense of frustration and betrayal that black veterans (and, indeed, the black community in general) felt after World War II. Returning home to second-class citizenship seemed hardly a fitting fate for American patriots who risked life and limb for their country. But back in the States, precious little had changed by the war's end.

Tulsa continued to prosper long after World War II ended. The defense plants spawned auxiliary industries. Those industries spurred the growth of ancillary manufacturing concerns. Workers transitioning from war industries found employment in new factories. Attractive employment conditions lured rural Oklahomans into Tulsa. But Tulsa's African-Americans did not partake equally in the economic boom their city experienced. Despite persistent labor shortages, African-Americans faced rampant employment discrimination. They remained largely in unskilled, low-wage positions, if employed at all, with little prospect of advancement. The African-American community in Tulsa and with it the vital Greenwood District, home to scores of bustling black-owned businesses, had to compete with incompatible land uses, particularly industrial development in the area, as a result of a zoning change dating back to 1923. Community development suffered.[24]

Socially, Tulsa remained segregated. Retired University of Tulsa Professor of Sociology and attorney Nancy Feldman recalls an incident at a 1947 bar association meeting in Tulsa. Women and African-Americans, scarce amongst the ranks of the bar at the time, felt isolated within their own profession. Ms. Feldman, then a young, Jewish, Chicago-trained lawyer, invited her dear friend, Primus Wade, a well-known African-American attorney, to have lunch with her prior to this particular bar association meeting. Mr. Wade anxiously agreed. But the pair soon realized that there were few public eateries in Tulsa where a white woman and a black man could have lunch together. After giving the matter some careful thought, Ms. Feldman and Mr. Wade decided to have a picnic lunch down on the banks of the Arkansas River. At the time, there were no benches, picnic tables, or other amenities. But the Arkansas River knew nothing of color. It would be an acceptable meeting place.

After a pleasant lunch, the two headed for the Mayo Hotel in downtown Tulsa, the site of the bar association meeting. The gathering, they discovered, was being held on the sixteenth floor. As they approached the elevator, the attendant intervened. She refused to transport Mr. Wade to the sixteenth floor. African-Americans were not welcome on the Mayo Hotel elevator, it seemed. Undaunted and ever polite, Ms. Feldman and Mr. Wade stepped back and evaluated the options. Mr. Wade, noticing a large pin that adorned Ms. Feldman's dress, got an idea. He asked to borrow the pin. Ms. Feldman surrendered it. Mr. Wade then asked a member of the hotel staff if he could borrow a white linen napkin. Having secured both pin and napkin, Mr. Wade dexterously wrapped his head with the napkin, then affixed the pin to hold his makeshift headdress in place. On the second approach to the elevator, the operator obliged, assuming Mr. Wade to be some important foreign potentate, not just an ordinary "Negro." Ms. Feldman and Mr. Wade made their way to the bar association meeting, perhaps indignant, but with dignity intact.[25]

Despite black-white economic disparities and a gradual decline beginning in the mid-1940s, Tulsa's Greenwood District remained, relatively speaking, a sight to behold. Rev. Calvin G. McCutchen, pastor of Mt. Zion Baptist Church, arrived in Tulsa in 1953. He had lived previously in Louisville, Kentucky, Cincinnati, Ohio, and Nashville, Tennessee, yet he had never seen anything like the Greenwood District. Lined with bustling business, the Greenwood District seemed to have everything— drugstores, movie houses, groceries, pharmacies, and more. But Reverend McCutchen noticed that most of the shops were "one-horse" operations. He quickly discovered, through a personal experience just after arriving in Tulsa, that segregation played an important role in the viability of the black-owned Greenwood District businesses.

Fond of neckties and new to Tulsa at the time, Reverend McCutchen set out one afternoon on a downtown Tulsa shopping expedition. A tie on a mannequin in the window of a well-known local downtown clothier caught his fancy. He went into the store to get a closer look. Staring intently at the tie and that man-nequin, Reverend McCutchen waited for assistance from a clerk. But too much time elapsed. There was something amiss. Reverend McCutchen finally realized, after being ignored for twenty minutes, that he simply was not welcome there. It was not a matter of money. It was a matter of race. When he told an African-American friend about the experience, the friend replied matter-of-factly: "You weren't supposed to be in that store." Reverend McCutchen, the friend implied, needed to learn to play the social game by Tulsa's cultural rules. Because segrega-tion had not been so strictly enforced in Nashville, his prior home, he was simply unprepared.[26] Reverend McCutchen went on to take a leading role in future civil rights activities in Tulsa.

The emotion, pride, and goodwill associated with the Greenwood District continued unabated. These passions notwithstanding, the 1950s were a time of continued decay and decline for the Greenwood District. Many of the pioneers who had made it all happen were by now aged, retired, or deceased. Sam and Lucy Mackey, owners of one of the Greenwood

District's showplace residences, had divorced. The Williams Dreamland Theater, an early landmark, fell on hard times and closed. By the end of the decade, more than half of the businesses were abandoned or closed. Stable employment during the war years had provided new opportunities for home ownership. The rooming house, a source of progress just after the turn of the century, became virtually obsolete in the 1950s. Ironically, the civil rights actions of some Tulsans that broke down racial barriers helped to break the back of the Greenwood District.

As part of the struggle to gain a measure of economic equality for African-American Tulsans, plans for the establishment of an affiliate of the National Urban League began to take shape in 1951. The National Urban League, established in 1911, is an interracial organization committed to dismantling race-based social and economic disparities in America. Its original mission was to assist African-Americans who were migrating to large urban centers in increasing numbers. Dr. Norvell Coots spearheaded the drive to establish a National Urban League affiliate in Tulsa.

The National Urban League conducted a feasibility study of the proposed Tulsa affiliate. Community leaders formed the National Urban League Project Council on April 9, 1953, as a "trial run." The council received contributions for operational expenses from supportive individuals, but two organizations, the Prince Hall Masons and the Greenwood Chamber of Commerce, provided sizable donations—$2,000 each. Marion M. Taylor served as the executive director of the council and council members included: L. H. Williams (president); J. T. A. West (vice-president); Dr. Norvell Coots (treasurer); E. W. Clarke; Father Cecil Cowan; E. L. Goodwin; Amos T. Hall; and Lynn Holderness.

The National Urban League officially chartered the Metropolitan Tulsa Urban League, Inc., in 1954. The Tulsa affiliate began with a board of directors numbering twenty-eight, evenly split between whites and blacks. Initial officers were James P. Malone, president; Lloyd H. Williams, first vice-president; Julius Livingston, second vice-president; and Mable Lynch, recording secretary. To this day, the Metropolitan Tulsa Urban League champions the cause of social and economic justice in the Tulsa community.[27]

Like the Metropolitan Tulsa Urban League, Inc., the NAACP played a prominent and pivotal role in shaping Tulsa's African-American community. Its span of influence on the Tulsa community, however, is perhaps twice as long. Though the precise date on which the Tulsa chapter of the organization was founded remains uncertain, the actions of the NAACP have enhanced the lives of African-American Tulsans since the organization came to Oklahoma in 1913. Part of the strength of the NAACP in Oklahoma has been its ability to bring local chapters together in pursuit of common goals and objectives.

Since its start in Oklahoma, the NAACP battled violence and racism. The organization came to Oklahoma four years after its 1909 founding in New York. Henry A. Berry, a teacher at Douglass High School in Oklahoma City, conceived the idea of an Oklahoma branch of the NAACP. At the time, Berry sold *Crisis* magazine, the official publication of the NAACP, in the Oklahoma City area. Berry and the principal of Douglass High, J. H. A. Brazelton, convened a conference at Avery Chapel Methodist Church in Oklahoma City during which plans were made for the establishment of an Oklahoma branch. In 1913 the branch was formed with an initial complement of twenty-eight members. Dr. A. Baxter Whitby was elected president. The branch targeted Jim Crow laws and various forms of discrimination in the early years.

World War I brought its activities to a virtual halt, but in 1918 the Oklahoma City chapter reorganized at Calvary Baptist Church. That reorganization brought about new energy, thanks in no small part to the involvement of Roscoe Dungee and his newspaper, *The Black Dispatch*.

Roscoe Dungee was the heart and soul of the NAACP in Oklahoma. He began publishing *The Black Dispatch* in 1915, and for fifty years thereafter he used the paper to promote the cause of social justice for African-Americans. Dungee sat on the national board of directors of the NAACP, served as president of the Negro Business League, and was a member of the Executive Council of the Association for the Study of Negro Life and History.

Dungee organized the State Conference of Branches of the NAACP. The conference idea—bringing together a group of chapters organized on a statewide basis in service of a common goal—gave state groups additional flexibility in terms of their ability to file civil rights lawsuits. That masterstroke gained Dungee favor with the NAACP leadership and propelled the Oklahoma NAACP into the national spotlight.

With Dungee's active support and with the backing of *The Black Dispatch*, the NAACP scored a number of impressive victories in Oklahoma. In 1915 the United States Supreme Court, in *Guinn v. United States*,[28] sided with the NAACP in a voting rights case, ruling against an Oklahoma "grandfather clause" designed to disenfranchise African-Americans. Oklahoma had amended its constitution to provide for a literacy test as a prerequisite to voting. But individuals who, on or before January 1, 1866, were entitled to vote under any form of government or resided in a foreign nation were exempt from the literacy test requirement. So were the lineal descendants of those "grandfathered" individuals. In effect, Oklahoma had disenfranchised African-Americans. The U.S. Supreme Court found a violation of the Fifteenth Amendment to the United States Constitution, which prohibits such denials of the right to vote on account of race, color, or previous condition of servitude.

Another case spearheaded by the NAACP, *Hollins v. State of Oklahoma*, is significant because the U.S. Supreme Court found that the exclusion of "Negroes" from jury service simply based on race and color is a violation of the equal protection clause of the Fourteenth Amendment to the United States Constitution, at least in those cases where the criminal defendant is African-American. In the 1935 *Hollins* decision, the defendant, Jess Hollins, stood accused of raping a white woman with whom he had allegedly maintained an affair. Okmulgee County, Oklahoma, the county in which the trial court was situated, had a longstanding policy of excluding African-Americans from jury service. Hollins was convicted by an all-white jury. The U.S. Supreme Court reversed the conviction. Famed African-American attorney Charles Hamilton Houston led the team of attorneys presenting Hollins' case to the U.S. Supreme Court.

In *Lane v. Wilson*,[29] decided in 1939, the NAACP convinced the U.S. Supreme Court to void a post-grandfather clause restriction on the right of African-Americans to exercise the franchise. Oklahoma had passed a statute to circumvent the decision in the *Guinn* case. Persons who had not voted in the general election preceding the enactment of the statute because of the Oklahoma grandfather clause were required to register within a twelve-day period in order to be entitled to vote at any time in the future. By definition, this new, albeit limited, "opportunity" to register to vote applied only to African-Americans. After all, they were the ones denied the vote under the literacy test requirements from which whites were exempted under the grandfather clause. Again, the U.S. Supreme Court found a violation of the Fifteenth Amendment to the U.S. Constitution.

In the 1940s and 1950s, the Oklahoma NAACP achieved significant triumphs in the field of education. Amos T. Hall, a prominent African-American Tulsa lawyer, joined Dungee, Jimmy Stewart, and others in Oklahoma City and elsewhere in spearheading these efforts.

Sipuel v. Board of Regents of the University of Oklahoma[30] is perhaps the most celebrated of the Oklahoma education cases handled by the NAACP. Amos T. Hall joined Thurgood Marshall, then of New York City, in arguing the case. (Thurgood Marshall would later become "Justice Thurgood Marshall," a jurist on the U.S. Supreme Court.) Ada Lois Sipuel had sought and was denied admission to the University of Oklahoma School of Law. There was no question as to Ms. Sipuel's qualifications for admission, and the University of Oklahoma School of Law was the only state-supported law school in Oklahoma. Ms. Sipuel was denied admission solely on account of race. The U.S. Supreme Court found a violation of the equal protection clause of the Fourteenth Amendment to the U.S. Consitution. It declared that since Oklahoma maintained a law school for white students, the State should also make legal education available to "Negroes" on equal terms.

The NAACP used litigation and education as its primary tools, yet many whites considered it a "militant" organization. As a consequence, NAACP members often endured threats, harassment, economic discrimination and, in some cases, physical violence. Nonetheless, they would not be moved.[31]

The NAACP worked hand in glove with the African-American church. Tulsa's African-American ministers began actively cultivating an organized local civil rights movement in the 1950s. The likes of Rev. B. S. Roberts, Rev. Ben Hill, Rev. G. Calvin McCutchen, and Rev. T. Oscar Chappelle, among others, using Rev. Martin Luther King, Jr.'s nonviolent, pacifist strategies, took on the establishment in Tulsa. Rev. B. S. Roberts knew Dr. King personally, having met him in Atlanta in 1944. Some white ministers and several white students from the University of Tulsa (including Rodger Randle, who would later become mayor of the city of Tulsa and, still later, president of Rogers University) participated in this new and exciting social justice movement.

African-American youth played an integral role in Tulsa's civil rights movement. Youth participation ran the gamut from conceptualization to implementation. The youth chose their battles. They simply wanted what all the other kids in Tulsa back then wanted: to be able to play in public parks; to be able to swim in public pools; to be able to try on the latest fashions before they purchased them; to be able to eat in the hole-in-the-wall diner or the elegant restaurant of their choosing. That they were denied the opportunities other kids took for granted propelled them to action. They staged sit-ins, "wade-ins," and voter registration drives. It was an experiential lesson in good citizenship—a lesson not without some considerable risk to personal safety and security.

The youth civil rights brigade, trained in the art of non-violent protest, also learned how to protect themselves from harm in the event of a physical attack. Mere words could be ignored. But "sticks and stones" were quite another matter. They perfected the art of peaceful, lawful picketing by watching, listening, and learning from the masters. A. Phillip Randolph, Dick Gregory, and Rev. Martin Luther King, Jr., all visited Tulsa at one time or another. Dr. King's visit in 1960 aroused a level of enthusiasm and passion seldom seen in Tulsa.

Oklahoma City's civil right warriors, led by Clara Luper and somewhat stronger than the Tulsa group, provided training for the Tulsa contingent of civil rights crusaders. At the height of the civil rights movement in Tulsa, some 600 Tulsans were arrested and jailed in one day. Gradually, the tall walls of segregation began to crumble. Eventually, those walls came tumbling down.[32] Beyond the dust lay an island of promise amidst a sea of uncertainty.

Tulsa Metropolitan Ministry (T. M. M.), a Tulsa ecumenical and interfaith organization founded in 1937 as the Tulsa Council of Churches, also played a significant role in Tulsa's civil rights movement. From its inception, T. M. M. sought to improve community race relations and eliminate discrimination in housing and employment. African-American churches took seats at the T.M.M. table almost from the beginning. In 1963, T.M.M. asked Tulsa congregations to commit to the acceptance of people in their houses of worship irrespective of race or national origin. T.M.M. collected the signatures of 160 congregations.[33]

As a result of the efforts of civil rights pioneers in Tulsa and beyond, the 1960s heralded the beginning of the end of legal segregation (i.e., *de jure* segregation) and the relaxation of rigid social customs. Legal rights and remedies were put in place to combat discrimination. Some upwardly mobile African-Americans seized the opportunity to move out of the black community and into integrated neighborhoods. African-Americans could by now shop in (and line the coffers of) some of the chic, previously off-limits white business establishments in town.

Not all racial barriers came down of their own force. A case in point is the initial brush with integration at Tulsa's prized Philbrook Museum. Tulsa educator, attorney, and community activist Nancy Feldman served on Philbrook's education committee in the early 1960s. The committee funded scholarships for children, but the recipients had to be children of Philbrook members. Since Philbrook had no "Negro" members, African-American children were effectively frozen out of the competition for its scholarships. Troubled by this discrimination, Ms. Feldman and Claudia Baker, a Philbrook staffer, conspired to break through the race barrier at Philbrook. Ms. Feldman asked an African-American friend, Jeanne B. Goodwin, a prominent educator and community leader who then lived at 51st Street and Mingo Road (in southeast Tulsa), to apply for a membership at the museum. Ms. Goodwin agreed. No one at Philbrook (save the co-conspirators) suspected that the application was that of an African-American woman. After all, the address on the application indicated a "white" part of town. The application sailed through. When the issue of allowing "Negroes" into the membership ranks of Philbrook Museum next arose, Claudia Baker calmly and politely indicated that the issue was moot: Philbrook already had a "Negro" member. To the board's chagrin, Ms. Goodwin had been accepted for membership. The color barrier shattered; the case was closed.[34]

Segregation turned out to be a double-edged sword, at once a curse and a blessing, for the African-American community. Segregation's central, racist premises—that African-Americans were by birth inferior and that "race-mixing" tainted and tarnished whites—fell gradually into disrepute. As minds changed, so did economic interests and incentives. The "black market," the mass of African-American consumers not previously cultivated by white merchants, suddenly became fair game in a desegregated marketplace. As segregation ended, white merchants broke the virtual lock on black dollars that the once-insular African-American community held.[35] Ultimately, the outflow of black dollars from the Greenwood District, first drip by drip, then in a steady stream, and finally in torrents, left a parched, barren wasteland—failing businesses, deserted streets, and vacant buildings. The opening up of the Tulsa economy afforded African-Americans choice. At the same time, it eliminated self-sufficiency by forcing the smaller, often undercapitalized, sometimes marginal African-American businesses out of the market.

By 1961, more than ninety percent of African-American income—some $12-15 million—was spent outside the Greenwood District.[36] To go "outside" for needs was to add another hole in the dike that surrounded the closed economy of the district, whether or not anyone intended that result. It was also to exercise the liberating power of choice. The issue of African-Americans investing in their own communities remains as critical now as it was then.[37]

Contemporaneously, America as a whole was moving away from "Mom and Pop" type businesses toward larger, nationally based operations and franchises.[38] The trend bode ill for the small shops of the Greenwood District. Once again, the central issue became competitive business advantage. "The Black Wall Street of America" was no high-flying financial district like its namesake. Its entrepreneur-driven small businesses looked much more like "The Black Main Street of America."

Like many American main streets, Greenwood Avenue faced rough roads ahead. Riotous mobs decimated the Greenwood District in 1921. In ironic and like fashion, desegregation and free market economic forces in the 1950s and 1960s ran rough-shod through the African-American community, leaving behind only traces of the entrepreneurial spirit that once seemed endemic.

Race relations in Tulsa improved during the early 1960s, at least superficially:

> On the surface, the intense racial enmity of the past has been replaced by racial amity. A Negro minister heads the Tulsa Ministerial Alliance. The mayor sponsors an Equal Opportunity Day. White business leaders participate in Urban League programs. A few department stores have hired Negro sales clerks. A few Negro white collar workers are employed in the municipal government offices. A private all-white children's medical clinic employes [sic] a Negro social worker. The Oklahoma State Employment Agency recently abandoned its Negro branch agency for an integrated one. Public schools carry on moderate programs of interracial communication. One assistant county investigator is Negro. And the City Water Department employs a Negro in its chemistry department.
>
> However, despite the appearance of racial harmony in present-day Tulsa [1961], evidence of discrimination is rampant in employment, in housing, and in public facilities such as parks, restaurants, movie theaters, hotels, and hospitals. It is true that there have been gains made by Negroes which others before them had not the opportunity to make; but credit for improved living conditions among Negroes, while not unwillingly given to a progressive Tulsa, must be given to it with reserve: it is not yet clear how solid these gains are which Negroes have made.[39]

"Urban renewal," conceived as a means by which to rehabilitate and redevelop deteriorated or distressed urban areas, often missed the mark. Many of the inner-city areas targeted for

Interstate 244, which bisects the heart of the Greenwood District. (Photo courtesy of Goodrum Photography, 1997)

urban renewal were poor, black, or both. As a result, urban renewal had significant implications for race relations. Dr. John Sibley Butler observed: "'Urban renewal' did little to enhance race relations. Indeed, combined with the expansion of expressway systems, urban renewal added further stress to an already unstable community."[40]

Others shared Butler's sentiments about the destructive capacity of urban renewal. Barbara Baer Capitman, former president of the Art Deco Societies of America and the Miami Design Preservation League, visited the Greenwood District after the commencement of urban renewal initiatives and noted: "I must confess I was shocked at the degradation of North Tulsa—the brutal results of past eras of city planning that allowed expressways to be cut through what is probably one of the most potentially interesting sections, and the wholesale destruction of entire neighborhoods."[41] Noted Tulsa attorney James O. Goodwin, publisher of the African-American community weekly *The Oklahoma Eagle*, recalled: "What was characteristic of urban renewal authorities across the country was that right through the core of the black business community, like an arrow through the heart, came the expressways."[42] Tulsa was no exception. Hugh Hollins remembered: "When Urban Renewal came through there and bought us black business people out, I had to move out to the 46th and Cincinnati area of Tulsa. It was alright out there. I had a nice little [barber] shop, but it was nothing like the shop I had on Greenwood all those years. I sure did love Greenwood in the old days."[43]

The future of the historic Greenwood District hung perilously in the balance.

As the 1970s approached, only the law offices of E. L. Goodwin, Sr., and *The Oklahoma Eagle* (both located at 122 North Greenwood Avenue) and Georgola's Fried Chicken remained on Greenwood Avenue. Urban renewal (or "urban removal," as it was commonly called) ultimately drove these businesses away. After several moves, Goodwin and *The Oklahoma Eagle* wound up at 624 East Archer.

By 1978, a report by Tulsa's Neighborhood Regeneration Project described the Greenwood District as an area "that is left today [with] generally abandoned and underutilized buildings, sitting in a sparse population of poor and elderly black[s] awaiting the relocation counselors of the Urban Renewal program."[44]

Goodwin, one of the refugees carted off to an internment camp during the Riot, had by this time acquired several properties actively sought by the Tulsa Urban Renewal Authority. Goodwin refused to sell except on condition that he gain outright title or an option to purchase the remaining buildings on once-famous Greenwood Avenue. The Tulsa Urban Renewal Authority agreed.

Thanks to Goodwin and others who fought long and hard to save their community, "Deep Greenwood," the 100 block of Greenwood Avenue located between Archer Street and the Interstate 244 overpass, remains an African-American business district. Yet it is but a skeleton of its former self. The Greenwood District at its peak in 1942 was home to 242 black-owned and operated businesses in a thirty-five-square-block area.[45] Now only a handful of businesses remain in the Greenwood District.

The decay and decline of the Greenwood District was slowed

and, to a degree, reversed through the gallant efforts of Tulsa civic and political leaders of both races beginning in the early 1970s. At a meeting called by Tulsa's Mayor James Hewgley and the Tulsa City Commission, in compliance with a mandate for citizens' participation in the federal Model Cities Program, local African-American leaders urged the special treatment for a truly special area of the city: the Greenwood District. In the end, these visionaries helped create what is now one of Oklahoma's—and the nation's—showplaces: the Greenwood Cultural Center.

Long an integral part of the planning for the Greenwood District, the Greenwood Cultural Center was part of the initial Model Cities proposal submitted to the federal government by the City of Tulsa. It is located on the site of the original Mackey house on Greenwood Avenue.

The historic Mackey house was scheduled for demolition by the City of Tulsa. The original white frame structure was destroyed in the Riot, and its new brick replacement was built in 1926. It had initially been preserved during the tenure of Tulsa Mayor Robert LaFortune, but eventually fell prey to vandals and profiteers. It stood dilapidated, abandoned, and decaying for years. J. Homer Johnson, Oklahoma State Representative Don Ross, Thelma Whitlow, and Mabel B. Little led a chorus of African-American community leaders in a din of opposition to the demolition. These leaders contended that far too much of the heritage of Tulsa's African-American community had been lost to decay, decline, and demolition. The old Mackey house, they argued, must be saved and enshrined for future generations; the past had to be appreciated and preserved.

A cornerstone of the Greenwood District revitalization, the Mackey house symbolized the rich history of the community and the toll that time and transition take if left unchecked. The Business and Industrial Development Corporation (BIDC), an African-American community service and development agency, created the North Tulsa Heritage Foundation, Inc., to restore the historic landmark with the assistance of a ninety-nine-year lease from the City of Tulsa and a commitment financially to assist in the renovation. The house was moved from 356 North Greenwood Avenue to its present location at 322 North Greenwood Avenue. BIDC engaged Oklahoma State Representative Don Ross, then a Gary, Indiana, newspaper editor, as a program consultant for the venture. Working closely with city officials, Representative Ross moved full throttle toward the reestablishment of a significant African-American presence on Greenwood Avenue.

In early February of 1980, the City of Tulsa, together with a diverse array of civic, professional, business, civil rights, and social organizations, convened to discuss economic development in the Greenwood District. Remarkably, representatives from all principal federal departments (i.e., labor, commerce, transportation, energy, housing and urban development, and health and human services) joined Greenwood community leaders and corporate Tulsa decision-makers for the unique and historic conference. United States Senator James Inhofe, then Tulsa mayor, challenged those assembled to come up with a way to reverse the decline of the Greenwood District:

> Times really have changed. There was a time in the City of Tulsa when what we had referred to as the Black Community, which was in the area of Greenwood and Archer, really was booming at one time. They had commerce going there, there were businesses that were prospering, and then in the mid-20's, there was [t]his horrible devastating riot that killed countless numbers of people, and just as things were starting to get rebuilt, the depression came in. And now when you stand at the corner of Archer and Greenwood, you can see the physical signs of urban decay. . . . I think it is reversible here in the City of Tulsa.[46]

The February 1980 conference indicated the Tulsa's community's heightened awareness of the importance of the Greenwood District. Finally, it seemed that the district had become more than simply a concern for African-Americans.

Later in 1980, the Greenwood Chamber of Commerce secured a $3.5 million grant from the Economic Development Administration to develop the Greenwood Cultural Center. The renaissance of the Greenwood District had begun.

THE RENAISSANCE

Renaissance: A new birth; rebirth; revival; renascence.[1]

The Greenwood District is in the midst of a renaissance. But it is a renaissance of spirit, not of bricks and mortar. New hotels, cafes, and shops are not being built. Those businesses that exist still struggle to survive. Physically, the Greenwood District today pales in comparison to the same area in its prime. But the soul of the Greenwood District remains deeply embedded in its people. Visitors from all walks of life, from all around America, now know of the Greenwood legacy due in large part to the creation of the Greenwood Cultural Center and its constituent organizations—the North Tulsa Heritage Foundation, Inc., the Business and Industrial Development Corporation (BIDC), and the Oklahoma Jazz Hall of Fame. This heightened awareness and renewed interest, if backed by investment, could bring about an economic resurgence the likes of which have not been seen since the boom days of the 1940s.

The birth of the Greenwood Cultural Center, a tax-exempt, nonprofit corporation, heralded the dawn of a renaissance for the Greenwood District. The Greenwood Cultural Center focuses on African-American history and culture and seeks to enhance race relations. It is a monument to the ideal of interracial cooperation that made its very existence possible. That same type of cross-cultural collaboration will be necessary if the economic clout of the Greenwood District is to be recaptured.

Inspired by Katie Duckery, who during a town meeting convened by Tulsa Mayor James Hewgley in the early 1970s pushed for the establishment of a community-oriented African-American cultural center, the Greenwood Cultural Center represents the realization of a dream. Duckery, the daughter of a family sold into slavery and a long-time Tulsan, lived through the Riot and became a staunch civil rights advocate and community activist. She remained in many ways a simple woman, working for years as a domestic and, later, in the Junior League of Tulsa Tea Room.[2] A true believer in the possibilities of her community and possessed of the spirit of the Greenwood pioneers, Duckery inspired and motivated all who knew her. She wanted her rich heritage and culture celebrated, not merely for herself, but for all of us. And she would eventually get her wish.

The Target Area Action Group, Tulsa's citizen participation component of the Model Cities Program then led by J. Homer Johnson, acquired title to the Mackey house and developed and refined Duckery's proposal. The Mackey house, saved from scheduled demolition by the Tulsa Urban Renewal Authority, sat abandoned and in ruin. It had passed from one organization to the next until the BIDC gained the title in 1983. That group embraced Duckery's idea of a cultural and children's center and made plans for the development of a million-dollar cultural complex. Plans to locate the University Center at Tulsa (now "Rogers University," a consortium of four state universities—Langston University, the University of Oklahoma, Northeastern University, and Oklahoma State University) in the Greenwood District gave rise to renewed discussions about moving and preserving the Mackey house, located near what would be the entrance of the then-proposed University Center at Tulsa campus. Rogers University now occupies the site on which the original Booker T. Washington High School sat before and during the Riot. This tie to Tulsa's African-American history did not go unnoticed. Today, only two streets run through the Rogers University campus—Greenwood Avenue and John Hope Franklin Boulevard.

The City of Tulsa provided two and one-half acres of land and $275,000 for future development of what would become the Greenwood Cultural Center. In less than one year, the African-American community raised in excess of $100,000—some $7,000 in just one week—for the project thanks to the efforts of individuals such as Oklahoma State Representative Don Ross, community activists Mable Rice, Shirley Johnson, Opal Dargan, and Thelma Whitlow, and a host of others who simply gave what they could spare in the fund-raising effort. Fully furnished, restored to its original construction and appearance where possible, and renamed the Mabel B. Little Heritage House, the old, history-filled Mackey home was dedicated in 1986.

The house's namesake, Mabel B. Little, is a Tulsa legend. Born Mabel Bonner on October 4, 1896, in Spring, Texas, she attended school in Boley, Oklahoma, and graduated from Boley High School. She then attended Madam C. J. Walker Beauty College. (Madam C. J. Walker earned a fortune in the beauty business, and became the first African-American female millionaire in the United States.)

Mabel Bonner moved to Tulsa in 1913 and promptly mar-

Interior of the Mabel B. Little Heritage House, the restored and renamed home of Greenwood District pioneers Sam and Lucy Mackey. (Photo courtesy of Goodrum Photography, 1997)

ried her beau, Pressley Little. She and her husband suffered substantial financial losses in the Riot, and subsequently she became
Tulsa's "civic-minded beautician." Active in a host of church
activities, Little organized the first church "Woman's Day" in the
state of Oklahoma. In her more than 100 years of living, Little
has been actively involved in numerous community organizations and is a published author.

Three organizations operate under the umbrella of the
Greenwood Cultural Center: the North Tulsa Heritage Foundation, Inc., BIDC, and the Oklahoma Jazz Hall of Fame. Each
of these affiliated organizations functions independently with a
combination of paid staff, consultants, and volunteers. Together
they form separate and distinct spokes of a unified hub, the
Greenwood Cultural Center. That hub has become the centerpiece of Tulsa's African-American community.

The North Tulsa Heritage Foundation, Inc., is committed
to the preservation and documentation of the history of Tulsa's
African-American pioneers, past and present. The organization
strives to share the rich heritage, legacy, culture, and arts of
African-Americans with the Tulsa community. The North Tulsa
Heritage Foundation maintains the Mabel B. Little Heritage
House, that historical monument to Greenwood's past.

The Business and Industrial Development Corporation,
formed on August 1, 1974, represents the consolidation of two
"Model Cities" programs, Model Neighborhood Loan, Inc., and
the North Tulsa Development Corporation. BIDC initially made
loans to individuals and businesses to promote business development and improve employment opportunities. At the outset,
BIDC worked closely with the City of Tulsa and was funded
through federal grants. Currently, BIDC works to promote,
develop, and sustain minority businesses and enhance economic opportunities, primarily in the African-American community,
but no longer makes loans. BIDC owns real estate and purchas-
es, rehabilitates, and sells affordable housing for first-time
homeowners. Though limited in terms of financial resources,
BIDC remains an active participant in the Tulsa community. The
North Tulsa Heritage Foundation, Inc., was spun off from BIDC.

The Oklahoma Jazz Hall of Fame seeks to educate the public about the significant, often-overlooked contributions of jazz

musicians with Oklahoma ties (and performers of music closely related to jazz, such as blues and gospel) to the cultural heritage of the state of Oklahoma, the Midwest, and America as a whole. The Oklahoma Jazz Hall of Fame's educational and entertainment programs throughout the year provide opportunities to look back through Oklahoma's unique window on America's music world.

The Greenwood Cultural Center is a multipurpose education, arts, and humanities complex for people of all races, with an emphasis on the positive development of children and youth, promoting programs that: (1) address African-American history and culture; (2) explore, recount, and review the varied contributions of Tulsa's African-American artists and scholars; (3) foster improved race relations; and (4) focus on the preservation and promotion of Tulsa's historic Greenwood District. Constructed in three distinct phases and located proximate to downtown Tulsa, it is a fitting and proper tribute to Tulsa's African-American pioneers. Groundbreaking ceremonies in August of 1985 drew participation from notables such as Oklahoma Governor George Nigh, Oklahoma Congressman Jim Jones, Tulsa Mayor Terry Young, Oklahoma Speaker of the House Jim Barker, and Oklahoma Senate President Rodger Randle.

Two individuals deserve special recognition for securing funding from the State of Oklahoma for the Greenwood Cultural Center. Without them, and without the firm foundation they laid, the Greenwood Cultural Center simply could not and would not exist. Oklahoma State Senator Maxine Cissel Horner and Oklahoma State Representative Don Ross both lent their considerable legislative skills and influence to the cause of erecting and maintaining the Greenwood Cultural Center as a showplace for African-American culture and history. Their presence in the Oklahoma Legislature and their success in convincing that overwhelmingly white body to support the development of the Greenwood Cultural Center is a testament to the spirit of inter-cultural cooperation that the Center itself represents. Senator Horner, a life-long Tulsan and daughter of Greenwood District entrepreneur Earl Cissel, and Representative Ross, a native Tulsan, continue to advocate on behalf of the Greenwood

Cultural Center and are stalwart champions and defenders of its purpose, mission, and significance.

Phase I of the construction of the Greenwood Cultural Center involved the restoration and opening of the historic Mackey house, now the Mabel B. Little Heritage House, complete with antique furnishings, in September of 1986. The Mackey house, listed on the National Register of Historic Places and perched on a lot at 322 North Greenwood Avenue, has special significance because it is the only home built in the original Greenwood residential district of the 1920s that still stands.

The very existence of the Mackey house is a testament to the working-class African-American family that history so often ignores. The Mackeys were simple folk. They did domestic and yard work for prominent white Tulsans. The Mackeys proved, however, that with hard work, perseverance, and ingenuity African-Americans could succeed against the odds. The Mackeys rose above the prejudice and discrimination heaped upon them and built a home with as much character as the mansions of Tulsa's prestigious Maple Ridge neighborhood.

The first home of Sam and Lucy Mackey was a frame structure located at 327 North Greenwood Avenue. The home was reduced to ashes in the Riot. In a 1967 interview with *The Oklahoma Eagle*, the Mackeys' only child, Mrs. Vernon Wilson Prince, recalled the days of the Riot. Mrs. Prince's uncle (her mother's brother) was none other than Barney Cleaver, the first African-American law enforcement officer in Tulsa. Cleaver had the distinction of being the only African-American who could safely walk the streets of Tulsa during the Riot. Cleaver warned the Mackeys of the encroaching white mob during the height of the Riot. Fearing for their safety, the Mackeys fled. When they returned, the home was a total loss. But the Mackeys vowed to rebuild. And they did. Though the record is not entirely clear on the matter, the Mackeys probably obtained financing for the home from out-of-state sources.

In 1926 the Mackeys built a stately two-story brick house. The new house contained a number of features unusual at the time, including spacious walk-in closets and lights that could be turned on at the base of the stairs and turned off at the top of the stairs. The well-appointed Mackey home became one of the social centers of the African-American community, playing host to weddings and all manner of social events. Though the Mackeys are both deceased, their home, steeped in African-American culture and history, remains. The home escaped destruction at the hands of the Tulsa Urban Renewal Authority, and is now maintained by the North Tulsa Heritage Foundation, Inc. Group tours, historical lessons, and an archive of mixed-media memorabilia are now available to the public.

Phase II of the Greenwood Cultural Center project centered on the construction of the Goodwin-Chappelle Gallery. The Gallery opened on April 23, 1989. The Goodwin-Chappelle Gallery, named in honor of two of Tulsa's most prominent African-Americans, publisher and attorney E. L. Goodwin and minister T. O. Chappelle, Sr., showcases African-American art, history, and artifacts and is available for private showings.

Phase III included the construction of facilities to house the Oklahoma Jazz Hall of Fame and the Opal L. Dargan Renaissance Hall. The Oklahoma Jazz Hall of Fame celebrates the achievements of musicians with Oklahoma connections. The Opal L. Dargan Renaissance Hall is a multipurpose facility named in honor of one of Tulsa's leading African-American community activists.

The Oklahoma Jazz Hall of Fame celebrates America's music—jazz. Jazz, according to author James Haskins, is an outgrowth of spirituals, ragtime, and the blues—uniquely African-American musical styles.[3] Like the "economic detour" that racism, discrimination, and segregation forged, those same factors, it could be argued, created a "cultural detour"—an environment that allowed African-Americans to develop distinct musical idioms like jazz. Jazz, like the other musical styles rooted in the African-American community that preceded it, went "mainstream" over time. Rather than being played solely by black musicians in black establishments, all manner of artists and all types of venues eventually became purveyors of jazz.

Like ragtime and the blues, jazz developed in major towns along the Mississippi River, most notably New Orleans. It had its beginnings near the turn of the century. New Orleans, because of its unique, rich admixture of cultures, provided fertile field for the creation of jazz. In New Orleans, blacks, Creoles, and

Bettie Downing, administrator for the Oklahoma Jazz Hall of Fame. (Photo courtesy of Goodrum Photography, 1997)

whites were the primary racial/ethnic groups. Creoles, individuals of mixed heritage, were considered black by whites, who sat atop the prevailing racial hierarchy.

An 1897 New Orleans ordinance restricted prostitution to an area in the black and Creole section of the segregated town. Saloons and gambling houses flourished in this area, known locally as Storyville. These establishments employed bands, and brought together black and Creole musicians for the first time. A new standard of musical ensemble evolved from this union. The trumpet or cornet carried melody lines and brasses, piano and drums, bass and banjo, or a combination of these provided the rhythm. The rhythm section became one of the hallmarks of early jazz. Storyville musicians played in funeral processions (as was common in New Orleans) and at amusement parks. Music could be heard round-the-clock in the black sections of New Orleans.[4]

Jazz gained in popularity in 1919 with the passage of the Volsted Act, which outlawed the sale, manufacture, and transportation of alcoholic beverages. Speakeasies, private clubs that sold illegal liquor, sprang up everywhere. These clubs needed live entertainment, and jazz artists filled the bill.[5]

Sound recording and the invention of the radio made jazz accessible to many who would not have otherwise had access to it. Since jazz is largely an improvisational art, recordings and radio allowed young jazz musicians to study the masters and afforded jazz buffs the opportunity to hear performances that, by virtue of their improvisational nature, could not be replicated.[6]

Oklahoma musicians helped further develop the jazz idiom, and contributed greatly to the artform. For that reason, the Oklahoma Jazz Hall of Fame honors the premier artists from among this group.

The Oklahoma Jazz Hall of Fame owes its existence primarily to the leadership of State Senator Maxine Horner and the support of Oklahomans throughout the state. Leadership, like jazz, is a performance art. According to Max DePree, "[Both depend] on so many things—the environment, the volunteers in the band, the need for everybody to perform as individuals and as a group, the absolute dependence of the leader on the members of the band, the need of the leader for the followers to play well."[7] Senator Horner's love of jazz and jazz history struck a chord with the Oklahomans, and under her leadership the concept of the Oklahoma Jazz Hall of Fame resonated throughout the state.

Senator Horner discovered Oklahoma's contributions to music generally and to jazz particularly while reading *Singing Cowboys and All That Jazz* by William Savage, Jr., a University of Oklahoma historian and author. The book recounts the contributions of musicians with Oklahoma ties to America's homegrown music—jazz.

Jazz greats like Jimmy Rushing, Count Basie, Sr., Charlie Christian, Lester Young, Oscar Pettiford, Chet Baker, Jay McShann, and so many others were influenced by and/or played with Tulsa musicians like big band leader Ernie Fields, Sr. (who produced a "Top 40" hit in the 1940s with "In the Mood"), bassist and nightclub owner Clarence Love, and saxophonist Al

Dennie. Tulsa's Greenwood District offered an outlet for blossoming jazz talent and served as an incubator for up-and-coming jazz bands.

Trumpeter Julian Northington, a graduate of Langston University in Langston, Oklahoma, and a long-time music teacher in the Tulsa area, played with many of the bands of the jazz era, including those of Clarence Love and Ernie Fields. He listened to the likes of Fields, Al Dennie, and James Lark, a graduate of Howard University and a music teacher at what was once all-black Carver Junior High School in Tulsa. Northington recalled fondly:

> They put emphasis on music back in those days, a little more than now. It was a thing to be a member of an organization and try to develop your musical talents.
>
> [W]e had Florence's Chicken Plantation, in which [Florence] kept a trio at all times, and people would come from all over the country. Dinah Washington sang there.
>
> Sometimes we would go all night having a good jam session. She had a pact with the church next door that she would have to cut it off by 8:00 o'clock, because they would start Sunday school at 9:00.[8]

So inspired was Senator Horner that she proceeded to set in motion the forces which created and enshrined in law the Oklahoma Jazz Hall of Fame in 1988. A joint legislative resolution sponsored by Senator Horner and other legislators passed in the Oklahoma legislature in the spring of 1988. The resolution recounts the history of jazz in Oklahoma and authorizes the creation of the Oklahoma Jazz Hall of Fame:

> WHEREAS, in the music world the State of Oklahoma is well known for its many outstanding country and western artists but is little recognized for producing many of the world's greatest jazz artists; and
>
> WHEREAS, many, many great jazz musicians were born in the State of Oklahoma or became well known while practicing their craft here and from the earliest territorial days the State of Oklahoma has been an important stop on the nation's jazz scene; and
>
> WHEREAS, when black slaves owned by the Five Civilized

Tribes were relocated here with the Indians by the federal government, their work songs and field hollers evolved into a form of rural black folk music known as the "blues"; and

WHEREAS, after the Civil War two black slaves working at a Choctaw boarding school were overheard singing a spiritual song, "Swing Low, Sweet Chariot" which was transcribed by a minister who sent it to the Jubilee Singers of Fisk University in Nashville, Tennessee, who performed the song on a tour of the United States and Europe, thereby sharing one of Oklahoma's first musical gifts with the world; and

WHEREAS, it is another little-known fact that the "blues" song entitled "Dallas Blues" was written and published in Oklahoma City in 1912, and in a matter of weeks it could be heard playing up and down the Mississippi River thereby helping to popularize this form of music that had been played regionally for years; and

WHEREAS, the entire northeast section of the State of Oklahoma was especially fertile ground for producing many great jazz musicians, including Jay McShann, Claude Williams, Samuel Aaron Bell and Barney Kessel all born in Muskogee and Ernie Fields and Earl Bostic from Tulsa. Each of these men went on to become quite famous in the music industry; and

WHEREAS, so many fine Oklahoma born and bred jazz musicians, far too many to mention here, are deserving of special recognition by their proud home state; and

WHEREAS, in his book *Singing Cowboys and All That Jazz*, Dr. William W. Savage, Jr., associate professor of history at the University of Oklahoma, has written a brief history of music in Oklahoma and points out that our state has produced more jazz musicians than any other type of musician; and

WHEREAS, there is a tremendous desire by many Oklahoma music fans to publicly recognize the accomplishments of our state's jazz artists and to achieve that goal there will hereby be created the "Oklahoma Jazz Hall of Fame."

The resolution was approved by Oklahoma Governor Henry Bellmon on April 12, 1988, and filed with the Oklahoma secretary of state on the same date.

Senator Horner, moreover, secured a state grant of some $750,000 to provide a permanent home for the Oklahoma Jazz Hall of Fame. Dedicated on June 17, 1989, it is physically located in the Greenwood Cultural Center. Each June the Oklahoma Jazz Hall of Fame inducts new honorees into its ranks.[9]

The Oklahoma Jazz Hall of Fame recognizes Oklahoma music and musicians, and serves as a repository for the treasured artifacts, recordings, musical scores, and memorabilia that are relevant to the history of gospel and blues and the roots of jazz. It also reaches out to the community through workshops featuring notable musical artists and provides scholarship assistance for collegiate music education majors.

June marks the Oklahoma Jazz Hall of Fame's "Juneteenth Heritage Festival" on Greenwood Avenue. Some 30,000 patrons attend the Juneteenth Heritage Festival annually. ("Juneteenth" represents June 19, the date on which slaves in Texas, Oklahoma, Arkansas, and some other southern, southwestern, and midwestern states received word that President Abraham Lincoln had indeed signed the Emancipation Proclamation. The word came on June 19, 1865, when federal troops landed at Galveston, Texas. The news traveled quickly to Oklahoma and other states. President Lincoln actually issued the Emancipation Proclamation in September of 1862, effective as of January 1, 1863. The Oklahoma legislature has by resolution recognized Juneteenth as an official holiday.)

The now-traditional Greenwood Jazz Celebration began in August 1989. The free event features regional and local musicians as well as national entertainers. Headliners to date have included the likes of talented and celebrated stars such as Natalie Cole, Lou Rawls, Spyro Gyra, Ramsey Lewis, Kirk Whalum, and Cab Calloway.

The Oklahoma Jazz Hall of Fame is but one-half of the "Phase III" construction of the Greenwood Cultural Center. The other half, the Opal L. Dargan Renaissance Hall, is the centerpiece of the Greenwood Cultural Center. The Hall, named for the late Opal Long Dargan, an African-American pioneer, community activist, and volunteer in Tulsa, hosts community banquets, stage productions, and other large events. Few African-American communities anywhere in the nation boast such an impressive facility. Its namesake is equally impressive.

Opal Long Dargan possessed a special sparkle that enlightened and warmed all those fortunate enough to know her. She had the uncanny ability to emerge from the depths of adversity unscathed, and to bring others up with her.

Dargan was born in 1916. As a child in 1921, she and her family were forced to evacuate their Greenwood home in the face of the Riot. Dargan would never forget that day—the devastation, the brutality. But she always kept countervailing positive images of Greenwood in mind. She fondly recalled Greenwood, the cradle of African-American families; Greenwood, the incubator of a new brand of jazz; and Greenwood, the mecca of black business. For Dargan, there was always a silver lining for those who would take the time to seek it out.

Dargan earned bachelor's and master's degrees and chose teaching as her profession. Teaching was Dargan's gift and her most obvious legacy to the Tulsa community. She taught thousands of elementary school children during her thirty-five-year teaching career with the Tulsa Public Schools, earning "Teacher of the Year" honors in 1975. To her own children and all the children she taught, she was a motivator extraordinaire. "If you are going to be a ditchdigger," Ms. Dargan would tell her kids, "then be the best ditchdigger in the world!"[10]

Often honored for community service, Dargan seemed never to tire of working on behalf of Tulsa's African-American community. As a founding member of the North Tulsa Heritage Foundation, Inc., and the Greenwood Cultural Center, Dargan reinvested her time, talent, and treasure in old Greenwood, her home and her heart since childhood.

Dargan was blessed to be able to witness the opening of the Greenwood Cultural Center, and even gave guided tours of the facility that made her so proud. Visitors from near and far heard Dargan's personal account of the Riot. Her message invariably found amidst disaster and despair a lingering glimmer of hope. On a tour in October 1993, Dargan moved her audience with a personal account of the events surrounding the Riot that was equally bloodcurdling and heartwarming.

>   That riot was a terrible thing and I have never forgotten it; the memory of it is engraved in my thoughts as if it happened yesterday! I was home from school May 31, 1921 because I had the measles. The first day we tried to ride out

the riot, but that second day, June 1, 1921, things got so bad that it became obvious that the black people could no longer remain in their homes and businesses on Greenwood Avenue or in the Greenwood area. There was burning and looting everywhere. Most of the men had been taken to the old Convention Center on Brady or to the Fairgrounds. Others were dead and in temporary morgues while some bodies had been unceremoniously dumped into the Arkansas River. Some of the women were taken that first day too, and were housed in schools and churches. Others like my mother had remained in their homes hoping that things would "soon blow over." When the women saw that they were not going to be able to stay in the area, they reluctantly took their children and headed for safer ground. I remember that we all walked paralleled to the Frisco Railroad tracks heading south and east. What a sight we were—black mothers with babies in arms, and children of all ages by their sides, all of them walking down dusty paths try-ing to get to safety. We did make it to safety thank God. We reached a lovely three-story house in which a white doctor and his family lived. I will never forget that doctor as long as I live. He made the whole bottom floor of his house into a shelter for us hungry, scared, dispossessed and homeless riot refugees. I will never forget the kindness of that man and his family.

When we got to our house, my mother was overjoyed, for our house was still standing. It had been looted however and the drapes, lamps, and my mother's "pretty things"—vases, jewelry, hats, etc., taken. But the house had not burned and when we went into my parents' bedroom, we found out why. The white mob had tried to burn down the house. In the mid-dle of the bed was a pile of burned papers and debris. But the fire had gone out because Mother had a feather mattress on the bed. The feather parts burned but the stem parts did not; they just melted together in a big blob. Oh it was a mess but that mess saved our house. Thank God for that feather mat-tress! We were happy about the house, but we were still sad because we didn't know whether my dad was dead or alive. Thank God, he was alive and he returned to us when the riot was over and order was restored. People were able to rebuild and restore their lives to order, but that terrible riot left marks on our minds that will never be erased.[11]

A bit of Opal Long Dargan lives in each of us. Dargan's abil-

Aerial view of "Deep Greenwood," the 100 block of Greenwood Avenue, look-ing south. (Photo courtesy of Goodrum Photography, 1997)

Looking north on Greenwood Avenue from Archer Street. (Photo courtesy of Goodrum Photography, 1997)

The Brady Theater, formerly "Convention Hall" in Tulsa. (Photo courtesy of Goodrum Photography, 1997)

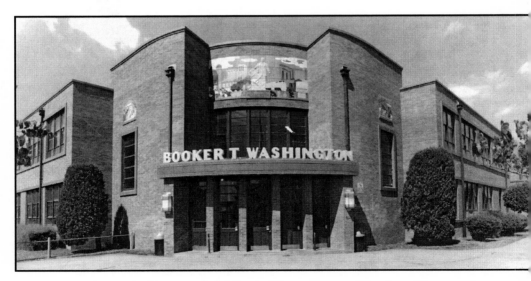

Booker T. Washington High School. (Photo courtesy of Goodrum Photography, 1997)

Memorial service held on June 1, 1996, at Mt. Zion Baptist Church on the occasion of the seventy-fifth anniversary of the 1921 Tulsa Race Riot. Standing and approaching the podium is Dr. Benjamin Hooks, the former executive director of the NAACP. (Photo courtesy of Goodrum Photography)

Jerry Goodwin, assistant to the publisher, The Oklahoma Eagle *(foreground) and James O. Goodwin, his father, publisher of* The Oklahoma Eagle *and principal in the law firm Goodwin & Goodwin. (Photo courtesy of Goodrum Photography, 1997)*

Author Hannibal B. Johnson at the corner of Greenwood Avenue and Archer Street. (Photo courtesy of Goodrum Photography, 1997)

ity to find something positive in all life situations, her perseverance, her willingness to give any individual the benefit of the
doubt until experience dictated otherwise, and her fundamental
sense of integrity are a model for us all.

Like Opal Long Dargan, many African-American Tulsans
made significant contributions to the Greenwood District. In
1992 the North Tulsa Heritage Foundation, Inc., began induct-
ing into its "Hall of Memories" those African-American Tulsans
who have throughout the years invested immeasurably in their
community. Appropriately, these individuals are honored with
a tribute to their achievements and contributions and presented with the "Image Builder Award." The Opal L. Dargan
Renaissance Hall provides the ideal venue for the event.

The Greenwood Cultural Center completed an expansion
in 1996, and now boasts some 25,000 square feet of multipurpose space with banquet rooms, classrooms, office space, museum, a gift shop, and an art gallery. The renovated Greenwood
Cultural Center represents some $2.7 million in total capital
investments. Supported with capital funding from both the City
of Tulsa and the State of Oklahoma, it raises its own operating
funds through tours, facility rental, grant awards, and program-
ming. It is self-sustaining.

The Greenwood District in its heyday was sustained in large
part by a system of legal segregation that forced a large measure
of black economic independence—an "economic detour."
Segregation, despite its obvious ills, generated black prosperity
as dollars from black residents of the Greenwood District stayed
in the community. As segregation fell into disfavor, economic
markets opened up and dollars began to flow outside the community. Ultimately, the community declined. By contrast, the
Greenwood Cultural Center, a monument to the Greenwood
District at its peak and a center for black culture and history, is
the product of integration and interracial collaboration. State
and local officials and citizens of various racial and ethnic backgrounds lent moral and financial support to its creation and
maintenance. This broader support base, if sustained, should
ensure the viability of the Greenwood Cultural Center. Indeed,
inter-cultural collaboration may provide a model for the revitalization of the Greenwood District as a whole.

Tulsa skyline with Greenwood Cultural Center in the foreground. (Photo courtesy of Goodrum Photography, 1997)

The Greenwood Cultural Center places Tulsa's African-American community squarely in the cultural, economic, social, and intellectual mainstream of the city, the state, and the nation. Improving race relations and removing barriers to equal opportunity are vital parts of its mission.

Letters from the Smithsonian Institution and from noted historian and native Tulsan Dr. John Hope Franklin to the Greenwood Cultural Center make clear its significance. The undated letter from Wilton S. Dillon of the Smithsonian Institution commends the Greenwood Cultural Center on its efforts to educate the public about African-American history and culture and promote intercultural exchange:

To the Board of Directors of Greenwood
Cultural Center

Dear Colleagues:
I am delighted by the civic energy and pride being poured
into the Greenwood Cultural Center in Tulsa, a new complement to Gilcrease and Philbrook. Since my childhood in the
nearby village of Yale, I have looked up to Tulsa's cultural institutions for their style and substance. Tulsa was one of my first
windows on the bigger world, and now, from a larger world
perspective, I am still looking to Tulsa for innovations which
will help to draw people together. Cultural and ethnic pluralism are what make the United States a mosaic society, each
group enriching the lives of others. The Smithsonian wel-
comes partners in our efforts to celebrate the cultural gifts of
all people. *E pluribus unum* takes on new meaning.

Jim Crow laws and customary practice kept people apart
in the Oklahoma and Alabama of my childhood. These arbitrary barriers inspired my wartime signing up for membership
in the National Association for the Advancement of Colored
People, and my later civil rights actions in the 1950's as a dis-
ciple of Martin Luther King and Mahatma Gandhi. They
inspired many of us to seek out the potentials of all persons,
and to realize that the rights of blacks, whites and other citizens were all being violated. Good luck took me to live in
Africa, ancestral home of at least 12% of all Americans. My
only son was born there. So I have an enduring interest in
African and Afro-American cultural experience and the institutions which help transmit that experience to all citizens.

Americans of African ancestry, such as the world famous
historian John Hope Franklin, who grew up in Tulsa are
among the people known as "old Americans." Some came
before the revolution and fought in it. They are citizens who
can welcome all the later cultural influences coming in from
Europe and Asia as well as the Africa from which they were so
cruelly cut off by slavery. Greenwood Cultural Center has an
opportunity to reflect these cosmopolitan interests, as well as
the uniqueness of "Africans in the New World." Oklahoma has
become a crossroads of many cultures. All of us have much to
learn from the Native Americans who preceded us all, and
adapted to us newcomers without losing their identities. (A
prime practitioner of learning from each other is found in my

Smithsonian colleague, John W. Franklin, son of John Hope Franklin.)

Another great Tulsan, Daniel J. Boorstin, the Librarian Emeritus of Congress, and author of many books on American and world civilizations, had to go to Harvard before he could meet John Hope Franklin. Franklin and Boorstin later became professors in the same department at the University of Chicago. They both should be on hand to celebrate the Greenwood opening and the symbolism of its location in the handsome though once divided city where they both "came of age." Boorstin has written about "boosterism" in American society, inspired by the boosting of Tulsa. There is something new to boost and boast about. And I am proud of the interest my brother, Jerry Dillon, is taking in this marvelous new experiment in enjoying the cultural gifts of all. Tulsa must be on the threshold of a Renaissance, facing a bright future without ignoring her history.

Congratulations,
WILTON S. DILLON,
Director of Interdisciplinary Studies
Smithsonian Institution

Dr. John Hope Franklin, son of legendary Tulsa lawyer B. C. Franklin, moved to Tulsa from the nearby community of Rentiesville, Oklahoma, in or about 1925. His father had moved to Tulsa some four years earlier. B. C. Franklin operated his law office out of a tent after the Riot. Meanwhile, young John Hope graduated from Booker T. Washington High School, then Fisk University in 1935, and finally Harvard University in 1936 and 1941, with a master's degree and a doctorate, respectively. The much-honored Dr. John Hope Franklin is the James B. Duke Professor of History Emeritus at Duke University and chairs President Clinton's advisory task force on race relations.

Dr. Franklin, who figures prominently in Wilton S. Dillon's letter to the Greenwood Cultural Center, penned a similarly moving letter. The letter, dated April 4, 1989, and addressed to the Board of Trustees of the Greenwood Cultural Center, reads as follows:

Please accept my heartiest congratulations on the occasion of the dedication of the Greenwood Cultural Center. I am confident that this new facility will enhance the quality of life not only for the citizens of North Tulsa but for those in other parts of the city as well.

Shortly after Dr. W. E. B. Du Bois visited Tulsa in 1926, he wrote, "Black Tulsa is a happy city. It has new clothes. It is young and gay and strong. Five little years ago fire and blood and robbery leveled it to the ground, flat, raw, smoking. . . . Yet it lived. . . . Scars are there, but the city is impudent and noisy. It believes in itself. Thank God for the Grit of Tulsa." This is the spirit that has helped North Tulsa survive, and I hope that this spirit will drive the Cultural Center to become a powerful force in the community. Best wishes.

> Sincerely yours,
> JOHN HOPE FRANKLIN
> James B. Duke Professor Emeritus
> [Duke University]

The Greenwood Cultural Center offers healing to a community too long divided, too long afraid to peer behind the closed doors of its past. It is a repository of historical information and artifacts on the African-American experience. More profoundly, however, it is a storehouse of knowledge about our collective past, present, and future. African-American history is an integral part of American history.

In March 1997, eighth-grade students from Monte Casino, a private, predominantly white Catholic school in Tulsa, visited the Greenwood Cultural Center and the Mabel B. Little Heritage House. These students took the time to mail postcards of thanks to Carmen Pettie, administrator coordinator for the North Tulsa Heritage Foundation, Inc., who took them on a tour of the facilities. What these children said should inform and inspire us all. Following are two of the postcard comments:

> Dear Carmen,
> Thank you for showing us around the Greenwood section of town and the Jazz Hall of Fame. It was interesting to see how prosperous Greenwood was until it was burned. I think Greenwood would have been a great part of town and a

wealthy part of town if it had not been burned. I would like to return and see it again sometime. Thanks a lot. . . .

Dear Carmen,
Thank you so much for teaching us about Greenwood's society before, during and after the race riot. I never would have even known about the terrible incident in Greenwood's history or what they had gone through if I hadn't have visited the Greenwood Cultural Center and studied about it. . . .

These are remarkable tributes to the power of accurate history. If we share our history, there is hope.

Outside the Greenwood Cultural Center stands the "1921 Black Wall Street Memorial," a proud monument to those individual and business causalities of the Riot. The lustrous black granite memorial, inscribed with a partial listing of the names of individuals and businesses lost in the Riot, was unveiled in 1996 to coincide with the seventy-fifth anniversary of the Riot. Beneath the listing on the memorial is a fitting literary tribute to Greenwood penned by Wyonia Murray Bailey, a Riot survivor, in May 1967. Ms. Bailey's moving lament recalls Greenwood's glory and implicitly beckons to those who so loved the Greenwood of old to come to the aid of its shattered remnants.

O GREENWOOD!
LEST YOU GO UNHERALDED

She held the hopes and future of her own
Others heard and came to pay her homage
She was a showcase for the industrious
Here stood the monuments of the proud
And now, men falter midst her rubbles
She symbolizes progress no more.
A crone stripped of her finery
So slowly changed so lowly bowed.

Many, who she praised to dignity
Pass quickly by, all favors forgotten
Ignoring the sight of her deterioration,
Aborting all thought of a second chance.

The 1921 Black Wall Street Memorial. (Photo courtesy of Goodrum Photography, 1997)

Few remain to dignify her disgrace
Or fight to rescind her demise
The ghosts of her better days await,
Death rattles to intone the macabre dance.

O Greenwood lest you go unheralded,
I sing a song of remembrance
While sons of your bounty loyal still
Place a head stone at the site of your victory.

Without doubt, Greenwood has come miles along the road to rejuvenation since 1967, the year Wyonia Bailey penned "O Greenwood." Just as surely, it has miles yet to go if it is to rise to the heights of its bright past.

EPILOGUE

Things ain't what they oughta be,
Things ain't what they gonna be,
But thank God things ain't like they was.[1]

Tulsa's Greenwood District may never reclaim its title as "The Black Wall Street of America" (or even "The Black Main Street of America," a more historically accurate reflection of what once was), but she will remain one of the most interesting, provocative places in America and a vast repository of African-American history and culture. History can neither be undone nor relived. But it offers lessons for the present and future that we ignore at our own peril.

One great truth to be gleaned from the storied Greenwood District is the ability of time to heal and renew. Healing and renewal, however, come only when we use time wisely—when we use time to reflect on our history and tailor our current and future actions to what we know about our past.

The story of the Greenwood District is tightly interwoven with the history of race in America. The Greenwood District has come a long way. So, too, has America. But there is work yet to be done. Race still divides us—unnecessarily so. As we move toward the twenty-first century, we can, we should, and we must continue to seek common ground.

Artificial barriers such as segregation sent Tulsa's African-American community on an "economic detour" and prompted the establishment of the Greenwood District, an insular, self-contained community that prospered for decades. The same

145

barriers, it may be argued, led African-Americans on a "cultural detour," and occasioned the creation and refinement by talented artists, Oklahomans among them, of the musical idiom we know as jazz.

Integration (or, more accurately, desegregation), achieved only after hard-fought civil rights battles, had unintended negative economic consequences. One of the rights that African-Americans fought for and attained—the right to spend their dollars in the greater Tulsa community rather than solely in the Greenwood District—proved a hollow victory indeed. "Integration" turned out to be a one-way street. Black dollars flowed out. But white dollars did not contemporaneously flow in. Additional stresses from enhanced competition, fluctuating economic conditions, and changing demographics made it virtually impossible for black businesses to survive without successfully reaching out to the entire community. That did not happen. The Greenwood District declined. The welcome demise of segregation ultimately doomed the economic and cultural vitality of the Greenwood District.

The detours—temporary diversions—from American society's main economic and cultural arteries forced upon African-Americans are considerably diminished, but not wholly eliminated. *De jure* segregation (i.e., segregation by law) no longer exists. True integration, the free and equal association of all people, should be viewed as the vehicle through which we establish economic and cultural interchanges—common points along the way at which all societal traffic intersects, and may enter or exit voluntarily, subject to universally applicable rules of the road.

Realization of the full potential of a Greenwood District renaissance demands recognition of a simple proposition: The Greenwood District can only be truly independent if and when it recognizes and celebrates its interdependence with the greater community. The Greenwood Cultural Center, a collaborative effort among diverse interests, grew out of just such a model of interdependence. While its orientation is African-American, the Greenwood Cultural Center sees itself, and is generally seen, as an asset of the community at large. There is an increasing realization that Tulsa must view itself as a single community composed of distinct, interrelated, and valuable facets. Learning about, understanding, and celebrating those facets is ultimately in the best interest of the community as a whole.

Perhaps the new sense of cooperativeness stems from a desire to preserve the history of previously marginalized groups—a desire to encourage cultural pluralism. Perhaps it emanates from the growing clout of such groups (and African-Americans in particular) in an increasingly diverse society. Whatever the reasons, the spirit of cross-cultural cooperation comes better late than never.

Cultural cooperation is a laudable goal in and of itself. But revitalization of the vaunted entreprenurial character of the Greenwood District will demand more than that. Viable public-private partnerships built on sound economic, sociological, and demographic data must be part of the equation. When the Greenwood District is viewed as an asset of the greater Tulsa community (or, deservedly, a national treasure), such public-private partnerships seem both prudent and feasible.

The present Greenwood District, with the Greenwood Cultural Center as its crown jewel, stands as a proud and living monument to the scores of African-Americans whose unsurpassed faith, hope, and courage are an inspiration to all. They are the individuals who planted its roots, persevered its Riot, promoted its regeneration, and precipitated its current renaissance.

The torch now rests in the hands of new leaders. There are new challenges to be met, new alliances to be forged. But the original torch-bearers, the Greenwood pioneers, will never be forgotten. To these heroes we are forever indebted and eternally grateful. It is upon their shoulders that we stand today. In tribute to them, and as a legacy to our own children, born and yet-to-be-born, let the renaissance live on.

APPENDICES

APPENDIX A

INDUCTEES INTO
THE OKLAHOMA JAZZ HALL OF FAME

(PROFILE INFORMATION COURTESY OF THE OKLAHOMA JAZZ HALL OF FAME)

1989 JAZZ HALL OF FAME INDUCTEES

ZELIA N. PAGE BREAUX

Zelia N. Page was born in 1880 in Jefferson City, Missouri, where she finished college at Lincoln Institute. She received her master's degree from Northwestern University in Evanston, Illinois. She taught at Langston University, where she served as head of the Music Department, and in the Oklahoma City Public Schools as Supervisor of Music. Ms. Breaux conducted many musicals throughout the United States. She became a legend in Oklahoma City because of her superior musical talents and her complete musical education. Oklahoma City became a center for music education in black schools. Its Douglass High School band became one of the best high school bands in the entire southwest among black schools.

She never lectured. Instead, she encouraged students to learn about and play jazz through ensembles. At that time, and as late as 1954, she was not allowed to teach a class called "Jazz" in high school. Musical greats John Anglin, Sherman Sneed, Al Dennie, Alva Lee McCain, Edward and Charlie Christian, Lloyd and Malcolm Whitby, Juanita Burns Bolar, Leon Nelson, Francis "Doc" Whitby, Cornelius Earl Pittman, and Jimmy Rushing were among those on the long list of talents nurtured by Zelia Page Breaux.

Before her death in 1956, she was recognized as the spirit of the

new day for Negro history in America, which came to be known as
"The Dawn of a New Day." This movement embraced the use of the
Negro national anthem, "Lift Every Voice and Sing."

CHARLIE CHRISTIAN

Charlie Christian was the man who introduced single-string solos
on the amplified guitar. Talent scout John Hammond heard of
Christian and arranged for him to audition with Benny Goodman. He
got the job.

Christian, born and reared in Oklahoma City, showed talent for the
guitar early and became an admired local musician. He was not the first
to use the electric guitar, but was the first to put it in the solo spotlight.
He played mostly single lines, like horn players. Christian had a warm,
full sound, and that, along with other things, set the sound standard
for future jazz guitarists. He helped Dizzy Gillespie, Thelonious Monk,
Charlie Parker and others build a good portion of modern American
jazz. Some of those who knew him called him a "natural" who did not
realize that what he was doing was truly something special.

On March 2, 1942, at the age of 24, Charlie Christian died of
tuberculosis.

ERNIE FIELDS

Ernie Fields is known nationwide alternately as "The Gentleman of
Swing" and "Mr. In The Mood." His Tulsa-based orchestra was formed
in the mid-thirties and made its debut at the famed Apollo Theatre in
New York City in 1939. Texas born, but Taft, Oklahoma-raised, Fields
toured across the United States for over 30 years. He recorded several
hits: "T-Town Blues," "Butch's Blues," "Lard Stomp," and others during
the '30s and '40s. His rock and roll version of "In The Mood" topped the
Billboard and Cashbox charts in 1959-60. "In The Mood" earned Fields
a gold record, designating over a million record sales.

In *Big Band Blues*, author Albert McCarthy notes Fields' recordings "suggest that the band possessed the potential for a greater success than it ever achieved." Jazz scholar Gunther Schuller noted in his
book, *The Swing Era*: "In terms of medium-tempo relaxed swing and,
in general a wonderful sense of rhythmic well being, the band was hard
to match, let alone beat."

Fields and his wife of over 50 years, Bernice Copeland, both
retired, made Tulsa their home. They raised three children, Ernie Jr.,
Charles, and Carmen. Ernie Fields died in May of 1997.

LOWELL FULSON

Lowell Fulson, one of the greatest treasures ever produced by Oklahoma, is known throughout the United States and Europe for his pioneering blues style. His compositions influenced the likes of B. B. King, Magic Sam, and Ray Charles. Charles and Stanley Turrentine were members of his band. "Reconsider Baby" was perhaps his best known hit.

Born in Tulsa in 1921, Lowell moved to Atoka, Oklahoma, when he was about five years old. There he learned to play the blues from local guitarists. His style was also influenced by listening to recordings of Blind Lemon Jefferson, Peetie Wheatstraw, and Blind Boy Fuller. His uncle introduced him to a West Texas style of blues. By the time he was 18, he was playing professionally at country balls, clubs, and juke joints.

After meeting and playing with the legendary Texas Alexander, a country blues singer, Lowell began his trek away from Oklahoma. He moved to Texas, then after the war, to California. In Los Angeles, he recorded on the "Big Time" label, then on "Swingtime."

He recorded several hits, including "Guitar Shuffle," "Low Society Blues," "Blue Shadow Falling," and "Everyday I Have the Blues." Musical greats who have paid tribute to Lowell by recording some of his over 100 compositions include Elvis Presley, Sam Cooke, Leon Russell, B. B. King, T-Bone Walker, and Otis Redding.

JAY MCSHANN

Jay McShann, born in Muskogee in 1916, heard music from an early age. Both his mother and father played an old upright piano in their home. Self-taught, McShann began playing blues piano at age 12 after hearing a Bessie Smith recording. When he was 19, he formed his first band. He hired Charlie Parker, who played with him until the early 1940s. After a stint in the military, McShann returned to his music and recorded on the West Coast.

McShann was the subject of a documentary in 1978, "Hootie Blues," and was proclaimed the "last" Blue Devil as a result of Bruce Rickers' documentary film, "The Last of the Blue Devils," a study of Kansas City music which also focused on the Oklahoma City Commonwealth band. His renewed popularity began following this documentary.

After the death of Count Basie in 1984, Jay McShann stood alone as the greatest practitioner of the Kansas City jazz piano style. His magical blend of Oklahoma blues, powerhouse piano, and rich voice has generated a worldwide following.

He is the recipient of the 1987 Jazz Masters Fellowship from the National Endowment for the Arts. He has received awards from the Smithsonian Institution and a citation from Congress.

McShann travels extensively, appearing at music festivals worldwide. During his last visit to Tulsa, Jay McShann conducted a two-day workshop at the jazz lab of the McLain High School Fine Arts Center and performed at the Greenwood Cultural Center.

JESSIE MAE RENFRO SAPP

Among the vast array of brilliant performers of African-American sacred music produced by Oklahoma is Jessie Mae Renfro Sapp. The soloist ranks alongside such greats as Mahalia Jackson, James Cleveland, and Shirley Caesar. Her professional career spans over 50 years.

Born into a musically-inclined family, she was immersed in gospel music-playing and singing from an early age. "Looking for something different," she sang jazz as a teenager in Dallas, but after two years, she returned to the gospel music that was such an important part of her childhood.

Beginning in 1951, Jessie Mae Renfro Sapp recorded with Peacock Recording Company of Houston, Texas, which was in those days one of the most important purveyors of African-American sacred music. One of her albums, "He's So Wonderful," remained on Billboard gospel charts for almost three years. In her many years as a performer, she appeared in churches and auditoriums in almost every one of the United States.

CLAUDE WILLIAMS

Claude "Fiddler" Williams is often referred to as the "inventor of the jazz violin." A veteran of early bands fronted by Count Basie and Nat King Cole, Williams is proof that music can improve with the age of the performer. Williams toured nationally and internationally well into his eighties.

Williams got his start with road shows traveling in the southwest and moved to Kansas City in 1929 with Andy Kirk's Clouds of Joy. In 1936, he joined Count Basie's band, becoming its first guitar player. The band journeyed to New York and cut several sides for Decca. This was the first recording for Count Basie.

After leaving Count Basie's band, Williams returned to playing the violin. He recorded with Jay McShann, B. B. King, Budd Tate, Paul Quinichette, and the Claude Williams Quintet.

Williams performed at the 1992 "Juneteenth on Greenwood" Heritage Festival in Tulsa.

1990 OKLAHOMA JAZZ HALL OF FAME INDUCTEES

THE BLUE DEVILS

The Blue Devils are perhaps Oklahoma's most famous jazz band. Having roots in Oklahoma City in the early 1920s, they went on to become nationally acclaimed, influencing scores of musicians along the way. Count Basie said that the first time he heard the Blue Devils "was probably the most important turning point in my musical career—once a Blue Devil, always a Blue Devil." The Blue Devils produced such great artists as Walter Page, Oran "Hot Lips" Page, James Rushing, Eddie Durham, Buster Smith, Lester Young, Abe Bolar, and Alvin Burroughs. They recorded only one session. That was November of 1929. The personnel from that band became the nucleus of the Bennie Moten band in the early 1930s, which later formed the core of the Count Basie Band.

Part of the reason for their vast influence came from the new verve that they brought to jazz through their many innovations. Walter Page brought the string bass into prominence in big bands. James Rushing permanently changed the big band vocal style. Buster Smith became the prominent influence on a cadre of musicians in the mid- and late-thirties, including the young Charlie Parker. Many people credit the Blue Devils with beginning the "riff" structure which has become one of the hallmarks of jazz. With these innovations and the abundance of talented soloists, the Blue Devils have become legendary among the "territorial bands."

AL DENNIE

Al Dennie was born near Arcadia, Oklahoma, on September 27, 1903. He was one of many great musicians introduced to music by Douglass High School teacher Zelia Breaux. Dennie moved to Kansas City and received further training from a Tuskegee graduate, Professor Dawson. His professional beginnings go back to his days with such seminal Kansas City bands as Chauncie Downs and the Rinky Dinks, George Wilkerson's Musical Magnets, Jessie Stone's band, and Bennie Moten's band.

Along with Bennie Moten, he organized the Jap Allen Band. This group toured extensively throughout the Midwest, soon becoming featured in many of the historic band battles which were such an important part of Kansas City's daily musical menu. He also played a prominent role in the Paul Banks Orchestra, another important early territorial band.

Dennie was one of the first people to notice the developing talent of a seventeen-year-old piano player named Jay McShann. Jay's first lessons in big band music were taken from Al Dennie in Tulsa. Dennie spent much of his life in Kansas City, playing and keeping company with jazz legends from Kansas City and all across the country.

CLARENCE LOVE

Clarence Love was born on January 25, 1908, in Muskogee, Oklahoma. His family moved to Kansas City, where he first began his music studies. His first influence was Charlie Watts, a protege of ragtime genius Scott Joplin. He attended Kansas City's Lincoln High School, forming a jazz band there before he graduated. He was inspired to become a full-time professional musician after hearing George Lee's Band performing at Kansas City's Lyric Hall. By 1928, he had formed the Clarence Love Orchestra which included some of Kansas City's finest musicians. Love's band rivaled Bennie Moten's and George Lee's for local and regional popularity.

In 1933 he moved to Dallas and formed a new band. The group was an immediate success, soon broadcasting over Dallas KRLD radio station. After hearing Love's group over KRLD, a Decca records agent scheduled them to record in New York. The band broke up before they reached New York, with Love ending up in Indianapolis. Love helped start one of the largest African-American booking agencies in the business. He founded an all female group called the Darlings of Rhythm, managing and touring with them over all the world. When his father died, Love moved back to Tulsa and began another Clarence Love Orchestra. In 1948, he opened his own club, The Love Lounge, where locally and nationally prominent musicians congregated and played. He owned and operated clubs until 1957, when he returned to the booking business. A key figure in Oklahoma's legacy of jazz greatness, Clarence Love died in 1998.

James "Jimmy" Rushing

Born in Oklahoma City, Oklahoma, on August 26, 1903, James Rushing developed musical skills that earned him honors as both a jazz and blues great. Rushing has been called "one of the greatest of all big band singers." It has also been claimed that his blues career "reached the furthest and spread the appeal of the blues on a wider area than anyone."

Jimmy was first encouraged to play the piano by his uncle, Wesley Manning, a sporting house pianist. As a child, he became involved as a singer at school and church functions in Oklahoma City. In his teenage years, he became restless and roamed across the United States, meeting such musicians as Blind Lemon Jefferson and Jelly Roll Morton. When he returned to Oklahoma City, he joined the Blue Devils. By doing this, he began to bridge the gap between itinerant street singing and the blues-based lyrical swing which became the standard singing style for most big band singers for the next four decades. He recorded with the Blue Devils on their first and only recording. Later he joined the Bennie Moten Band, the foundation for the Count Basie Band. His excellent intonation and robust, yet sensitive, manner perfectly complemented the Count Basie Band and helped to shape its identity. He stayed with Count Basie from 1935 until big bands began to wane in the early 1950s. He also recorded frequently with Benny Goodman's band.

Jimmy Rushing is regarded as the father of the "blues shouters," a style that arose in the 1940s. He became famous within this idiom, touring (until his death in 1968) with the likes of Count Basie, Dave Brubeck, and Earl Hines. His influence has been strongly felt in the fields of jazz, rhythm and blues, blues, and rock and roll, reaching a range of artists from Lowell Fulson to Chuck Berry.

C. C. Skinner

Claude Columbus Skinner was born in Clarkesville, Tennessee. In his early teens, he began his commitment to religious music. By 1920, he had become the musical minister for the Paradise Baptist Church of Tulsa, a position he held for the next thirty years. He taught piano and other music lessons in his home, instructing and inspiring dozens of musicians in the Tulsa area.

Known affectionately as "Uncle C.C." by his students, he founded the North Tulsa Singing Convention in 1975. He served as its president for ten years. Uncle C.C. traveled across the United States teaching choirs in every part of the country. He was a prolific songwriter, composing such songs as "Back to the Dust," "Jesus In My Heart," and "Working for the Lord." He died in Tulsa on September 22, 1989.

1991 Oklahoma Jazz Hall of Fame Inductees

Chesney "Chet" Baker

Born in Yale, Oklahoma, on December 23, 1929, Baker moved with his family to Oklahoma City where he sang in the church choir but, at the time, did not play an instrument. At age thirteen, his father gave him a trombone. Thinking the trombone too large for him, Baker exchanged it for a trumpet. Best known for his trumpet virtuosity, Chet Baker also was a flugelhorn player and a gifted vocalist.

And the rest, as they say, is history.

His widow, Carol, described him as "the dearest and most sensitive man I ever knew. In spite of his many troubles . . . over the years, he never changed."

His "many troubles" included losing his teeth from a street beating in 1966 and having to teach himself to play again with dentures. After this unfortunate incident, Baker did not play professionally for three years, but made his comeback on the *Steve Allen Show* late in 1968. Baker's career was revitalized when Dizzy Gillespie arranged a booking in 1972 for him at the Half Note in New York City.

From then until his death in Amsterdam, Netherlands, May 13, 1988, Baker again played in Europe and the United States, including appearing at Carnegie Hall. Chet's national and international reputation is reflected in the fact that his three children were born in three different venues: London, New York, and Los Angeles.

Joey Hobart Crutcher

Born in Tulsa, Oklahoma, on December 11, 1947, Joey Hobart Crutcher sports a biography that reads like a "Who's Who" in music. This despite the fact some of his music teachers tried to discourage his early devotion to the gospel genre.

Cruthcer's mother reports that when the delivery men brought a piano to their home, he showed versatility when he sat down and played "My Country 'Tis of Thee." It was Reverend John Henry Johnson and Don O'Banner who had an outside influence on Joey's development of his dynamic gospel style.

In school, Crutcher was pianist for the Boy's Glee Club. During his stint in the Army, he was the chapel organist. After the military, he came back to Tulsa and attended Tulsa Junior College, Oklahoma Business College, and the Oklahoma School of Religion, where he studied sacred music.

In 1970, he joined musical forces by marrying his childhood sweetheart, Leann Johnson. The couple has four children and specializes in building mass choirs and helping churches build quality music programs.

Crutcher serves as minister of music for the New Heights Christian Center, the director of the Love Connection Community Singers, music director of the Gospel Music Workshop of America, and music coordinator at The University of Tulsa for the Unlimited Praise Gospel Choir.

BARNEY KESSEL

Born in Muskogee, Oklahoma, on October 17, 1923, Barney Kessel is known for his blues-like, hard-driving, earthy style. He is a model of brilliant harmonic improvisation.

Kessel became a guitarist by accident. In 1935, while selling newspapers on a street corner, he saw a guitar in a pawn shop window. He bought it, along with a "how to" book for a dollar. His mother issued a mandate—either play it or get rid of it—after learning that the instrument was stashed in a broom closet. He chose to play it.

For three months, four hours a day, six days a week, Barney struggled with the instrument as he took advantage of free lessons offered at a government-sponsored school.

At the age of thirteen, Kessel discovered the jazz of Benny Goodman, the Dorseys and Jimmy Lunceford. He said, "It was almost like a mist lifted. . . ."

In 1940, he moved to Los Angeles. From there his career led him to New York. Kessel continued playing for film and television until 1969. He then moved to London, playing European clubs and concerts. Barney Kessel played and taught in Sweden, Italy, France, Germany, Spain, Austria, Canada, Japan, and the United States.

CECIL MCBEE

Cecil McBee was born and reared in Tulsa, Oklahoma. He began his musical career as a clarinetist in his high school band. He traveled the state playing duets with his sister in concert and marching bands.

But by age seventeen, he began experimenting with the bass and played steadily at local night clubs. Working his way through Central State University in Wilberforce, Ohio, he was inspired by the jazz tradition. He focused on the bass and jazz composition.

While in the Army, he conducted the military band at Fort Knox, Kentucky, and began to probe his bass composition. By graduation from college, he was deep into jazz improvisation.

After a stay in Detroit, he joined the Paul Winter Group and moved to New York City and commenced a book project, *The Techniques of Improvised Bass.*

His virtuoso-composer accomplishments have been recognized by "ASCAP"—the American Society of Composers, Authors, and Publishers. McBee joined ASCAP in 1975.

In 1985, he received his second National Endowment for the Arts award for experimental composition. In 1989, McBee received a Grammy Award in the category "best group recording" for "Blues for John Coltrane."

His compositions have been recorded by Charlie Lloyd on the "Forest Flowers" album, by Charlie Tolliver on "Live at Slugs Volume I and II," by Pharaoh Sanders on "Thembi," and by Norman Conners on "Love From the Sun."

Roy Milton

Roy Milton, an internationally famous bandleader, conquered Europe after his band catapulted into national prominence in the United States in the 1940s and 1950s. A Paris, France, newspaper critic described Milton's drumming as "terrific" and his singing "often languorous," making Milton the ultimate "Swing Man."

Milton, born in Tulsa, Oklahoma, became a featured drummer and vocalist with the Ernie Fields Orchestra before settling in Los Angeles in the mid-1930s. His combo, "The Solid Senders," was composed of an array of strong artists who furnished pulsating rhythms and exciting solos. Musical director of Milton's group was Bobby Smith, the saxophonist who composed "Tippin' In" and was also an alumnus of the Erskine Hawkins Orchestra. Milton was a night club and recording star with million-record sellers "R.M. Blues," "Best Wishes," "Red Light," and "So Tired," which has become a standard.

When rock music began to flourish, his albums reflected it with titles like "The Roots of Rock" and "Instant Groove." As a singer, his voice was described as "of exceptional quality, his diction is clear, and his moving simplicity touches you deeply."

He died in 1983 following a stroke.

1992 OKLAHOMA JAZZ HALL OF FAME INDUCTEES

AARON BELL

Aaron Bell, a multi-faceted jazzman of extraordinary and diverse accomplishments, was born in Muskogee, Oklahoma in 1921. He was the fifth of ten children of James Aaron Bell and Bridelle Beatrice Bell, a music teacher who saw to it that all eight sons and both daughters played musical instruments.

Bell began his musical journey on the piano, but shifted to trumpet when he discovered jazz on radio broadcasts from Chicago. Performances by such legends as the Earl Hines and Fletcher Henderson swing orchestras mesmerized him.

Bell entered Xavier University in New Orleans in 1938 and was introduced to the bass violin. He showed an immediate and natural affinity for the instrument, and at once startled and impressed his teachers. He graduated from Xavier in 1942, spent the next four years in a United States Navy band, and returned to Muskogee to teach music at Manual Training High School. This career phase ended abruptly. Bell sat in with Andy Kirk's Clouds of Joy band in Tulsa, and so impressed Kirk that he was hired on the spot. Bell toured with Kirk for a year, then left to enter New York University and earn his first of three advanced degrees.

Bell then resumed performing, first with Teddy Wilson, then with such luminaries as Lester Young, Stan Getz, Miles Davis, J.J. Johnson, Cab Calloway, Lucky Millinder, and Jimmy Lunceford. While working one night with pianist Billy Taylor at the Hickory House in New York, Bell attracted the attention of Duke Ellington, who subsequently hired him for a two-year stint with the band. Bell and Ellington maintained a close association for a total of six years. They recorded together and collaborated on several original compositions and arrangements.

For years, Bell maintained an active performance schedule. In recent years, he toured Europe with trumpeter Clark Terry and the "Ellington Spacemen," led a seventeen-piece orchestra at Carnegie Hall in a recreation of the renowned Ellington concert performed there by the Duke in 1941, and, in 1985, composed "The Edwardian Suite," introduced on the occasion of Ellington's birthday and commissioned by the Duke Ellington Jazz Society. Bell is considered the foremost academic authority on Ellington's music.

Dr. Bell, even in "semi-retirement," continued to teach at Essex Community College where he began teaching in 1969.

RUTH BROWN

Ruth Brown relishes her career and the sure knowledge that "overnight sensation" or "one-hit wonder" can never be applied to her.

Brown's career began in the late 1940s when she switched from what she had been doing—pop-singing for U.S.O. shows and big bands in the South during World War II—to rhythm-and-blues music. Her recording of "So Long" skyrocketed in 1949, and she became one of the giants of this idiom.

But her brilliantly successful early career was followed by eventual decline and near-retirement, then re-emergence. Recent achievements solidly underscore her stature as a brilliant, widely-recognized blues artist.

In 1989, Ruth Brown won a Tony Award as "best actress in a broadway musical," "Black and Blue," and followed that in 1990 with a "best female jazz vocalist" nod for her "Blues on Broadway" album.

Born in Portsmouth, Virginia, Ruth Brown made her musical debut as a teenager singing spirituals in her church choir, but eschewed the blues that her father called "the devil's music." Then came the war and her late '40s decision to try rhythm and blues, that paid off so handsomely.

She became one of the premier recording artists of the 1950s whose work influenced singers as diverse as Aretha Franklin and Bonnie Raitt.

Ruth Brown had five number one hits and two-dozen top ten hits on the R&B charts during the 1950s, including "Teardrops From My Eyes" and "5-to-15 Hours." She recorded more than 80 songs for Atlantic Records and sold so many records that Atlantic was called "The House that Ruth Built."

Ruth's 1992 induction as an honorary member of the Oklahoma Jazz Hall of Fame and her spectacularly popular performance two nights later at the Juneteenth Festival in Tulsa was followed by her induction into the Rock and Roll Hall of Fame.

DUKE ELLINGTON

Edward Kennedy Ellington, "Duke," was born in Washington, D.C. on April 29, 1899. He died in New York City on May 24, 1974. He was a citizen of the world.

Duke Ellington despised categories. He did not want to be restricted. He mistrusted the word "jazz," preferring to focus on the concept of "freedom of expression."

Categories of class, race, color, creed, and economic status were obnoxious to him. He made his subtle, telling contribution to the civil rights struggle in his musical statements—"Jump for Joy" in 1941, in "The Deep South Suite" in 1946, and in "My People" in 1963. Long before black was officially beautiful—in 1928, to be precise—he wrote "Black Beauty" and dedicated it to a great artist, Florence Mills. With "Black, Brown and Beige" in 1941, he proudly delineated the African-American contributions to American history. Asked if he would ever retire, Ellington used to reply scornfully, "Retire to *what?*"

The Duke Ellington standards "Mood Indigo," "Sophisticated Lady," "Caravan," "Solitude," "Don't Get Around Much Anymore," "I'm Beginning to See the Light," and "Satin Doll" are part of the fabric of twentieth-century life. But the popular hits are only a small part of Duke Ellington's priceless legacy to mankind. His music has been and will be interpreted by others, but never with the significance and tonal character given it by his own band and soloists—those for whom it was written. Duke Ellington's records are the greatest of his gifts to us. He possessed the uncanny ability to bring out qualities in his musicians they did not always know they possessed.

Kenneth E. Kilgore & The Ambassadors' Concert Choir

Kenneth E. Kilgore, now the minister of music of St. John Missionary Baptist Church in Oklahoma City, Oklahoma, and, at the time, administrative assistant and music coordinator, organized the Ambassadors' Concert Choir in 1979 as a component of the music department of the church.

The first performance by the forty-two-voice group was a Christmas Eve concert that offered an audience of more than 1,000 selections from Handel's *Messiah,* as well as light classic, spiritual and gospel selections.

The first concert was well-received and attracted a number of singers from other churches. The Choir moved into the broader Oklahoma City community, attracting more talent and expanding its musical repertoire.

Choir membership is based totally on singing ability and members' availability for the rehearsals that prepare the Choir for its major performances each year. Membership includes school teachers, church musicians, professional performers, ministers and housewives.

Its first performance with the Oklahoma Symphony, "An American Salute," took place in February 1985. This led to a 1986 collaboration presenting excerpts from Gershwin's "Porgy and Bess," and a 1987 performance as part of the Symphony's Pop series.

The Ambassadors' Concert Choir was invited to Mexico in July 1987 to perform with the Mineria Symphony Orchestra in Mexico City, bringing the group to the attention of a new and excited international audience and resulting in a recording contract.

In November 1988, Simon Estes, internationally known baritone opera singer, invited the Ambassadors to perform with him in Tulsa in a benefit for the Simon Estes Educational Foundation, Inc.

The State Arts Council of Oklahoma sponsored a 1990 tour of the state by the Choir. John Rutter's "Gloria," a contemporary work known for its rhythmic challenge, was presented in December 1990 to overwhelming critical acclaim.

JOE LIGGINS

The late Joe Liggins, Guthrie-born pianist, composer and bandleader, established his national reputation as an early 1940s rhythm-and-blues musician and leader in California.

He rose to prominence at age twenty-nine with two instrumental compositions he wrote and recorded with his band for Exclusive Records. The tunes were "The Honeydripper" and "I've Got a Right to Cry."

"The Honeydripper" (signifying a virile man popular with the ladies) was an unusual, two-part 78-rpm record that sold more than a million copies during 1945-1946 and an eventual two million copies. "I've Got a Right to Cry" eventually hit 1.8 million copies.

In Chicago, record buyers stood in blocks-long lines to obtain "The Honeydripper." According to William W. Savage, Jr. in his book, *Singing Cowboys and All That Jazz*, copies were "in short supply in the Midwest, and Pullman porters, knowing this, would purchase discs in California, carry them on trains to Chicago, and sell them to rhythm-and-blues fans for ten dollars apiece. . . ."

Liggins organized his band in 1944 in the home of Little Willie Jackson, one of his sidemen. He wrote "The Honeydripper" in 1942 but was unable to persuade big bandleaders to record it. Their lack of foresight opened the way to Liggins' own huge success.

Liggins and his band toured the country into the 1970s, when he tired of the grind and settled down in Compton, California, with his wife and family. He continued to perform in local southern California venues and to record occasionally for most of the rest of his life. He died July 31, 1987.

1993 OKLAHOMA JAZZ HALL OF FAME INDUCTEES

EARL BOSTIC

The late Earl Bostic, best known as an alto saxophonist, composer, and arranger, but also an accomplished trumpeter and guitarist, was born in Tulsa, Oklahoma, on April 25, 1913.

He played clarinet and alto saxophone in high school and Boy Scout bands, then studied harmony, theory, and various instruments at Xavier University in New Orleans before touring with Charlie Creath, Fate Marable, Marion Spears, and Clyde Turpin.

Moving to New York City, Bostic played with Edgar Hayes, Don Redman, Leon Gross, Hot Lips Page, and Cab Calloway. He arranged for the Paul Whiteman orchestra, as well as Louis Prima and the Ina Ray Hutton all-girls' band.

Bostic headed his own band in Harlem in 1941 at the Mimo Club. He then joined Lionel Hampton's band for two years, before starting again on his own in 1945. He recorded first with a big band on the Majestic label, then with a smaller group for Gotham records.

Bostic achieved extraordinary success later on King records, but not in jazz music. Instead, his big-toned, extroverted alto saxophone solos found favor with rhythm-and-blues audiences. His hits included "Flamingo," "Sleep," "Moonglow," "Cherokee," and "You Go to My Head."

Bostic was elected to the 1959 Playboy All Star Band in a readers' poll. He appeared at the Playboy Jazz Festival in Chicago in August of that year.

Bostic scored as a songwriter with "Let Me Off Uptown," the Gene Krupa band's novelty hit featuring Anita O'Day and Roy Eldridge on vocals, "The Major & the Minor," recorded by guitarist Alvino Rey, and "Brooklyn Boogie," recorded by Louis Prima.

Bostic died October 28, 1965, in Rochester, New York.

ELMER L. DAVIS, SR.

The late Elmer L. Davis, Sr., the gospel music inductee into the Oklahoma Jazz Hall of Fame in 1993, made a significant and indelible impression on the Tulsa community with a brilliant dual career as a director of sacred music for his church— Paradise Baptist—and Tulsa Public Schools, where he directed the entire system of vocal music for ten years.

A 1944 graduate of Tulsa Public Schools, Davis was also a well-known graduate of Langston University's class of 1950 and, additionally, studied at Oklahoma State University.

His first teaching positions were with the racially-segregated Bristow and Anadarko, Oklahoma, public schools. He spent a brief time in Bristow, then moved to Anadarko, where he spent four years as director of music for Lincoln High School. He returned to college— this time to The University of Oklahoma, on scholarship—and was awarded a master of arts degree in 1957. He then applied for and received a position with the Tulsa Public Schools as an elementary teacher of music. He taught at Ralph Bunche, E. W. Woods, and Barnard until 1971, when he was made supervisor of music for kindergarten through sixth grades, system-wide. He held that position for two years, then rose to the directorship of the Tulsa Public Schools vocal music system, a position he held until his death in 1983.

He began his long tenure with Paradise Baptist Church in 1950 as assistant music director, the same year he founded the "Chorus of Angels" there. Initially a young people's choir, the Chorus matured as its members did, became a community organization, and achieved a longevity that terminated only after Davis' death in 1983. Peaking at the membership of 35-40 at any given time, the Chorus of Angels cumulatively numbered in the hundreds. Members of the Chorus of Angels learned from their director and took those lessons with them to other church choirs, a number serving elsewhere as music directors.

Davis spent most of his life singing for something or someone. After his high school graduation, he spent the summer in California working for Warner Brothers and appearing at the old Palace Theater under the stage name "Lee Lane," a sojourn he repeated the next summer following his first year at Langston University.

He was blessed with a beautiful tenor voice akin to those of Nat King Cole and Billy Eckstine.

Davis performed at the famed Skyline Club in Oklahoma City on the same bill with Jimmy Witherspoon, by whom he subsequently was selected to travel for several months as an opening act. Davis' other forte was serious concert music. He performed for many groups around Tulsa and throughout the state.

But gospel music was his greatest love, and he soon returned to that discipline and to the more stately messages of spiritual music, which he believed to be a dying art.

As a composer and writer of music, Davis was noted for songs he wrote as signatures for the various schools at which he taught and for music created for several all-school music concerts, including "We Are the Future of Tulsa."

Later on in life, Davis developed an interest in journalism. He covered sports and special projects for *The Oklahoma Eagle*, where he also served as an advertising sales assistant.

Elmer L. Davis, Sr., died on June 24, 1983.

DIZZY GILLESPIE

Bebop, the first jazz played publicly for art's sake rather than entertainment, exploded out of New York's 52nd Street in the later years of World War II.

Bop enchanted jazz musicians. But its complexities puzzled many before it soared in popularity.

Bop's co-creator, John Birks "Dizzy" Gillespie, died in his sleep in January of 1993 at the age of 75 in a New Jersey hospital where he was being treated for pancreatic cancer. Early Dizzy was an enigma, but soon audiences learned to enjoy him and his huge and spectacular artistry.

Dizzy Gillespie visited Tulsa a number of times. On his 1991 visit for an appearance at the Mayfest celebration, the Oklahoma Jazz Hall of Fame made him an honorary member. Gillespie was presented with a plaque that incorrectly spelled his first name: "Dizzey." Gillespie said he wanted to keep it to go with a Kennedy Center plaque that also misspelled his name, but the Oklahoma Jazz Hall of Fame insisted on replacing it.

His formal and posthumous induction into the Oklahoma Jazz Hall of Fame took place June 16, 1993, in connection with that year's Juneteenth on Greenwood Heritage Festival. The ceremony was also dedicated to Hosea Martin, an Oklahoma Jazz Hall of Fame founding member and officer, who passed away in July of 1992.

Dizzy and Charlie Parker ("the other side of my heartbeat," in Dizzy's words) co-led the first bebop band on New York's 52nd Street in the mid-'40s. In the next five years, Gillespie made the first bebop record, took the first bebop band to California, and with a big band, introduced Europe to bebop. With Parker's death in 1955, the bop revolution ended and the legends began.

Dizzy's obituary was long and eloquent: "Along with Charlie Parker, Thelonious Monk, John Coltrane and Miles Davis, Gillespie stood as one of the towering figures of modern jazz. He turned jazz in new directions in at least two ways—as a founding Father of . . . bebop and when he collaborated with Cuban musicians (most importantly, conga player Chano Pozo) to give African-American music a Latin beat." (Associated Press)

He was the last of the four great American musical revolutionaries, the other three being Louis Armstrong, Duke Ellington, and Charlie Parker. (Armstrong and Ellington died in the early seventies and Parker many years before.) Gillespie, like Armstrong and Ellington, had become a new kind of American personage: a Universal Performer, who spent his last thirty years traveling up and down the world spreading the gospel of his music and the light of his amiable, quicksilver personality.

. . .

In his last years, the poles of Gillespie's professional life stretched from a one-night stand in a seedy New York club where the sound system had a high hum, the audience was indifferent, and Gillespie himself, just back from a grueling European tour, was exhausted—stretched from that to an early-evening concert on the South Lawn of the White House, which ended when Gillespie, calling President Jimmy Carter "Your Majesty," invited him to sing "Salt Peanuts" with him. Carter did, and Dizzy asked him to go on the road with his band. He was smiling when he said it, but he meant it.

WHITNEY BALLIETT
New Yorker magazine

JIMMY LIGGINS

Jimmy Liggins joins Joe Liggins, inducted into the Oklahoma Jazz Hall of Fame in 1992, as the Hall's first brother act. They seem to have had little else in common.

According to Specialty Records, Joe, the elder of the two brothers, was born in July of 1916 in Guthrie, Oklahoma. Joe wrote and recorded music which was organized—that of a schooled musician. Jimmy, born October 14, 1922, in Newby, Oklahoma, wrote a rougher, more primitive style of music. Both made exiting, danceable music which was very popular in its time—the heyday of urban jump blues, that important link in the evolution between swing and rock-and-roll.

The work of the two brothers foreshadowed rock-and-roll in the views of Specialty and other observers. Guitarist Jimmy Liggins had a smash hit on Specialty called "Cadillac Boogie" in 1947. Jackie Brenston had a Number 1 hit in 1951 with what is often referred to as the first rock-and-roll record, "Rocket 88" on Chess. Brentson, however, reportedly admitted that he based "Rocket 88" on "Cadillac Boogie."

The Liggins family moved to San Diego when Jimmy was about

nine and Joe was fifteen. Pianist Joe organized his band in 1944 and recorded "The Honeydripper," which sold more than a million copies during 1945-1946 and eventually sold two million copies—huge sales figures for that era. The band quickly became Joe Liggins and the Honeydrippers, their careers were successfully launched. Their record company, Exclusive, became the dominant independent rhythm-and-blues label in the United States.

Jimmy did not immediately follow Joe's path. He was a disc jockey for a while, a professional boxer very briefly, then worked for a year as Joe's driver when the band was on the road.

Impressed by the kind of money Joe was earning from "The Honeydripper" and another classic, "I've Got a Right to Cry," Jimmy started writing songs himself and formed his own band in 1946. Neither Joe nor Leon Rene's Exclusive Records showed any interest, however, so Jimmy turned to Specialty Records, which had been having some success at that time with Roy Milton.

Jimmy's Drops of Joy Orchestra recorded for Specialty from 1947 to 1952. The relationship yielded a number of *Billboard* top ten R&B hits—"I Can't Stop It," "Teardrop Blues," "Don't Put Me Down," and, of course, "Cadillac Boogie."

Jimmy Liggins and the Drops of Joy toured widely throughout the southern states, where Jimmy's brand of blues and rocking boogie—quite different from brother Joe Liggins' more urbane music—proved popular with record buyers and influential with the young post-war generation of southern blues and R & B musicians.

Jimmy's success did not parallel Joe's. In Specialty's account: "Misfortune hounded Jimmy, in spite of his successful records, in the form of bad bookings, canceled engagements and continuous union problems. . . . Then, on April Fool's Day 1949, Jimmy was accidentally shot in the mouth and badly hurt during a fracas at an engagement in Jackson, Mississippi. . . ." He recovered and bounced back with recordings of "Saturday Night Boogie Woogie Man," "Shuffle Shuck," and "Drunk," his last song and biggest hit at number four on the *Billboard* charts in late 1952. Jimmy and the Drops of Joy left Specialty in 1954 and recorded briefly for Aladdin before disappearing from the national scene.

Jimmy established his own label, Duplex, in 1958, and continued to release singles sporadically over the next 20 years while moving his headquarters from city to city—Los Angeles, San Diego, El Dorado, Arkansas and Madison, Florida among them—before settling in Durham, North Carolina, in the mid-'70s. In Durham, Jimmy stayed busy with his record shop, studio, and nightclub promotion. When the

Swedish Route 66 label released a collection of Liggins' 1947-52 recordings in 1981, his own Duplex label served as Route 66 distributor for the southeastern United States.

Jimmy died in Durham on July 18, 1983, preceding brother Joe's death by four years and two weeks.

LEE SHAW

Lee Shaw studied classical music from the age of five and continued without interruption—even during the summers—until she had earned a master's degree. Established as a classical accompanist and teacher, she had achieved her dream. But something was missing. She was not entirely fulfilled.

Then Shaw heard jazz and decided to pursue a career as a jazz pianist. This abrupt shift was triggered in the late 1950s when she was working as an intermission pianist at Mr. Kelly's in Chicago, where she was exposed to singers like Ella Fitzgerald and Billie Holiday appearing with their own trios. Friends took her to see and hear Count Basie at the Blue Note. She decided to learn to play the wonderful music she heard.

"I have never regretted it," she told an interviewer, "although the cost of playing only the music I believed in has been very great and I had to adjust my style of living to the income of a dues-paying jazz musician."

Shaw lived in New York state for years, performing frequently with her trio, including husband Stan Shaw on drums. They were married in 1963, two years after establishment of the trio.

Shaw was born in Cushing, Oklahoma, and reared in Ada, Oklahoma. She earned a bachelor's degree from the former Oklahoma College for Women and a master's degree from the American Conservancy of Music in Chicago. She did further graduate work at the Conservatory of Music in Puerto Rico, and later, after she had made her transition to jazz music, studied privately with jazz giant Oscar Peterson. She asked him to take her on. Also conservatory-trained, he agreed after he heard her play. Given her abilities—high critical praise for her work follows virtually every appearance, and her musical peers have deep respect for her—Shaw is a comparative unknown.

The new trio seemed to have great opportunities but, one after another, they evaporated. Their timing was significantly off. She told an interviewer: "We had just begun working at Birdland—great exposure—when it closed. We had been at The Embers in New York three times when it closed. Joe Franklin wanted us for the trio on his show if it became syndicated. We appeared on his show several times, then the syndication fell through.

"We played Harlem many times and would have gone back, but the riots occurred. Joe Glaser, head of Associated Booking Agency and mentor of Louis Armstrong, and others, had just begun to take an interest in us, and he died. Columbia Records was interested but it was at a time during the 1960s when jazz was not selling so they didn't sign us. . . . and on and on and on."

The Shaws lived for a time in Florida but returned to Albany, New York, in 1980. They have performed frequently since then, but have primarily stayed close to home base.

Her physical power (she is often told she "plays like a man") seems incompatible with her small stature. "I sometimes must play hard because my temperament makes me do that. And I must have developed a lot of strength in my hands, arms and back, for my size."

She appeared on "Marion McPartland's Piano Jazz" program in 1989, the long-running feature broadcast over National Public Radio. She is ranked with McPartland and the late Mary Lou Williams among the premiere pianists in jazz.

1994 OKLAHOMA JAZZ HALL OF FAME INDUCTEES

HOBART MELVIN BANKS, SR.

The late Hobart Banks was born in Rentiesville, Oklahoma, August 17, 1907. His family always had a piano in the home, and he took to it with complete naturalness and an astounding sense of how to play it. He was a child prodigy on the instrument. "He began playing the piano when he was about three years of age," his mother said, and reached the point very soon where he could play any composition once he had listened to it.

The family moved from Arkansas City, Kansas, to Muskogee, Oklahoma, fertile ground for such other Oklahoma jazz greats as Jay McShann, Claude Williams and Barney Kessel. Young Hobart obtained all of his education in the Muskogee public school system, participating in all of the music programs offered.

He played regularly as a teenager at Muskogee's Grand Theater before the advent of talking pictures. He loved music dearly and had the gifts to perform it strikingly. He was blessed with perfect pitch. According to his harmony teacher, "he could reproduce any musical sound that he heard."

Banks worked with many bands—Ben Johnson's and Leonard

Howard's Muskogee bands, Bucky Coleman's band in Oklahoma City and Ernie Fields in Tulsa—and traveled all over the Southwest to perform. He played with a "Who's Who" of well-known musicians—Jay McShann, Clarence Love, Ernie Fields, Jr., Don Byas, Earl "Supreme" Jackson, Barney Kessel, and Aaron Bell. During the Harlem Renaissance, he played at the famed Cotton Club in New York.

Dr. Lowell Lehman, music professor at Northeastern State University at Tahlequah, Oklahoma, recalled: "I came to Muskogee in 1954 and Hobart Banks took me under his wing. We played lots of club dates together. It was a fascinating time because black and white musicians were integrating bandstands for the first time. The musicians, themselves, made it happen."

Hobart Banks absorbed the influences of all the greats—Art Tatum, Fats Waller, Oscar Peterson, Count Basie—and molded them into his own unique style.

Hobart Banks passed away in 1957.

DOROTHY DONEGAN

Dorothy Donegan, literally a jazz piano artist for the ages and a master of all idioms of the art form, is a 1994 honorary inductee into the Oklahoma Jazz Hall of Fame and the recipient of the organization's first "Living Legend" award.

Born in Chicago in 1922, Donegan has played seemingly forever and has gotten better with the passing years in the judgments of leading critics. Leonard Feather, perhaps the nation's foremost jazz critic, wrote in *Jazz Times* magazine that "Dorothy Donegan is the unfairly forgotten woman of jazz. A pianist of extraordinary talent . . ." John Wilson of *The New York Times* wrote: "She can be the lustiest, most exciting, hard-swinging and virtuosic jazz pianist in the world . . . one of the most brilliant pianists, male or female, that jazz has ever known."

Dorothy Donegan is considered the master of a staggering range of piano-playing styles—jazz, ragtime, boogie-woogie, gospel and blues, as well as classical music. In this stage of her long career, she is a "staple" on the national jazz music circuit and can perform virtually as often as she wants.

Donegan was recognized as a child prodigy and began her piano training at the age of eight in Chicago. She made her concert debut at Orchestra Hall at eighteen, playing selections that included Mendelssohn and Chopin as well as jazz standards. She became a prominent figure on the Chicago jazz scene in the 1930s, so prominent, in fact, that Art Tatum sought her out to become her mentor.

She went on to nightclub appearances and recording, film work, and a Broadway play. She married in 1948 and raised two sons while continuing her career. During the 1950s, she played the top supper clubs in the country. And in the 1990s, although the club names have changed, she is still a regular as well as a major attraction at jazz festivals abroad and in the United States.

Donegan, together with her trio, highlighted the 1994 Oklahoma Jazz Hall of Fame induction ceremonies.

THOMAS A. DORSEY

Thomas A. Dorsey is recognized as the founding father of gospel blues, a blending of sacred texts with blues or blues-inspired tunes—which originated in the 1930s in Chicago's African-American, old-line Protestant churches largely because of Dorsey's blues-influenced composing and singing.

Thomas Andrew Dorsey, known as "Georgia Tom" at the time, enjoyed considerable success in the 1920s as pianist, composer and arranger for prominent blues singers including Ma Rainey. He was drawn to sacred music, which he was eventually instrumental in revolutionizing, but he was torn between secular blues and gospel blues until a personal tragedy struck him like a thunderbolt in August of 1932.

In St. Louis for one of the first gospel conventions, Dorsey lost his wife in childbirth while he was gone and his new baby boy the night he returned to Chicago. The loss was the inspiration for Dorsey's best-known gospel song, "Take My Hand, Precious Lord."

Dorsey was immensely influential in blues-oriented gospel music that swept African-American churches and their services and in the gospel music conventions that he popularized. Resistance to the roots of his style of music triggered significant controversy within the church community first, however.

The basis for the music in blues was offensive to many: "We don't want that mess in our church," according to one well-known pastor. But the music galvanized church musicians, singers, and publishers, and the influence that Dorsey introduced eventually overwhelmed the naysayers.

"Wade in The Water," a National Public Radio series produced with the Smithsonian Institution, recently focused on Dorsey and the gospel blues legacy that he left. "He wrote simply in words that could be sung readily by every-day people," according to one observer, "but his music was naturally powerful and elevating."

Dorsey was instrumental in the organization of the first blues gospel choir at Chicago's Ebenezer Baptist Church in 1931, contributing the "down-home blues-man's" perspective to the musical conceptualizing of two churchmen from the deep south. The result was a chorus given status by the fact that it was established within the context of an old-line Chicago church, but possessed of a sound unlike any in memory.

A Public Broadcasting System special, "Somebody Say Amen," keyed on Dorsey and his vast contributions to the Chicago foundations of gospel blues as a sacred song style. After Chicago, gospel blues spread like wildfire to St. Louis, Detroit, Cincinnati, and Philadelphia, everywhere that established African-American church congregations had been flooded with deep-south black migrants.

In addition to "Take My Hand, Precious Lord" (sung by Mahalia Jackson at the funeral of Dr. Martin Luther King, Jr. in 1968 and by Aretha Franklin at the funeral of Mahalia Jackson in 1972), Dorsey is noted for his "How About You," "I've Got Heaven In My View," "God is Good To Me," "Peace In The Valley," "Someday, Somewhere," "It Don't Get There," and "If You See My Savior," his first published gospel piece, which dates to 1928. The native Georgian published more than 400 gospel songs and, along with two associates, chartered the National Convention of Gospel Choirs and Choruses in 1933. That organization sent out agents to metropolitan areas from the late 1930s until the middle 1950s to organize choruses which, in turn, became the predecessors of the gospel choral groups found in most black churches today. Dorsey presided over the National Convention until very late in his life.

VERBIE GENE "FLASH" TERRY

Flash Terry is a legend in his own time and, simultaneously, a completely down-to-earth man. Verbie Gene "Flash" Terry drove Metropolitan Tulsa Transit Authority buses for years while at the same time fronting the Uptown Blues Band. He is a constant in the North Tulsa African-American community, where his name is synonymous with the blues.

Early influences in both his guitar and blues playing were, first, his father, then, bluesmen Blind Lemon Jefferson, T-Bone Walker, Gatemouth Brown, and Butch Lucky. He came to Tulsa in the late 1940s from Inola, Oklahoma. He sat in occasionally with Ernie Fields, but it was 1953 before he got his "first real gig"—with Jimmy "Cry Cry" Hawkins—and he did his first national tour in 1955, with Floyd Nixon.

Terry played with blues and R&B idioms: Bobby Blue Bland, B.B.

King, Albert Collins, Curtis Mayfield, Otis Redding, and James Brown. "They (years back) were just like I am now, just hangin' out and giggin' in local clubs. . . . Yeah, I was on the same shows as Otis and James Brown and a lotta those guys before they made it big. We were makin history and didn't even know it." He also coached a young Leon Russell. "Leon used to hang around with me at the old Flamingo Club, him and Chuck Blackwell and J.J. Cale and David Gates. They used to come out and learn the blues. Those guys really made it, but Leon's still my favorite. . . . He's rich and famous now, but to me he's never changed, he's my friend."

FLOYD RICHARD WILEY

The late Floyd Wiley was a native Tulsan who taught music, voice and elementary education in the Beggs, Oklahoma, and Tulsa Public Schools for 23 years. He served both Mt. Rose Baptist Church and Friendship Missionary Baptist Church in various musical capacities.

Wiley was widely known in gospel music circles as singer, composer, director, arranger, pianist, organist and accompanist. And, like Flash Terry, he was widely known and celebrated in Tulsa as a warm, giving human being.

Wiley was born in April of 1939, and attended elementary school in Tulsa. He graduated from Booker T. Washington High School in 1957, and received a degree in music from Langston University.

A child prodigy, Floyd was a known pianist by the age of three and served Paradise Baptist Church as its youngest musician ever. He played for weddings, funerals and reunions all over the United States and won acclaim as an accompanist for such luminaries as Mahalia Jackson and the Reverend James Cleveland. He worked with the late Thomas A. Dorsey for three years in National Singing Convention Workshops in Chicago, St. Louis, and Oklahoma City.

Wiley served four years in the U.S. Army, organizing many gospel choirs in that environment. On discharge he joined Mt. Rose as minister of music. Then he became a member of Friendship Missionary Baptist, where he used his incredible range of talents with the Master's Choir, Missionettes, Mission Chorus, Special Edition, Pastor's Choir, Brotherhood Chorus and the L.L. Tisdale Singers.

Wiley died in March 1993, leaving an indelible legacy as a choir director and a vastly gifted gospel musician whose talents God obviously wanted him to share, in the words of one admirer.

1995 OKLAHOMA JAZZ HALL OF FAME INDUCTEES

OSCAR PETTIFORD

Okmulgee, Oklahoma, native Oscar Pettiford was born into a large musical family, began playing the bass at fourteen, and toured with the family band until 1941. Two years later he was co-leader, with Dizzy Gillespie, of an early bebop group. He subsequently led his own band and spent several periods with Duke Ellington and Woody Herman before settling in Europe in the 1950s.

Pettiford was the first jazz bass player to develop fully within a be-bop context, which started his swift rise to fame among musicians. He made his recording debut in 1943. In about 1950, he transferred his solo style to amplified cello, which he played dexterously and with a bouncy manner reminiscent of guitarist Charlie Christian.

Together with Ray Brown and Charlie Mingus, Pettiford was influential in establishing the double bass as an important jazz solo instrument. He spent his last years in Europe. He was based in Copenhagen when he died in 1960.

JOHNNY ROGERS

Blues guitarist Johnny George Rogers was born in Tulsa, Oklahoma, and mastered his instrument as a youngster. He constantly amazed his listeners with his skills and command of the guitar. Early in his career, Rogers played with the Clarence Love Band. He was later recruited by Roy Milton and toured extensively with him. Playing with a noted band leader was remarkable for a seventeen-year-old, but even more remarkable were songs he wrote, "Junior Jives," and "Junior Jumps."

Rogers' distorted tonal style was reminiscent of Willie Johnson, guitarist for Howlin Wolf. Rogers was from a family of noted musicians. His parents, Robert F., Sr., and Lucy Rogers, and his brothers, Lee Daniel and Robert, Jr., were all musicians.

MARSHALL ROYAL

Another internationally renowned artist, Sapulpa, Oklahoma, native Marshall Royal, is perhaps best known as Count Basie's lead saxophonist, on alto, in the new big band the Count formed in 1950. He remained with the band for twenty years. He left Basie to settle in Los Angeles, where he performed with Bill Berry's big band and the Capp-Pierce Juggernaut.

Born in 1912, Royal learned violin and guitar as well as reed instruments as a child, and first performed professionally at thirteen. He played with Les Hite during most of the 1930s, with Lionel Hampton in 1940-1942, and with Eddie Heywood after wartime service in a Navy band.

Royal's eloquent sound, both on solos and as reed-section leader, provided ample evidence of his incomparability. His style was firmly rooted in swing, and was both harmonically and rhythmically solid.

Royal died in May of 1995.

MILT HINTON

Bassist Milt "The Judge" Hinton was inducted into the Oklahoma Jazz Hall of Fame as the recipient of the organization's second "Living Legend" award.

Born in Vicksburg, Mississippi, in 1910, he moved to Chicago when he was nine and was encouraged by his mother, a pianist, to pursue a musical career. He attended Wendell Phillips High School, famous as the alma mater of many noted jazz musicians, and then Northwestern University. Following fifteen years of playing with Cab Calloway, Hinton worked as a freelance artist in New York, and was soon one of the most sought after jazz musicians. He launched a studio, recording, and touring career that made him world-famous. Hinton was also involved in teaching and photography, but he focused his career on his studio activities in recording and television.

"The Judge" played with groups including Count Basie, and Louis Armstrong's All Stars, and it was in the 1940s when his playing with Dizzy Gillespie made him a forerunner of modern jazz bass players.

MAHALIA JACKSON

Gospel great Mahalia Jackson was inducted into the Oklahoma Jazz Hall of Fame as an honorary member for her dazzling feats in sacred music. She was gospel's first true superstar, carrying her music from African-American churches to the world's concert halls.

Born in New Orleans, Louisiana, young Mahalia Jackson listened to the records of Ida Cox, Bessie Smith, and Mamie Smith. But her heart was always in gospel music instead of the blues.

After moving to Chicago, Jackson led a quartet of church singers and attracted attention at various Baptist churches. National recognition began for her in 1945 when she began recording with Apollo. Her first million seller was "Move on Up A Little Higher." "Silent Night" was overwhelmingly successful in Denmark, prompting her continental tour in 1952. She performed at the Newport Jazz Festival in 1957 and again in 1958 with Duke Ellington. They performed the expanded version of "Black, Brown, and Beige." She also sang at the White House in 1959 at President Eisenhower's birthday celebration.

Associated mainly with sacred music, she refused many lucrative offers to work in night clubs and bars because of her religious convictions. Her singing illustrates the close link between Negro religious music and fundamental origins of jazz.

1996 Oklahoma Jazz Hall of Fame Inductees

Ernie Fields, Jr.

The induction of Ernie Fields, Jr., gives the Oklahoma Jazz Hall of Fame its first father-and-son team. Ernie, Sr., was inducted into the Oklahoma Jazz Hall of Fame's first "class" in 1989.

A highly successful music producer and studio musician in Los Angeles, the younger Fields was thoroughly grounded with bachelor's degrees from Texas College and Howard University in music education and applied music, awarded following graduation from Tulsa's Booker T. Washington High School, and instrumental studies and work in other disciplines at Oberlin University, the National Symphony in Washington D.C., Mannheim University in Germany, and the University of California at Los Angeles.

He has recorded with everyone from Lionel Richie and Aretha Franklin to Ray Charles, Nancy Wilson, Barry White, and Earth, Wind, & Fire. He has conducted for Bobby "Blue" Bland and Lou Rawls, as well as symphony orchestras, and has had a long, varied musical involvement with films, television shows and videos. He has played (on sax, flute or clarinet) with Count Basie, the Duke Ellington Orchestra under direction of Mercer Ellington, Louis Jordan, and countless others, including, of course, the Ernie Fields orchestra.

Hal Singer

Hal Singer, noted saxophonist and vocalist, performed as a young man in Kansas City as well as New York's 52nd Street at the birth of bebop. He started his career with big bands primarily in the southern United States, including that of Fields, then began touring with the Jay McShann band. He became famous for his hit, "Cornbread," played for Billie Holiday and many other big names including Roy Eldridge,

Coleman Hawkins, Don Byas, and Charlie Shavers, and joined the Duke Ellington orchestra at the age of 29. Singer's hits from the 1950s are included in many rock-and-roll anthologies, but his development also reflects modern jazz, blues, swing and R&B, and modern jazz characteristics. He studied at both Juilliard and Berklee as a young man.

In the later stages of his career, he became an institution in France, recorded all over Europe, and in South Africa and Ethiopia as well.

MELVIN MOORE

Melvin Moore, originally of Tulsa, Oklahoma, and later a New Yorker, wanted to be a singer when he was eight years old and was barely seventeen when he ran away from home to pursue that goal. Just three units shy of high school graduation at the time, he greatly displeased his father when he dropped out. But he returned in a year, made peace at home, and finished high school before leaving again.

From 1936 to 1950, Moore sang and recorded with some of America's finest bands, including Ernie Fields' orchestra, and performed in front of such musicians as Billy Taylor, Terry Gibbs, Charlie Mingus, Neal Hefti and Zoot Sims. He left the Gillespie band in 1950 for the Billy Bowen Ink Spots, and stayed with them until 1962. Moore then joined Decca Records as a promotion and marketing executive and went to Brunswick in 1966 as national director of R&B promotion and artist development. In his later years, Moore became a consultant.

BILLY HUNT

Trumpeter Billy Hunt was born in Grove, Oklahoma, and graduated from the University of Oklahoma with a degree in music.

Career highlights include a dozen years in Woody Herman's bands, stints of seven and five years sandwiched around three years with Harry James' band. He won a Grammy for his recorded jazz solo of "Days of Wine and Roses" with Herman. His time with Woody included membership in the Third ("Four Brothers") Herd.

Hunt returned to Oklahoma and earned his master's degree in music at Northeastern State University. He played for some twenty years with Forrest Watson's orchestra in its storied run at the Shangri-La Resort, and became a festival performer and judge of music events.

WALTER "FOOTS" THOMAS

The late Walter Purl "Foots" Thomas, a native of Muskogee,

Oklahoma, played with and was associated with some of the most talented jazz performers of his era. He devoted much of his life to perfecting his skills and teaching others. Born in 1907, he laid down his musical foundation in school under the strict direction of a teacher who insisted that students master their instruments (Thomas was the saxophone) and learn the fundamentals of music theory.

Thomas accordingly could read and arrange music well early, which was vital to his getting established with Jelly Roll Morton, with whom he had played briefly in 1926. Morton sent for him from New York in 1927 because he needed an alto sax player who could read well.

In 1929, Foots joined the Missourians, playing tenor and baritone saxes and doing much of the arranging for the band, which was taken over in 1930 by Cab Calloway as leader and emcee. The band became a great success, broadcasting regularly from Harlem's Cotton Club. Thomas stayed with Calloway for thirteen years.

In 1944, Thomas and Cozy Cole shared a teaching suite in New York. Thomas was a splendid teacher and a sharp innovator. He played often on 52nd Street in New York with Cole, Emmett Berry, and Oscar Pettiford and, during the late 1940s, got involved in personnel management and music publishing. He suffered a stroke in 1975 that left him unable to play music, but he continued to teach and write until his death in 1981.

JIMMY NOLEN

Jimmy Nolen was born in Oklahoma City, Oklahoma, in 1934. He began playing in public as a teenager, inspired by the guitar-playing of T-Bone Walker, B.B. King, and Lowell Fulson. He launched his recording career after moving to California, performing and recording with Jimmy Wilson, Chuck Higgins, and others, most notably, Johnny Otis. Nolen played guitar on Otis' classic "Willie and the Hand Jive" in 1958, in addition to numerous other tunes with Otis and recordings of his own on Federal, Elko, and Imperial.

Nolen was closely associated with James Brown because his funk rhythms formed the basis of the Brown "groove" for almost twenty years. His first session with Brown in 1965 produced the first of a number of trend-setting number one hits, "Papa's Got a Brand New Bag." The immersion into the Brown band, however, kept him in near anonymity except for the blues solos he played at regular stops during Brown's live performances. Nolen died of a heart attack in 1983 at his Atlanta home.

JULIA LATIMER-WARREN

The late Julia Latimer-Warren was born in 1922 in Honea Path, South Carolina, the first of six children of Major and Maria Latimer. She was still a child when the family moved to Tulsa, where her father established his famous barbecue business.

She graduated with honors from Booker T. Washington High School, studied at Dillard University in New Orleans, then was awarded a full scholarship to study at the prestigious Juilliard School of Music in New York. On completion of her time there, she was named musical director for a U.S.O. company of "Porgy and Bess" that toured the South Pacific.

An accomplished accordionist, she served as music director for First Baptist Church of North Tulsa for 16 years, and taught piano for more than 40 years at the Latimer School of Music.

She served as a member of the board of Tulsa's Moton Health Clinic and the Metropolitan Planning Commission, was executive director of Tulsa's Hutcherson Branch YWCA, and became the first Tulsan to receive an honorary life membership from Camp Fire, Inc., where she served as district director for more than twenty-five years.

She married Robert M. Warren in 1947 and was the mother of seven children. She passed away in 1989.

1997 OKLAHOMA JAZZ HALL OF FAME INDUCTEES

DON BYAS

Born in Muskogee, Oklahoma in 1912, Don Byas played tenor saxophone with a variety of bands in the 1930s, including those of Lionel Hampton, Eddie Barefield, Buck Clayton, Don Redman, Lucky Millinder, and Andy Kirk. He made his first recording with Timme Rosenkrantz in 1938.

In 1941, Byas joined Count Basie's Orchestra, taking the chair formerly held by Lester Young until 1943. From 1943 to 1946, Byas played in small groups led by Coleman Hawkins and Dizzy Gillespie and led his own bands as well. He traveled to Europe in late 1946 with Redman's band, and soon took up permanent residence there—first in France and later in the Netherlands and Denmark.

Thereafter, he worked frequently as a soloist, also playing with Duke Ellington (1950), touring with Jazz at the Philharmonic and recording with Ben Webster (1968). During the last years of his life he undertook jazz and dance-based engagements throughout Europe.

He returned to America only once, in 1970, when he appeared at the Newport Jazz Festival. He died in Amsterdam in 1972.

OSCAR ESTELL

Oscar Estell was born in Tulsa, Oklahoma, in 1929 and began playing the alto saxophone when he was seven years old. The innovative young player was mentored by Tulsa band leader Ernie Fields, Sr., and Clarence Love. He was also mentored by music teachers Cleo Meeker, William Jett, and James Lark. By the age of twelve, he was playing regularly at the Boy Scouts Jamboree and with Tulsa's Vernon Chapel A. M. E. choir.

Estell played with Music Masters, the Booker T. Washington High School jazz band, and became a member of Musicians Local 808. He graduated from Booker T. in 1947 and began playing for dances and in Tulsa nightclubs, including Florence's Chicken Plantation, Love's Lounge, Tom and Jean's Supper Club, the Coronado Club, and the Flamingo. He formed a trio that played regularly in Tulsa. He also played with the likes of Tulsa's Sonny Gray and the Ray Miller Sextet and nationally-known musicians Lionel Hampton, Ernie Fields, Sr., Sam Cooke, Roy Milton, Bill Doggett, and Ernie Freeman.

In 1959, Estell married Helen Willis and began to play nearer home and family in Tulsa one-nighters and weekend gigs. Admirers compared his alto style to those of Johnny Hodges, a member of Duke Ellington's band. Estell's recordings included baritone sax performances with Art Farmer in the early 1950s. He died in 1968.

ELLA FITZGERALD

Ella Fitzgerald is an honorary inductee into the Oklahoma Jazz Hall of Fame. Born in Newport News, Virginia, in 1918, Ella Fitzgerald was raised in Yonkers, New York. Fitzgerald credits her aunt, Virginia Williams, with her upbringing.

Fitzgerald's "discovery" is the stuff of legend. Singing "Judy, Object of My Affection" in a 1934 amateur contest at New York's famed Apollo Theatre, Fitzgerald dazzled the crowd. She played many famous nightclubs and cabarets, including the Cotton Club and Levaggi's.

Her hundreds of recordings and hits—"Love and Kisses," "A-tisket, A-tasket," and, sung in classic "scat" style, "Oh, Lady Be Good," "How High The Moon," and others—earned her universal acclaim. Duke Ellington once told *Life* magazine: "She captures you somewhere through the facets of your intangibles, which had to mean that marvelous voice found you deep down where you live."

Fitzgerald performed with all the greats—Duke Ellington, Count Basie, Louis Armstrong, Louis Jordan, Stevie Wonder, Earl Hines, and more.

Fitzgerald is the most honored jazz singer ever, possessing a dozen Grammys, reigning for eighteen consecutive years as the best female jazz artist in *Down Beat* magazine polls, garnering the prestigious Kennedy Center Award, and receiving an honorary doctorate in music from Yale University. Hundreds of her recordings sold over twenty-five million copies.

MATTHEW MCCLARTY

Matthew McClarty has played for more than sixty years, dedicating the last thirty-five years of his life to gospel music that shows the strong influences of blues and R&B he learned and sang early on in his career.

The Ada, Oklahoma, native first learned music by listening to his older brother play the guitar. He practiced the instrument, though specifically instructed not to do so by his brother. The guitar hung on the wall, presumably (but mistakenly) out of the reach of young Matthew. Matthew climbed in a chair and played his brother's guitar without taking it down from its perch on the wall.

McClarty grew up playing gospel and blues and was widely heralded for his talents. In 1952, he joined Tony Wise and the Blue Notes and toured with the band throughout Texas and Oklahoma for the next several years. This was interrupted by a calling that took him back to his church, where he has practiced his art as a gospel artist and piano player for the Church of God in Christ in Ada. In 1982, McClarty and his two sons performed to great popular acclaim in Washington, D. C. and at the Oklahoma Diamond Jubilee (part of the Smithsonian Folklife Festival).

ANTHONY "TONY" MATHEWS

Anthony "Tony" Mathews was born in Checotah, Oklahoma, in November of 1941, and sang in church choirs and gospel quartets before first picking up the guitar at age fifteen. He began playing club dates in Wichita, Kansas, the next year, then played in Muskogee, Oklahoma, with Willie Wright and the Aces, and recorded with Don and Bob on Chess. When he was twenty, Mathews moved to Los

Angeles and toured the country with the Sims Twins on *The Jackie Wilson Show*, later touring with Little Jonnie Walker and Moms Mabley.

Mathews became a studio musician in Hollywood in 1966, and toured with Ray Charles in 1967, with Little Richard following that, and with Ray Charles again in the 1970s and 1980s. Mathews has an Alligator album to his credit ("Condition Blue") and recorded "Allen in My Own Home" on SDEG. He has several acting credits for work on television.

APPENDIX B

REPORT OF THE AMERICAN RED CROSS (DISASTER RELIEF HEADQUARTERS) TULSA COUNTY CHAPTER, TULSA, OKLAHOMA

[Selected excerpts from the original document]

INDEX

ORGANIZATION

Director of Relief,
Maurice Willows

RELIEF COMMITTEE
Chairman, Clark Field
Assistants, Jennie K. Beam,
L. C. Murray

REFUGEE CAMP
Director, N. R. Graham

NURSING SERVICE
Director, Rosalind Mackay
Assistants, Mrs. W. D. Godfrey,
Bessie Richardson

PURCHASING DEPARTMENT
Director, O.V. Borden
Assistant, L. R. Surber

FOOD SUPPLY
Director, Mrs. Wheeler
Assistants, Ora Upp
Mrs. A. W. Roth

RELIEF DEPOT
Director, J. T. Forster

MOTOR TRANSPORTATION
Director, A. C. Anthony

RAILROAD TRANSPORTATION
J. A. Hull, W. L. Walker

BEDDING SUPPLIES
Lilah D. Lindsay

CLOTHING RELIEF
Mrs. H. L. Henzman,
Mrs. J. A. Hull

BUREAU OF IDENTIFICATION
Robert H. Woods

STOLEN AND LOST GOODS
A. C. Doering

SHELTER
H. L. Henzman

CINNABAR HOSPITAL RELIEF STATION   DIRECTOR RELIEF STATION
Dr. Paul Brown   Booker Washington School
                                        E. L. Connelly

ORGANIZATION

Proclamation of Mayor of Tulsa
Instructions from Chairman of Red Cross,
        Southwestern Division
National Guard Field Orders
Orders to Physicians Committee
Orders to Boy Scouts
Employment Organization
        Identification Tags, Meal Tickets, etc.
Minutes of Meeting of Medical Committee

REPORT
TULSA RACE RIOT
DISASTER RELIEF
AMERICAN RED CROSS

This compilation contains copies and duplicates of the original texts now in the possession of Mr. Maurice Willows, Director of Relief, Disaster Relief Headquarters, American Red Cross, Tulsa, Oklahoma.

Besides the compilation made for Mr. Willows by Mrs. Loula V. Watkins, there are three others—one for Tulsa, one for Washington, and one for St. Louis Red Cross files.

The typing was done by Miss Cleda Timberlake of Denver, Colorado. Most of the snapshots [not included] were contributed by Mr. Clarence H. Dawson, of Chicago.

The Compiler
LOULA V. WATKINS

FAMILY RELIEF PERSONNEL
Clarence H. Dawson, Director, Chicago, Ill.

CASE WORKERS
Abbot, Mrs. Gretchen, Tulsa, Okla.
Fish, Mrs. Ruth G., Alamosa, Colo.
Mac Cartney, Mrs. C. B., Oklahoma City, Okla.
Prout, Miss Jeanne, Memphis, Tenn.
Scott, Miss Mary Porter, St. Louis, Mo.
Watkins, Mrs. L. V., Kirkwood, Mo.
Westendorf, Miss Katharine, Denver, Colo.

*The following workers served only during the emergency period immediately
following the riot.*

Adams, Mr. C. D., Tulsa, Okla.
Davis, Miss Dorothy, Houston, Texas.
Golay, Mrs. T. L., Tulsa, Okla.
Lefko, Mr. Louis, Tulsa, Okla.
Palmer, Miss Ada, Chicago, Ill.
Reed, Mrs. J. M., Tulsa, Okla.
Williams, Miss Margaret, St. Louis, Mo.

STENOGRAPHERS
Timberlake, Miss Cleda, Denver, Colo.
Leslie, Miss Mildred, Tulsa, Okla.
Beggs, Miss, Tulsa, Okla.
O'Brien, Miss, Tulsa, Okla.
Miss Marguerite Watkins, Tulsa, Okla.

OFFICE CHIEF EXECUTIVE
T. D. Evans, Mayor,
Tulsa, Oklahoma

To the Red Cross Society:

Please establish headquarters for all relief work and bring all
organizations who can assist you to your aid. The responsibility is
placed in your hands entirely.

(signed) T. D. EVANS,
6/2/21   Mayor.

THE AMERICAN RED CROSS
Southwestern Division
St. Louis, Mo.

June 1, 1921.

Mr. A. L. Farmer, Chairman,
Tulsa County Chapter,
American Red Cross,
204 Palace Bldg.,
Tulsa, Oklahoma

My dear Mr. Farmer:-

As I indicated in my telegram to you of today, I am sending you herewith a copy of the statement of policy of the Red Cross in race riots and strikes issued by the General Manager in November 1919. This policy still holds.

Unquestionably there is big opportunity for misunderstanding any action taken by the Red Cross in connection with race riots. One or another party to the situation usually misunderstands and it accordingly becomes necessary for the Red Cross to act with unusual caution. As outlined in the attached statement from the General Manager, Red Cross can best serve through meeting the needs in the form of First Aid, Medical Assistance, Nursing Service, etc., to those injured in disturbances, regardless of the faction to which they may belong.

Service should only be rendered to National Guardsmen on the specific request of the State Authorities in charge.

May I ask that you keep me fully advised of any action taken by your Chapter and particularly in the event that any border line question arises which, in your judgment, does not seem to be covered by the enclosed statement of policy.

Very sincerely yours,

James L. Fieser,
Manager, Southwestern Division.

JLF*S

(POSTAL TELEGRAM)   Washington, D. C., Nov. 4, 1919.

Alfred Fairbank,
American Red Cross, Frisco Bldg.,
St. Louis, Mo.

The various situations that have arisen in United States at this time of unrest and readjustment make it desirable we lay before our Division Managers for their personal guidance the attitude which should govern Red Cross in event of race riots and conditions arising out of lockouts and strikes. Red Cross stands in a peculiar position because of its close relationship to Federal Government and at same time because of its support by the American people as a whole, a position which involves both special responsibilities and special obligations. Red Cross must therefore very keenly have in mind its obligations to maintain a position of impartiality. Red Cross must also always be open to appeal to meet needs in form of First aid, medical assistance, nursing service, etc. to those injured in disturbances regardless of faction to which they may belong. This is the prime service of Red Cross. There are also possible situations where widespread distress may develop as result of conflict between elements in communities, affecting in some cases other than those a party to the disturbance. This type or question may demand action on the part of the Red Cross, but decision cannot be made in advance as the possibilities are too various and intricate. Situations do not develop so rapidly but that there remains time for discussion in each case as to the obligation if any on part of Red Cross. There remains a type of service less important but one which Red Cross must consider; this is an obligation to be prepared at all times to furnish certain types of service similar to those of our army. This is a type of service which should not be sought by Red Cross on its own initiative but a service which should be given in response to request of those in authority. If those in command United States troops make request upon Red Cross for canteen or other reasonable service for the troops themselves, Red Cross should endeavor to meet these demands, confining their efforts strictly to comfort for the soldiers. In the case of state troops our relations are by no means so well worked out and established by war time experience and charter obligation; however, upon request of govenor of any state, Red Cross should consider favorably a call for service similar to that which it would be our obligation to render Federal troops limiting service in same ways. Beyond this point Red Cross should consider very carefully before undertaking any form of comfort and aid to those engaged in general police duty, being very sure that any request upon them for service is made on behalf of governmental authority representative of the general public and that the type of service requested is limited strictly to giving personal comfort to servants of the public and that such service be closely confined to its proper purposes and not be enlarged in such extent as for practical purposes to amount to furnishing police service of any kind whatsoever. Under no circumstances should this service be rendered to any group in control of either party to a controversy no matter what the temptation, on contrary it should be our aim to make clear and definite the understanding that irrespective of the merits of any controversy Red Cross will avoid favoring either side to that controversy by acts either of commission or omission. It is evident any question of relief which grows out of conflict between different elements in the population a position of much delicacy to Red Cross with its desire to represent an entire public calls for closest consultation between Chapters and Divisions and Divisions and National Headquarters as to application particularly as such types of controversy affect more than local situations and often involve questions national in scope.

F. C. MUNROE.

Headquarters Oklahoma National Guard
Tulsa, Oklahoma
June 2, 1921.

Field Order No. 4

All the able bodied negro men remaining in detention camp at Fair Grounds and other places in the City of Tulsa will be required to render such service and perform such labor as is required by the military commission and the Red Cross in making the proper sanitary provisions for the care of the refugees.

Able bodied women, not having the care of children, will also be required to perform such service as may be required in the feeding and the care of the refugees.

This order covers any labor necessary in the care of the health or welfare of these people who, by reason of their misfortunes, must be looked after by the different agencies of relief.

BY ORDER OF BRIG. GEN. CHAS. F. BARRETT

Headquarters National Guard
City Hall, Tulsa, Oklahoma,
June 2, 1921.

Field Order No. 5.

To Commanding Officer, 3 Infantry. You will detail a Non-commissioned officer and 12 men to set as guard at Fair Grounds Detention Camp, this detail be armed and fully equipped will report to Clark Field at American Red Cross Headquarters. From and after 1 P. M, this date detention camp at McNulty Camp will abolish and camps will be removed to Detention Camp at Fair grounds.

By Command of Brig. Gen. Barrett.
Bryan Kirkpatrick
May A. G. Dept. Adj.

Chief of Police Gustafson: *June 2, 1921*

Will you kindly furnish us two white police officers, to report at Red Cross Headquarters, Fourth and Cincinnati.

Assist. Director.
Tulsa, Okla.
June 5th, 1921.

The Physicians Committee of the Board of Public Health recognizes and accepts the selection of Chief of Department as made by the American Red Cross as follows, i.e.:

Surgery, Dr. Ralph V. Smith
Obstetrics, Dr. George R. Osborn
Medicine, Dr. Horace T. Price

For immediate service the following Doctors may be called:

SURGERY
Dr. H. D. Murdock O-95
Dr. A. W. Pigford O-187
Dr. H. S. Browne C-1039
Dr. D. C. Johnson O-5011
Dr. G. H. Miller O-6669

MEDICINE
Dr. A. G. Wainwright C-497
Dr. C. S. Summers O-9160
Dr. W. J. Trainer O-8744
Dr. J. E. Wallace O-812
Dr. E. S. Wilson O-8727

OBSTETRICS
Dr. Geo R. Osborn O-2010

It is the purpose of this committee to work in harmony with the American Red Cross and the other organizations doing relief work.

In recognition of the valuable services performed by Dr. Paul R. Browne, we recommend that in case of need he be consulted by all chiefs of departments and this committee.

The committee requests that the various types of work outlined further on, at the places named be performed by the designated physicians.

Sanitation—Dr. C. L. Reeder, Dr. L. C. Presson and assistants shall be responsible for sanitation throughout the city and county.

Fair Grounds Camp—Dr. C. D. Johnson, A. G. Wainwright and assistants shall have charge of all medical and surgical cases at the Fair Grounds Camp, but sending all Major operative cases to the Morningside Hospital and others requiring hospitalization to the Red Cross Hospital.

Obstetrics—Dr. Geo. R. Osborn and Assistants shall take care of all obstetrical cases arising anywhere, which must be sent in time to the Tulsa or Oklahoma Hospitals.

Red Cross Hospital—Dr. R. V. Smith and Assistants shall have charge of all operative cases at the Morningside and Red Cross Hospitals. Dr. C. H. Haralson and assistants shall take care of all eye, ear, nose and throat cases arising anywhere which may require special attention and those now in or coming to the Morningside or Red Cross Hospitals.

Booker Washington First Aid Station—Dr. Geo. H. Miller, Dr. C. S. Summers and assistants shall be responsible for the first aid and after treatment of all cases applying to this despensary.

The Committee recommends that no attempt be made to rebuild the devasted area until a sanitary sewerage system has been installed, with connections to each building or that it shall at least be started and no building planned without such connections and accessories, within the corporate limits of the City.

We further recommend that the adjacent territory now situated in the county, be immediately included within the corporate limits in order that the health of the community may be protected by the installation of proper sewerage.

We further recommend that recognizing the extremely insanitary conditions existing within the devastated area, that if legally possible, the same be corrected through condemnatory preceedings and necessary destruction of all shacks that are now a menace to health.

In view of the fact that their building and equipment have been destroyed by fire, we recommend that temporary quarters be provided in the colored district for the use of the Tulsa County Public Health Association, that is work may be resumed at once and we further recommend that permanent quarters be provided as soon as possible. We further recommend that the tuberculosis and general public health work be resumed at once among the white population at the Public Heath dispensary, 15 West 11th St.

BY ORDER OF THE COMMITTEE

DR. C. L. REEDER, CHAIRMAN

DR. R. V. SMITH

DR. HORACE T. PRICE, SECY.

TULSA COUNCIL
BOY SCOUTS OF AMERICA
TULSA, OKLAHOMA

REQUEST FOR SCOUT SERVICE

Number of Scouts Needed

Nature of Service

Remarks

Washington School

INFORMATION ABOUT BOY SCOUT SERVICE

1. Each office will have a detail of scouts for service in the building consisting of a door orderly and one or more desk orderlies.
2. The door orderly shall not be ordered from his post by any one other than the scout director.
3. The desk orderlies are for service inside the building only.
4. Scouts are on reserve in the scout director's office for all other duties.
5. All requests for scouts should be made in person or by a written order stating the number of scouts desired and the nature of service requested.
6. No scout shall leave the building without a written order from the scout director.

(*SIGNED*)   F. D. CRAFTS.

EMPLOYMENT ORGANIZATION
DUTIES OF AGENCIES

Red Cross Representative
Refers calls of all kinds to proper agency.
Makes adjustments.
Forms contact with Red Cross Committee.
Special advertising.

Federal State Employment Bureau
Direct all employment work.
Fill all calls for permanent male colored.
Labor and day work for colored women.

Colored Y. M. C. A.
Fill all calls for day work for colored men.

Colored Y. W. C. A.
Fill all calls for permanent work for colored women.

General Activities
Committee meeting Tuesday, 2:00 p.m. Washington School.
Employment city survey for positions.
Placards all over colored district, calling attention to agencies operating.
Advertising by newspaper stories.

EMPLOYMENT ORGANIZATION

Red Cross Representative:
N. A. Thompson, Cedar 2300, Washington School House.

Employment Committee:
Chairman: W. B. Ellis, Osage 3540, 14 1/2 E. First St.
        Representing Federal State Employment Service.
G. A. Gregg, Cedar 613. Easton and Bxter.
        Representing Colored Y.M.C.A.
Edna Pyle, Archer and Cincinnati,
        Representing Y.M.C.A.
Miss Eloise Williams, Osage 8639, 4th & Cincinnati.
        Representing Y.M.C.A.
Mrs. Victor A. Hunt, Osage 8823, 5th & Cheyenne.
        Representing Y.W.C.A.
Barney Meyers, Osage 9593, 120 E. Third St.
        Representing Open Shop Assn.
G. F. James,
        Representing Central Labor Unions.
T. C. Hopkins, Osage 9720, 406 So. Cincinnati.
        Representing American Legion.

June 6, 1921.

Report from Medical Committee

Report on Financial matters. Arranged that Fields, Terrell and Avery should arrange handling of funds and distribution of funds.

Matter of feeding taken up. Decided all dependents should go to fair grounds and all mass feeding done there. Reported that arrangements had been made at Booker Washington school to feed all workmen over there for 15 cents per meal and deduct it from wages.

Graham suggested getting all superfluous people out of white residence section, and issuing permanent passes to and from the fair grounds to responsible working people and daily passes to others. Question of jitney service to and from fair grounds for working people, and question of supplies for semi-permanent camp taken up.

Kates moved that Graham and Maj. Fuller be instructed to confer with Executive Committee, with full power on the part of Graham and Fuller to act with the Executive Committee to get all excess people out of servants questers and move them to the fair grounds—to act with Central Committee and Mr. Terrell.

Mr. Fields asked Kates to include motion to feed refugees and issue passes.

Kates moved to give Graham and Fuller complete authority to work out any scheme that is advisable to them and the Executive Committee and police identifying refugees by card, keeping off streets, moving, etc.

Willows stated that was not a matter which should be settled by Red Cross themselves, and whatever action is taken should be taken conjointly, in order that a united front might be presented to the people.

Kates stated that motion included recommendation for jitney service and everything else.

Willows stated that this would be placed in the hands of these men, to report back tonight.

Motion seconded, and upon vote unanimously adopted.

Question of setting up stands and stores taken up. Chief Police stated Hopkins was handling that.

Mr. Fields: At first we had a clear understanding that the

regular funds of the Tulsa Chapter were not to be put with this relief fund, as St. Louis informed us that their manner of handling relief funds is to handle it as separate from Chapter funds until all other resources are exhausted and then, if necessary, use our Chapter funds and then go back to St. Louis.

Mr. Willows: Our understanding with the Committee was, get your bills together and when you need money to pay them, bring them to us.

Question of employment taken. Decided to consolidate with all other employment agencies and it was suggested that Chairman of State Federal Employment Agency be Chairman of such Committee. Mr. Ireland to handle this matter as he sees fit.

Question of payroll taken up. Any one who is to be paid out of Red Cross Funds to report to Murray or Willows.

Kates brought up question of fire protection at fair grounds and Police Chief said they were attending to it.

Fields stated he would like Central Committee put on record as requesting them to feed workmen.

Murray reported that Borden is going to put on an inventory man and going to take an inventory of all Red Cross stuff.

Willows asked police to take action on matter of supplying transportation for negroes backwards and forwards over and around town, and to take action to stop this transportation by whites.

STATEMENT OF THE PASTORS OF THE CITY OF TULSA

The fair name of the city of Tulsa has been tarnished and blackened by a crime that ranks with the dastardly deeds of the Germans during the Great War, provoked by the bad element of the negroes, arming themselves and marching through the streets of the city. Block after block of our city has been swept by fire applied by the frenzied hand of the mob. Many of our people are dead, while thousands of innocent, peaceable, and law-abiding citizens have not only been rendered homeless, but they have been robbed and despoiled of all their earthly possessions. The pastors of Tulsa blush for shame at this outrage which renders our city odious and condemned before the world.

We believe that the only bulwark of American safety for our liberties, our homes, the peaceful persuits of happiness, of law, order, and common decency, is found in the teaching and living of the high ideals of Jesus Christ,—that without Christ modern civilization cannot bear the weight that is being placed upon it, and the crash is inevitable.

We, the Pastors of this city, hold that there cannot be peace, security, happiness, moral conscience, to say nothing of religious development, so long as the following obtain:

1. The Bible, God, Jesus Christ, and the Christian Religion outlawed in Public Schools. It is only where Christianity has influence and power that the Jew and the Infidel are protected. We insist that they have no right to tear down in America that which not only protects them but protects us. The little sop thrown to the Christian forces at Commencement by Prayer and a Sermon is little more that an insult to Christianity.

While the Bible has been outlawed, the Dance has been put in the Public Schools over the protest of hundreds of fathers and mothers who have a conscience on the subject. Certainly it is an established fact that the dance weakens moral fibre. We therefore demand consideration.

2. A Wide Open Sunday. The amusement houses, parks, and anything else that desires is free to run wide open on the Lord's Day. It was respect for the Lord's Day and the Lord's House the built that sturdy New England civilization which gave the world the Declaration of Independence, the Constitution of the United States, the great Educational Institutions of the Eastern part of the United States, as well as the great Statesmen, Poets, Philosophers, and Philanthropists.

3. Motion Picture houses constantly showing films that are suggestive in Title, Poster, Advertisement, and in actual production on the screen where there is drinking, the use of weapons, the portrayal of lust, the portrayal of the eternal triangle, the breaking of homes, the

caracture of the Christian ministry—until the young and the ignorant get the idea that such is the common order of Society. That in 1919, Tulsa County gave the startling total of 56.8 divorces, and increase of 18.9% over 1917, two years, is food for solid thought.

4. Officials who can see a car parked a foot out of line, but who are blind to Choc-joints, boot-legging, and the like, said to flourish in and about Tulsa.

5. Officials who have already winked at two lynchings, and who had every opportunity of knowing that a third was contemplated hours before the trouble actually began.

6. Criminals who are given their freedom almost immediately after arrest either on worthless bonds, or through some powerful "Friend" at court, or through some other unlawful manner.

7. A certain type of citizenship which openly boasts of violating the Law with respect to the 18th Amendment.

These and other things have created in the minds of some, especially the younger ones, that the Law is nothing and may be violated with impunity and that punishment is a farce.

We, the Pastors of the City of Tulsa, urge that a thorough and complete investigation of this outrage be made immediately, and that wherever the guilty ones may be found, and whoever they are, white or black, that a full punishment be meted out. Good citizenship can not condone and tolerate vandalism, looting, and such other lawless acts as both black and white were guilty of May 31st, and June 1st. We believe that the possession of firearms and ammunition, especially rifles, revolvers, and such should be made a felony.

We call upon the officials, both County and Municipal for a full enforcement of the Law. We call for a readjustment of our Moral and Civic life, placing it on the plain of decency, righteousness and justice.

We appeal to the Christians of Tulsa to be more faithful in exemplifying the true meaning of Christianity in word and deed, to refrain from all questionable practices, and to give themselves over to the practice of Christian virtues and general Christian living.

We appeal to the unaffiliated Church members to take membership at once with their respective Churches, for in so doing they will strengthen the moral fibre of the Community. This is no time to hold aloof.

We also deem it the part of wisdom that there should be a closer cooperation between the religious and business forces of the two races in Tulsa, so that at all times there shall be a better mutual understanding making it possible for both races to work together to achieve the highest ideals. As an example of what we have in mind, we have invited the pastors of the Colored churches to associate themselves with the Ministerial Alliance in this city.

We believe most emphatically that the Church is the only hope for the City of Tulsa, and without her moral influence there can be no security no matter how many or what laws are enacted, or how well policed the city may be. The observance of all law depends upon the moral consciousness and the Church is the only Institution in our Society whose sole and only business is the creating of that Moral Consciousness.

The Church stands between Society and destruction. What are you doing for the Church?

TULSA MINISTERIAL ALLIANCE

REPORT

By Maurice Willows.

TULSA COUNTY CHAPTER AMERICAN RED CROSS
DISASTER RELIEF COMMITTEE.
PREFACE

The story of the tragedy enacted in Tulsa, Okla., on the night of May 31st, 1921, and the morning of June 1st, 1921, has been told and retold in the press of the country, with all sorts of variations as to causes, actual happenings and immediate results.

The unprejudiced and indirectly interested people have from the beginning referred to the affair as the "race riot," others with deeper feeling refer to it as a "massacre," while many who would saddle the blame upon the negro, have used the designation, "artfully coined," "negro up rising." After six months work among them, it has been found the majority of the negroes who were the greatest sufferers refer to June 1st, 1921, as "the time of dewa." Whatever people choose to call it the word or phase has not yet been coined which can adequately describe the events of June 1st last.

This report refers to the tragedy as a "disaster."

(Signed)
Director

Tulsa Tribune, May 31st, 1921

NAB NEGRO FOR ATTACKING GIRL IN AN ELEVATOR

A negro delivery boy who gave his name to the police as "Diamond Dick" but who has been identified as Dick Rowland, was arrested on South Greenwood avenue this morning by Officers Carmichael and Pack charged with attempting to assault the 17-year-old white elevator girl in the Drexel building early yesterday.

He will be tried in municipal court this afternoon on a state charge.

The girl said she noticed the negro a few minutes before the attempted assault looking up and down the hallway on the third floor of the Drexel building as if to see if there was anyone in sight but thought nothing of it at the time.

A few minutes later he entered the elevator she claimed, and attacked her, scratching her hands and face and tearing her clothes. Her screams brought a clerk from Renberg's store to her assistance and the negro fled. He was captured and identified this morning both by the girl and clerk police say.

Rowland denied that he tried to harm the girl, but admitted he put his hand on her arm in the elevator when she was alone.

Tenants of the Drexel building said the girl is an orphan who works as an elevator operator to pay her way through business college.

NARRATIVE REPORT AS OF DECEMBER 31ST, 1921

CHAPTER 1

The real truth regarding the underlying causes of the short-lived civil war which turned Tulsa, Oklahoma, into a bedlam on the morning of June 1st, 1921, may come to the surface in the future. The concensus of opinion, after six months intervening time, places the blame upon "the lack of law enforcement."

"Race Riot" it has been most generally termed, yet whites were killed and wounded by whites in the protection of white property against the violence of the white mob. The elements of race rioting were present, from all evidences, on the night of May 31st, but the wholesale destruction of property—life and limb, in that section of the city occupied by negroes on June 1st between the hours of daylight and noon, testifies to a one-sided battle.

Altho newspaper clipping attached indicates the apparent local cause of the trouble, subsequent developments have proven that the arrest of the negro boy was merely an incident. Both the negro boy and girl have dropped out of the picture, it being shown that there was no grounds for any prosecution of the boy.

Those persons desiring to satisfy themselves as to causes, are respectfully referred to newspaper accounts of the trial of the Chief of Police, which are contained in this volume.

It should be noted, however, that while the original shooting took place at the County Jail on the night of May 31st, the actual burning, pillaging and destruction was consummated during the daylight hours of June 1st in the district nearly a mile from the Court House.

All that fire, rifles, revolvers, shot guns, machine guns and organized inhuman passion could do with thirty-five city blocks with its twelve thousand negro population, was done.

Those interested in details bearing on locations, methods used, and the organization of the mobs, both black and white, should refer to newspaper accounts contained herewith.

DEAD

The number of dead is a matter of conjecture. Some knowing ones estimate the number of killed as high as 300, others estimates being as low as 55. The bodies were hurriedly rushed to burial, and the records of many burials are not to be found. For obvious reasons this report cannot deal with this subject.

INJURED

One hundred and eighty-four negroes and forty-eight whites were in hospitals for surgical care as charges of the Red Cross, within twenty-four hours after the disaster. Five hundred and thirty-one were given First Aid at the Red Cross stations during the first three days.

An adequate picture of conditions relating to the injured cannot be written. Eye witnesses will long remember the speeding ambulances, the crowded hospitals, drugstores, churches and First Aid Stations. While the records show 763 wounded, this does not include wounded people afterwards found on practically all roads leading out of Tulsa. Wounded people turned up at Muskogee, Sapulpa, and other adjoining towns, and as far north as Kansas City. Neither do records tell of the after-the-riot developments. The Red Cross records show eight definite cases of premature childbirth which resulted in death of the babies.

Subsequent developments also show that of the maternity cases given attention by Red Cross doctors, practically all have presented complications due to the riot.

Too much credit cannot be given to the white citizens of Tulsa for the care and treatment rendered the wounded. Especially should it be noted that the women and men at the First Aid Stations gave voluntary and gratuituous service. While several hundred were given First Aid at the hospitals free of charge, the hospitals themselves, which were crowded with patients, ultimately presented bills in full for all services rendered, by which bills have been paid out of relief funds. It should also be made clear that the attending surgeons almost without exception have been paid in full for the services rendered in the emergency.

BURNINGS

Thirty-five city blocks were looted systematically, then burned to a cinder, and the twelve thousand population thereof scattered like chaff before the wind. All evidences show that most of the houses were burned from the inside. Eye witnesses say that the methods used were, first, to pile bedding, furniture and other burnable material together, then to apply matches. Eye witnesses also claim that many houses were set afire from aeroplanes. (In this connection it should be noted that while many houses and buildings in the Greenwood and Fairview Additions were destroyed, other houses, evidently choosen ones, were allowed to stand untouched. During the months following the disaster the Relief workers have gathered interesting information as to the ownership of the houses left intact.)

PROPERTY LOSSES

Property losses including household goods will easily reach the four million mark. This must be a conservative figure in view of the fact that law suits covering claims of over $4,000,000. were filed up to July 30th. A large number of property owners were not at that time heard from.

Newspaper accounts accompanying this report and statements of eye witnesses, give vivid pictures of what happened.

Where were the police?

Where was the fire department?

Why the temporary breakdown of City and County government?

The accompanying newspaper reports and editorials will help to answer these questions.

STATE TROOPS

State Troops had arrived and had checked the rioting at noon of Wednesday, and Martial Law was in effect, with Adjutant General Barrett of the State in charge.

CHAPTER II

RELIEF AND THE RED CROSS

While "Little Africa" was still burning, while ambulances whizzed to the hospitals, while "dead" wagons were carrying off the victims, while refugees were being driven under guard to places of refuge; and the fiendish looting, robbing, and pillaging was still in progress, different scenes were being enacted "up town."

Realizing that an awful calamity was in progress of perpetration, the Red Cross immediately sprung into action. The women mobilized with incredible speed, and before midnight of Wednesday had made sufficient insignias of Red Crosses on a background of white, to placard ambulances, motor vehicles, trucks and other conveyances for the transport of nurses, doctors, supplies and relief workers. This insignia was a pass everywhere.

Mayor Evans early in the day, by written communication, designated the Red Cross as the official relief Agency.

It should be noted here that even before any official request has been made, the Red Cross had by common consent, sprung into action.

IMMEDIATE CARE FOR REFUGEES

Simultaneously refugee camps were installed at Convention Hall, McNulty Ball Park, First Baptist Church and the Fair Grounds. Indeed every available church and public building and many private homes were used to house the homeless.

DIVISION OFFICE CALLED

On the afternoon of Thursday, June 3rd, a telephone message to the St. Louis office summoned division help. On Friday morning assistant Manager, Maurice Willows, arrived in Tulsa, and went into immediate consultation with Red Cross officials, immediately after which a trip of inspection of refugee camps and hospitals was made.

PUBLIC WELFARE BOARD

It should be noted at this juncture that the Chamber of Commerce and other city organizations had unitedly appointed a Public Welfare Board consisting of seven of the strongest men of the city to temporarily take charge of the appalling situation. This Committee was in its first session when the division representative arrived. This committee met with representatives of the Red Cross and unanimously charged the Red Cross with responsibility for relief operations.

FINANCIAL POLICY

The Public Welfare Board announced that Tulsa would not appeal to the outside world for contributions. This announcement was given wide publicity, which policy apparently met with universal approval. It was understood that in view of the many local complications which would inevitably follow, that the National Red Cross should be asked to furnish expert leadership to direct and handle the problems of relief. In order to steer clear of local complications it seemed wise to ask National Headquarters for finances sufficient to cover such personnel. This contribution was acceptable to the Welfare Board and the local Red Cross officials.

Consequently, on the night of Friday, June 4th, a telegram was dispatched to the Division Manager, which brought forth the cooperation and funds asked for.

Immediate steps were taken to centralize the work of relief which was being done at many different points in the "up town" section, notably the Y.M.C.A., the First Baptist Church and the Red Cross office at 4th and Cincinnati. The Booker Washington School property situated in the heart of the burned area was selected, and by Saturday afternoon all relief operations with the exception of the refugee camps were directed from central headquarters. The following organization was announced on Saturday:

RED CROSS DISASTER RELIEF

General Headquarters and Relief Depot, Booker Washington School.
Refugee Camp, Free Fair Grounds, N. R. Graham, Director.
Emergency Hospital, 510 North Main Street.
Red Cross Home Service (ex-soldiers) 4th & Cincinnati.
Tubercular Clinic for whites, 15 West Eleventh St.

ORGANIZATION

Acting Chairman of Local Chapter, Clark Field.
Director of Relief, Maurice Willows.
Assistant, L. C. Murray.
Registration Bureau: This department handled all telegrams and mail, and furnished information about lost relatives.
"For tents and bedding apply at the north unit building, Booker Washington School."
"For lost or stolen property, apply at 703 East Archer, Mr. Doering."
Clothing Department, Second floor, main building.
"For employment apply at N. A. Thompson, first floor, main building."
"For nursing service, Miss Mackay: for treatment apply first floor, main building."
Purchasing Department, O. V. Borden, first floor main Bldg.
General Dispensary and Clinic (Negro tubercular, veneral and dental clinics, medical dispensary), unit building at north end of fair grounds.
Food Supply, Mrs. Wheeler, first floor Main Bldg.
Motor Transportation Department, first floor main building, J. C. Anthony.
Director of Relief Depot, J. T. Forster, Mr. Murray's office.

TELEPHONES

Main Headquarters in Relief Depot, Cedar 2300
Fair Grounds,   Cedar 2509
Commissaries,   Cedar 6158
Fourth & Cincinnati,   Osage 1772
Emergency Hospital,   Cedar 2128
Reconstruction Camp,   Cedar 2508

Volunteer workers please report at Fourth & Cincinnati for pass.
Report location of stolen goods and names of culprits to J. M.
Adkinson, City Hall.

FAMILY WORK PERSONNEL

During the first days of emergency work the use of many volunteers was imperative. The first person of training or experience to arrive was Mrs. L. V. Watkins, formerly Home Service Secretary at Fort Scott, Kansas. Mrs. Watkins was placed in charge of the registration bureau, where she was ably assisted by Mr. Louis Lefko, Secretary of the Better Business Bureau, Mrs. J. M. Reed, Mr. C. D. Adams and Mrs. T. L. Goley. A wired request for additional personnel was sent to the Division Office, and after a delay of ten days our family work forces were supplemented by Miss Joan Prout of Memphis, Tennessee, Miss Mary Porter Scott of St. Louis, and a little later by Mr. Clarence Dawson of Chicago, Miss Ada Palmer of Chicago, Miss Margaret Williams of St. Louis and Miss Dorothy Davis of Houston, Texas. The last three remained in Tulsa for a period of ten days only. Later the Division Office sent Mrs. C. B. MacCartney and Mrs. Gretchen Abbott. These workers were all supplied out of Division Funds.

MASS WORK

For the first ten days practically all relief work was conducted mass fashion. The refugee camp at the Fair Grounds had been well equipped with plumbing, a refrigerator system, a temporary hospital and first aid stations. Over 2,000 people were housed and fed there, under the supervision of Mr. Newt Graham, and a corps of volunteer assistants.

An additional 2,000 were fed and housed at the Booker T. Washington School properties, while the balance of the refugees were hastily housed in tents, surrounding the Booker T. Washington School.

These first relief operations involved the watering and sewering of both camps making both properties sanitary. In these operations full and ample assistance was rendered by the National Guard and the City of Tulsa. It should be noted that the disaster had wiped out practically every resource that the negroes formerly had. All relief to able bodied men was given in the form of work, at a wage rate of $ .25 per hour. The men were paid at the end of each day. There were, however, no boarding houses, lunch stands or grocery stores from which to obtain food. This food was supplied at the rate of $ .20 per meal, until the time when temporary lunch stands were erected. In the meantime, the women and children were fed at the Red Cross kitchens.

FAMILY SURVEY

From time to time as found practicable, house to house surveys have been made to determine the next immediate relief needs of the effected families. From week to week the emergency relief situation has been made according to the needs of the moment. The first survey was necessarily a partial one for the reason that literally thousands of negroes had left the country for parts unknown and other hundreds were crowded together in servants quarters throughtout the city. The first survey made during the week following the disaster showed 1765 families in Tulsa more or less seriously effected. There were 5366 persons in these families, 1620 of which were children under fourteen years of age.

As far as figures were obtainable, it was found that 1115 residences have been destroyed exclusive of stores, cafes and other business properties. It was ascertained that in addition, 314 residences had been looted of practically all household possessions and valuables, which houses were not burned. It was also found that 563 families were crowded into small quarters with other families.

No accurrate estimate was possible on the number of refugees that left the district during and immediately following the trouble. As a basis of calculation, after seven months of relief work, it is noted that a total of 2480 family case records have been opened, indicating that at least 715 Families temporarily left Tulsa, returning later for various reasons. All evidences show that most of the families returned to their old homes after the cotton picking season was over, in order to place their children in school and to reestablish where possible their old homes.

There is little indication that other cities were seriously burdened with Tulsa dependents. Indications also point to the fact that the majority of these families found employment for themselves and children in the agricultural districts.

HOUSING PRESSURES

During the week of the riot, 284 army tents, 16x16, with a few, 17x21, had been thrown up to accomodate the refugees. The provisions, however, did not meet the conjected conditions in servants quarters.

By June 18th, 184 of these tents had been provided with floors and sides of lumber, wire screening and screen doors. Housing measures were handicapped because of insufficient sanitation and because of the lack of sewerage and also of the impossibility of inducing the city authorities to quickly furnish enough sanitary toilets.

HEALTH

With every sanitary condition unfavorable, thru one device or another, typhoid and other epidemics were avoided. In many instances strict measures were taken to segregate a few of the worst cases of typhoid, and the liberal use of typhoid serum, together with lime and other disinfectants, played a part in this epidemic.

GENERAL RELIEF PROGRAM

In the early days it was generally agreed that the Red Cross would have functioned when the homeless were provided with shelter, laundry outfits, cooking outfits and stoves; when sufficient, simple, plain bedding was provided; when the families were reunited as far as possible; when the destitute women and children were cared for; and when the able-bodied were placed on a self-supporting basis.

RECONSTRUCTION

The problem of reconstruction will be dealt with elsewhere. Suffice it to say that the Red Cross has refused to involve itself with the problem of permanent reconstruction or the rebuilding of a new colored district. This obviously was a task for the city and county administrations.

The uninformed should know that approximately two thirds of the burned area is located beyond the city limits.

HOSPITALIZATION, NURSING AND MEDICAL CARE

There are no public hospitals in Tulsa, there is no tubercular sanitarium. Consequently, during the riot the wounded and sick were taken to the private hospitals, where they were crowded into every available space and given surgical and medical attention. When the private hospitals became over crowded, a large residence was commandeered and equipped. With incredible speed a hospital staff of doctors and nurses were mustered in. 163 operations were performed during the first week, 82 of these being major ones. At the end of two weeks the Red Cross had equipped four large hospital wards in the Booker T. Washington school house for hospital uses, and all of the patients were transferred to this central hospital.

FIRST AID AND THE INJURED

Following the riot the Red Cross established a first aid station with Mrs. Clark Fields and a staff of nurses in charge. 531 patients were given first aid care, during the first ten days.

A general dispensary was equipped by the Red Cross in one of the rooms at the Booker Washington School and turned over to the Tulsa County Public Health Association in charge of Miss Richardson and her staff.

A V. D. Clinic was equipped also and operated by the Red Cross and turned over to Mr. C. L. Reeder, County Health Physician.

HOUSING SURVEY

Immediately following the riot all medical, nursing and hospital activities were placed under the supervision of Miss Rosalind MacKay, State Supervisor of Red Cross Nursing.

She was ably assisted by Mrs. W. D. Godfrey of the Tulsa Red Cross and Miss Bonnie Richardson of the Tulsa County Health Association. The following Red Cross Nurses gave their services for two weeks:

Miss Miser, Tulsa, Okla.
Mrs. Cleveland, Cleveland, Okla.
Mrs. Tosh, Sapulpa, Okla.
Miss Weaver, Osage, Okla.
Miss Thomas, Oklahoma City, Okla.
Miss Swanson, Tulsa, Okla.
Miss Hatch, Tulsa, Okla.
Miss Robinson, Tulsa, Okla.
Miss Trotter, Tulsa, Okla.
Mrs. Watson, Tulsa, Okla.

The most important phase of the work of the nurses was the house to house survey made, with the following results:

Number calls made by Public Health Nurses	4512
Number of patients needing medical or nursing care	551
Classified as follows:	
Maternity	38
Infant Welfare	359
General	154
Sent to Dispensary for treatment	80
Number emergency calls by nurses	84
Nursing care given to out patients	169

VACCINATION

Early in the day the utmost precautions were taken to prevent disease. There were seven cases of small pox reported at the Fair Grounds before the refugees could be vaccinated. There was some delay in medical organization because of conflict in jurisdiction between the county and city physicians. It was necessary to coral all vaccine and typhoid serum in the state of Oklahoma. Approximately 1500 refugees were vaccinated and treated with serum. The doctors of the city took charge of the health situation through a committee composed of Doctors C. L. Reeder, H. T. Price, and R. V. Smith, with Dr. Smith as Chairman. In addition to this committee, Doctor Presson, City Health Physician, exercised his functions as sanitarian.

SUMMARY

Chronologically the medical and nursing phase of the relief work was as follows:

1. Immediate surgical and medical care of the wounded at six private hospitals.
2. The mobilization of all available nurses for hospital and field service.
3. Placing the State Supervisor of the Red Cross Nursing in charge.
4. The organization of a committee of doctors under whose direction the state supervisor was to supervise.
5. The mobilization of vaccine and the typhoid serum and the administering of same to the refugees.

6. A Field Survey by Public Health Nurses.
7. The equipping of a First Aid Station, a general dispensary and a V. D. Clinic.
8. Equipping and furnishing a central hospital.
9. The evacuation of the private hospitals.
10. The building of a suitable hospital for the more permanent care of those wounded during the disaster and all of the sick needing hospitalization because of the lack of suitable homes. An arrangement was made whereby the County Commissioners and the Board of Education jointly turned over for Red Cross uses certain properties located at 324 North Hartford. On this centrally located site a nine-room hospital building was erected, the Red Cross furnishing the building material and the East End Relief Committee (colored) furnished the labor. This made the hospital a cooperative enterprise. The property when built represented an investment of approximately $68,000.
11. The evacuation of the Booker Washington School property as relief and hospital headquarters on September 1st, 1921.
12. The formation of a Colored Hospital Association, which is incorporated under State Law. The purpose of this association is to take over the management of this hospital and to ultimately take title to the same. A full statistical report of hospital operations is given elsewhere. To the everlasting credit of Tulsa and the Red Cross, it should be said that the very best surgical and medical care obtainable has been given to the negro patients. Dr. H. R. Browne (white) has supervised the medical and nursing service since the first week following the disaster. A white nursing staff was maintained until the Colored Hospital Association began functioning, January 1st, 1922.

STATUS OF WHITES WOUNDED

Our files contain the names of 48 whites who have passed through the hospitals. The greatest secrecy has surrounded the status of these whites, probably for the reason that they do not wish to have their names among those involved in the rioting. All of the whites needing Red Cross assistance have been handled by Mrs. Jennie K. Beam, Secretary of the Local Chapter, with headquarters at 4th and Cincinnati Streets. The best information obtainable is contained in a statement rendered by a local private hospital where practically all of the white wounded were given attention. On attempting to check the hospital bills for payment it was found that there were an unknown number who were wounded, given First Aid treatment at hospitals and sent directly to their homes. The number of white wounded probably exceeded the number given in this record, as the figures given represent the cases whose medical care was actually paid for out of relief funds. (Many humorous instances might be cited of claims presented by "innocent bystanders" for the payment of doctors bills). All such claims were rigidly investigated and many were turned down for the reason that it could not be shown that the wounded parties were "innocent bystanders," or persons in the employ of the city or county for guard purposes. Quite early in the fall, a claim for $85.00, doctor bill, was presented by a young white man for gunshot wound treatment. The claim was of the "innocent bystander" kind. After lengthy explanation on the part of the claimant as to how the injury was incurred, but after his admission that he was not employed by the city or county, the Red Cross record-keeper confronted him with a full sized photograph of the same young man in the middle of the riot district with a shot gun over his shoulder and high powered rifle in his hand. Altho he did not deny the identity, he has not been seen at the Red Cross office since. After this experience, no further claims have been made by "innocent bystanders."

FINANCES

This chapter in its beginning harks back to the commitments of the Public Welfare Board which amounted to, "Go ahead and take care of the relief as it should be done and we will finance all Red Cross needs." The Red Cross preceded full speed ahead. The Public Welfare Board started a campaign for funds, collecting the sum of $26,000.00 during the few days at first. The Welfare Board had also received the promise from the County Commissioners of a fund amounting to $60,000.00 to be made available for Red Cross uses. Immediately after July 1st pending the time when this $60,000.00 would be available, 25 men had agreed to underwrite the Red Cross for $25,000.00.

Plans were also underway whereby the Welfare Board was to engineer a rehabilitation and housing program. They expected to raise immediately a sum of $100,000 to start with.

When everything was running smoothly, like a thunderclap out of a clear sky the Mayor of the City, T. E. Evans, declared the Welfare Board out of commission, and in its place appointed a new committee of seven which he called "The Reconstruction Committee."

Thus, the backbone of financial support had been broken, most abruptly. The original Public Welfare Board resigned office at a mass meeting and at the time of their resignation recommitted itself collectively and individually to stand by the Red Cross Relief Committee if their services should be necessary.

The Red Cross therefore was placed in a position of having to deal with a new Reconstruction Committee. It was understood, at first, that the new committee was to function as the agent of the city in the same manner as the old committee. Time, however, has proven that the new committee was politically constituted and was chiefly interested in maneuvering for the transfer of negro property and the establishment of a new negro district.

When it became apparent that the Reconstruction Committee was powerless to raise funds, the old committee members, together with Chairman Fields of the Red Cross, brought about a meeting of the County Commissioners and the Mayor.

The Mayor and Chairman Fields of the Red Cross Committee requested the County to allow the local Humane Society to relieve the Red Cross of its work. The County Commissioners, however, went into reverse and suggested to the Mayor that the Red Cross was the only organization competent to deal with the relief situation. The Commissioners and the Excise Board forcefully suggested that the Mayor include $40,000.00 in the 1921-1922 budget to be used by the Red Cross, in finishing its relief program. The Mayor promptly and gracefully acceded.

This left the appropriation status as of September 1st as follows:

Appropriation from County of Tulsa	$60,000.00
Appropriation from City of Tulsa	40,000.00
Private Donations to Relief Fund	24,865.36
Merchandise Contributions	6,000.00
	$130,865.36

The financial report and statement indicates full payment of the appropriation made by the county but a falling down on the part of the city. It should properly be said that there is no indication that the public has been aware of the failure of the city to meet its properly and legally made pledges of financial support. On the other hand there is every indication of disinterestedness and lack of sympathy on the part of certain city officials. It was deemed best by the Relief Committee not to press its claims upon city funds. This meant the curtailment and limitation of the relief program to the extent of $22,400.00. It should be said that the County officials have from the beginning shown a magnanimous spirit toward the sticken colored population, while on the other hand the city officials in control of the municipal policy, certainly for the period ending October 1st, were entirely out of sympathy with the relief program. In fairness to Mayor Evans it should be recorded that since October 1st, or more accurately speaking, since certain court decisions were made restricting the city from interferring in the rebuilding processes, he and other city officials have shown an increased and more sympathetic interest in the condition of the colored people.

PLANS FOR THE WINTER

From month to month as conditions changed and after conference with W. Frank Persons, the Vice-Chairman of the Red Cross, James L. Fieser, Division Manager, and local chapter officials December 1st, 1921, was set as the date for closing the relief operations of the American Red Cross. Certain conditions, however, delayed the closing date to December 31st. The primary reason for this delay in closing, was the lack of any modern, record-keeping, case-work agency dealing with dependent families in Tulsa. There are no public hospitals nor facilities for handling the problems remaining. Prior to the fire there was a small private negro hospital and a general dispensary for colored people, both of which were burned.

It should also be indicated most clearly that the County Commissioners, the City authorities, the white population and the negroes themselves, insisted upon the Red Cross continuing its relief work thru the winter, but that the best judgment of the Red Cross Relief Committee, Division and National offices, dictated the final decision to close on December 31st, 1921.

Arrangements have been made whereby the "Tulsa Relief Trusteeship" will maintain a nucleus of workers and an office in the colored district to carry on the work of salvage and relief until the same is deemed unnecessary.

RECONSTRUCTION

All that has been said in this report has had to do with emergency and temporary relief. Seven months have elapsed since the trouble started, and on this date, December 31st, no rehabilitation nor practical reconstruction program has been outlined by the city government.

Early in the day the Red Cross made it clear that it was not its function to engineer plans for the acquisition of a new negro district, nor for converting any portion of the burned area into a commercial wholesale or industrial district. It was recognized at once, however, that the most suitable action, from a civic and business standpoint, would be the acquisition of that part of the burned area bordering on the railroad tracks, for future industrial or commercial expansion. Public opinion seemed in favor of this general proposition. Any such plan, however, it was pointed out, would involve, (1) the organization of a Housing Corporation or Holding Company which would act for the municipality in appraising and purchasing from the negro property owners their holdings; (2) the raising of sufficient funds to back the enterprise; (3) the acquiring of a new residential district to be sewered, watered and lighted; (4) a committee or sub-committee to help the negroes clear up their property equities and to assist them in repurchasing and rebuilding.

The above general suggestions were, on June 4th, made to the representatives of the Public Welfare Board in session at the City Hall. This board concurred and Chairman L. J. Martin outlined in writing a plan which would virtually embody the above suggestions. All that was necessary for the first plans, which among other things included plans for sufficient funds to start the enterprise immediately. It was well known in this connection that several men connected with the Public Welfare Board had agreed to liberally finance the move.

A CONSTRUCTIVE PLAN UP SET

A close reading of the newspaper articles in this report will show that just at the time when the Welfare Board was ready to announce its plans to the public, Mayor Evans again took up the reins of positive authority at the head of the city government. His first act was to discharge the old Public Welfare Board. He immediately appointed a new committee which he named "The Reconstruction Committee." This new committee was politically constituted and did not have in its membership men of large financial power or influence. Later on this committee membership was enlarged sufficiently to include representatives from the banking interests. Seven months have elapsed. The so-called Reconstruction Committee has gone out of existance without recording any constructive results.

Because of the many complications, political and otherwise, the Red Cross has unsuccessfully steered clear of the so-called "reconstruction processes" which engaged the "committee" during the early and late fall.

EXTENSION OF FIRE LIMITS

One of the first acts of the new committee was to extend the fire limits to embrace practically all of the burned area within the city limits. This move automatically made it impossible for the rebuilding of frame houses on the old properties. Shortly after this action the Red Cross asked the city authorities to grant the negroes permission to build temporary wooden houses on their lots. This permission was granted, only to be recalled a week later when it was found that a startling number of houses were under erection within the newly-extended fire limits. The agitation for and against the permanency of the fire limits proceeded for two months and until the district court—three judges presiding—permanently enjoined the city officials from executing the provisions of the fire ordinance recorded immediately after the fire. During the interim the negroes were prevented from helping themselves by rebuilding. With the final court decision, the so-called Reconstruction Committee automatically went out of business and rebuilding processes began in earnest. The statistical report appended indicates the progress made since that time.

Summarized, the activities revolve around the creation of a public sentiment which would force the negroes to rebuild in a section somewhere outside the city limits. Concurrently, it was hoped by some that public opinion would become sufficiently strong in favor of a Union Station site or a Commercial District, to bring about the financing of some such project. The Committee did not, however, evolve or state any practical plan for helping the household situation.

THE NEGRO ATTITUDE

The negroes have consistently said to the City, "Pay us for what we have lost and we will talk to you about selling what we have left." The Insurance Companies have consistently refused to honor the payment of insurance moneys because of the riot clause in the insurance policies. No suits for damages have reached the local court dockets and that which has been done is the responsibility of the negroes themselves and their white friends who have stood back of them.

RED CROSS RELATIONSHIPS

The Tulsa County Chapter with the guidance of the Director of Disaster Relief, bore the responsibility for Red Cross policy and execution. The workers from the Division office have been supplied the local

chapter at Division expense. Altho using funds from the public trea-
sury, it maintained a strictly independent position in the handling of
such funds.

The accounting system has been under general supervision of the
Division Accountant and a firm of local Public Accountants.

ADDENDA

The newspaper clippings and pictures tell the rest of the story. All
local persons contributing valuable services are mentioned in these
articles.

Be it said, however, in this report, that the Red Cross has had the
united support and good will of the whole population, all political fac-
tions and both of the newspapers.

It has been taken for granted that the Red Cross was the only
organization which could minister to both black and whites and maintain a strictly neutral position on all political and racial questions.

RESPECTFULLY SUBMITTED,
DIRECTOR
DECEMBER 31ST, 1921

SUPPLEMENT TO GENERAL REPORT
July 30, 1921
Tulsa Disaster Relief Statistics.
Compiled as of July 31st, 1921.

(These records do not show figures for any but those whose records are actually known to the Red Cross office.)

Number of families registered for relief	1912
Number of persons in these families	5739
Number of detached persons	360
Number of families with no children	407
Number of families with no children (missing or dead)	222
Number of families with no mother (missing or dead)	87
Houses burned	1256
Houses looted but not burned	216
Families living in tents at present	245
Families living with other families	649
Families definitely relieved with clothing, beds, bed clothing, tentage, laundry equipment, cooking utinsels, dishes, material for clothings, etc.	941
Churches housed in Red Cross tents	8
Medicines furnished (outside of hospitals)	130
Medical service (in field) given to maternity cases, typhoid cases, and infant cases	69
Small property adjustments made	68
Transportation furnished (estimate)	475
Telegrams sent or received (relative to riot victims)	1250

MEDICAL AND SURGICAL

Hospital cases, definitely charged to Red Cross	183
First Aid cases—during riot	531
Cases still in hospital	32
Maternity cases in hospital awaiting confinement	3
Maternity cases—prospective hospital cases	4

Equipped: 1 general dispensary for Tulsa P.H. Asso.
1 V. D. Clinic for County Physician
1 Dental Clinic
4 Wards in hospital

Physicians in Employ of Red Cross   (colored) 1 (white) 1

Total number of nurses employed by Red Cross since riot:

In hospitals	36
In field	8
TOTAL	44
At present on Staff	5

Number of surgeons whose services were paid for from
Red Cross funds   11

SUMMARY OF ACCOMPLISHMENTS TO DATE

1. During the immediate days after the riot, over four thousand people were housed and fed in detention camps, mess fashion.
2. An unknown number, approximating 2,000, were given shelter and fed wherever houses could be found to accomodate them.
3. Five hospitals were supplied with emergency dressings and medical supplies for care of 183 patients. 531 First Aid cases were cared for at emergency First Aid stations.

Note: It should be noted that all of the hospitals charged their regular fees both for hospital care and surgical attention— the bills being presented to the Red Cross.

4. Anti-tetanic, typhoid and small-pox serums were administered to over 1,800 people.

Following the concentration of relief in the Booker T. Washington school, individual work has been done with 1,912 families in addition to many hundreds of detached persons of whom no records were kept. On account of the variety of services rendered, it is impossible to list the kind of services rendered.

5. A modern hospital, general dispensary, dental clinic, and a V. D. clinic has been equipped and put into service.
6. Over 200 temporary residence tents have been fully equipped with floors, sides, and screens, and the people made as comfortable as possible. 150 women have been supplied with laundry outfits, thus enabling them to partically make a living.

PROBLEMS STILL TO BE MET

1. Of first importance is the evacuation, in late August, of the Booker T. Washington school. This means that our four-ward hospital,

the general dispensary, V.D. clinic, dental clinic, supply rooms, lumber yard, and relief administration offices must find quarters elsewhere.

2. On account of there being no permanent rehabilitation and housing program officially stated or planned, the Red Cross or some other agency must act in a temporary rehabilitation capacity.

Attention is called to one or two items most important, of which is the preparation of over 1,400 school children for school in September. Probably one-half of these must be furnished from some source or other, clothing, headwear, shoes, stockings, and school equipment.

Next in importance is the probability of a long winter with more sickness than usual, and with no provisions for emergency hospital or nursing care.

I might also call attention to the fact that with fall comes relief needs in bedding which will be stupenduous. Practically none of these temporary homes are equipped with stoves, lighting or heating.

It would be insane to argue or assume that more than three-fourths of the negro population are in position to help themselves—with the more essentials in living without continued assistance. It is quite certain that with the present status of unemployment and reduced wages, with no lessening of the cost of living, that even some wage earners will need emergency assistance.

The solution of these problems cannot be met by a "let alone policy." To avoid chaos among the negroes before spring, these problems must be faced and tackled by the community with sufficient finances and personnel to handle them on a socially sound and economical basis.

A Still Larger Problem

Developments are showing that as the overflow from the old burned district in reaching beyond the city limit, living conditions are becoming worse and worse, especially in the Greenwood addition. Sanitary and sewer arrangements are entirely inadequate and the lack of any policing is fast leading to a probably worse condition than existed before the riot in the old burned area. There is a growing attitude on the part of the city to throw responsibility for moral and sanitary conditions on the County, and the County is unprepared to meet the new condition with the necessary speed.

I might also call attention to the fact that the roads condition leading into the County through the Greenwood section are such in the dry season as to make it a disease-breeding center. Dust and filth accumulates everywhere.

These are but a few of the problems presented for action during the next few months.

SUMMARY MEDICAL AND SURGICAL RELIEF

No. Wounded Whites Hospitalized During and After Riot at Red Cross Expense	48
No. Wounded Negroes Hospitalized during and after Riot at Red Cross Expense	135
No. Negro Cases Hospitalized since Riot	98
Total Number persons receiving hospital care	233
No. patients still remaining in hospital	22
Number persons died	18
No. persons who have from time to time been discharged	193
No. First Aid cases during and after Riot	531
No. Colored Physicians used by Red Cross in treatment of sick since riot	11
Total No. of White physicians whose services were paid for by the Red Cross	11
Total No. of Nurses employed by Red Cross during and after the Riot:	
a. Hospital 38	
b. Field 8	46

Up to and including December 28th, the hospital has been in charge of Dr. H. S. Browne, Attending Physician and Surgeon, and under him a staff of three of the best white nurses obtainable. The white nurses, Mrs. Edmondson, Miss Cisser and Mrs. Pendergraft, left the service December 28th, the nursing work being taken over by a staff of colored nurses. Dr. H. S. Browne is Supervising Physician and Surgeon.

A Colored Hospital Association has been organized and incorporated to take over the management of the hospital. A staff of colored physicians and surgeons has been organized by Dr. Buttler, County Physician, the plan being to have the hospital entirely under the management of the colored people, the property interests for the time being to remain in the hands of the Board of Trustees—three or five white citizens yet to be selected.

TULSA AMERICAN RED CROSS RELIEF

Recapitulation of Accounts As of Sept. 1, 1921.

HOUSING AND FEEDING

Kitchen Labor		1,046.31
Food	5,352.64	
Refund	91.07	5,261.57
Refugee Camp Labor		437.50
Shelter Labor		392.32
Lumber & Building Material		4,121.07
Construction Labor		178.60
Shelter (Tents)		6,142.10
		17,579.47

MEDICAL AND SURGICAL
Care of Riot Sick and Wounded

Emergency Hospital Labor	1,821.37
Medical Hospital Supplies	1,418.46
Nurses	3,570.92
Hospitals (Care of Wounded)	2,834.85
Hospital Laundry	220.00
Physicians and Surgeons	5,871.00
Plumbing and Fittings	1,244.11
	16,981.70

FAMILY REHABILITATION

Clothing Commissary Labor		298.01
Furniture (cots)		3,308.24
Blanket Supplies		1,725.51
Clothing Supplies		982.06
Kitchen Utensils		278.83
Household Supplies		1,925.22
Transportation Persons	4,334.07	
Refund	67.09	4,266.98
Telegraph & Telephone	250.52	
Refund	14.07	216.45
Miss Mildred Leslie—Salary	325.00	
		13,326.30

FULL SOCIAL AND MEDICAL RELIEF REPORT UP TO AND INCLUDING DECEMBER 31ST, 1921

RELIEF STATISTICS

Total No. families registered	2480
Total No. persons in these families	8624
Total No. detached persons	410
Total No. families with no children	462
Total No. families with no father (missing or dead)	322
Total No. families with no mother (missing or dead)	87
Total houses burned	1256
Total houses looted but not burned	215
Families definitely relieved with clothing, beds, bed clothing, tentage, laundry equipment, cooking utensils, dishes, material for clothing, etc	1941
Churches housed in Red Cross tents	8
Medicines furnished (outside of hospital)	230
Medical service (in field) given to maternity cases, typhoid cases, and infant cases	269
Small property adjustments made	88
Transportation furnished (estimate)	475
Telegrams sent or received (relative to riot victims)	1350

RECONSTRUCTION

As of this date, December 30th, 1921, the following list shows progress being made by the negroes in rebuilding in the burned area:

180 One-room frame shacks
272 Two-room frame shacks
312 Three rooms or more, frame
1 Large brick church
2 Basement brick Churches
4 Frame churches—one room
24 One story brick or cement buildings
24 Two story brick or cement buildings
3 Three story brick or cement buildings
1 Large Theater
1 Corrogated Iron Garage
2 Filling Stations

There are still 49 families residing in tent covered houses. All of these are unable to rebuild. The Red Cross has assisted, with the use of funds from the National Association for the Improvement of Colored People, in the erection of 13 homes.

The Red Cross on its own account has transformed 152 tent homes into more or less permanent wooden houses.

FAMILY TASKS YET REMAINING

1. There still remains 49 tent houses to be converted into all wooden ones. While the National Association of Negroes have agreed to cooperate in financing this rebuilding, it is improbable that they will carry out their agreement unless some white guiding hand is present.

2. There is still a number of a hundred families whose destitution is due to the riot still needing constant help of one sort or another.

3. The problems of overcrowding, sufficient bedding and clothing and minor sickness are still present in abundance.

4. The transfer of the hospital has not been completed. A Colored Hospital Association is being incorporated. A staff of colored physicians and nurses are working at the hospital, under the direction of Dr. H. S. Browne and Dr. Butler, but it is too early to throw full responsibility of management and control to the negroes.

The hospital can and should be made self-sustaining. Wise direction at this time is necessary to insure this.

5. The business end of Red Cross Relief operations cannot close until all December business is closed and the books and accounts audited by public accountants. Such an audit is complete up to September 1st. It is estimated that the final closing accounts will take until January 15th.

SOCIAL RELIEF SUPPLY SCHEDULES

During the first three days following the riot a vast quantity of food was supplied for refugees at the Y.M.C.A., the Fair Grounds, the churches, the Convention Hall, the McNulty Park and other places. Likewise, a vast quantity of bedding supplies, cots, blankets, etc.

These supplies are not listed in the following table, altho these articles were ultimately paid for from relief funds. The cost of these first relief supplies is included in the detailed financial classification.

This supply list is necessarily a partial one, it being impossible to list the endless number of small goods which make up building material, clothing supplies and household equipment. This list does, however, give an idea as to the variety and extent of social relief operations.

Preceeding the list, however, should be the following statement on the methods of distribution.

Beginning on June 3rd, all family relief supplies given, were incidental to the particular need of a particular family. By a flexible system of family case work each family was encouraged in helping itself to the limit of their ability. Where lumber was donated, for instance, the labor necessary to rebuild or build the tent house was supplied by the family or their negro friends. Exceptions were made only in the cases of widows, sick or helpless people.

Instead of issuing ready-made clothing, cloth was supplied, sewing machines were provided and the raw material turned into clothing by the negro women and girls.

A typical variation was made in the cases of school books for High School pupils. The girls in the High School classes who could not purchase their school books were furnished with work, making hospital garments, nightgowns, underwear, etc., thus enabling them to pay for their books. The High School boys were furnished manual labor, their wages paying for their books.

The same place was followed with bedding supplies. The raw goods have been furnished, power sewing machines have been provided and the women required to manufacture their own quilts, conforts, cot pads, sheets, pillow cases and pillows.

The following is a list of relief supplies purchased on requisition or donated on invoice as shown:

HOUSING

Article	Purchased	Donated	Made in Workroom	Total
Tents	303	10		313
Lumber	305, 160 ft	72,000 ft		377, 160 ft
Tent Poles	300			300
Paint	119 gal.			119 gal.
Shingles	41 bun.			41 bun.
Screen Doors	152			152
Screen Wire	16, 300 ft			16,300 ft
Roofing Paper	125 rolls			125 rolls
Lime	40 bbls.			40 bbls.
Nails	2,233 lbs.			2,233 lbs
Household Equipment				
Cots	1,222	160		1,382
Blankets	1,491	225 prs.		1,716 prs
Comforts	143		360	543
Mattresses	112	36	80	228
Pillows	349		240	589
Cotton Bats	1,540			1,540
Bed Springs	120	16		136
Stoves (cooking)	36	24		60
Stove Piping	1,400 ft			1,400 ft
Gas Stoves	54	8		62
Heaters (small)	68			68
Oil Stoves	25	10		35
Lamps	50			50
Chairs	48	26		74
Laundry Tubs	360	16		376
Boilders	360			360
Sets of Irons	350			350
Wash Boards	360			360
Variety Kitchen Utensils	8,272			8,272
Bedsteads	40			40

Clothing Materials	Purchased	Donated	Made in Workroom	Total
Children's Stockings	500 pr.			500 pr.
Thread	50 doz.			50 doz.
Men's Socks	300 prs.			300 prs.
Women's Stockings	200 prs.			200 prs.
Outing Cloth (for children's underwear)				
Unbleached Domestic (underwear)				
Ginghams				
Cheese Cloth				
Denims				
Gause for Surgical Dressings				
Sheetings				49, 982 yds
Material for Layettes				
Quilt Material				
Material for aprons				
Comfort Material				
Diaper Cloth				
Dress Cloth (Children's School Dresses)				
Boys' Suits	36			36
Boys' Caps	70			70
Girls' Caps	100			100
Children's Shoes	50			50

SCHOOL BOOKS

No. not know.

Total cash value of school books furnished $1,239.00

SUNDRY RELIEF SUPPLIES

Disenfectants, 24 gal
Working Tools
  (spades, wheelbarrows, hammers, saws, shovels, etc.), 204
Gas and Water Piping, 2,800 ft.

NOTE: Additional information on relief statistics is contained in the financial statement covering expenditures.

SUMMARY OF ACCOMPLISHMENTS

1. During the immediate days after the riot, over four thousand people were housed and fed in detention camps, mass fashion.

2. An unknown number, approximately 2,000, were given shelter and fed wherever houses could be found to accomodate them.

3. Five hospitals were supplied with emergency dressings and medical supplies for care of 183 patients. 531 First Aid cases were cared for at emergency First Aid Stations.

(Note: It should be noted that all of the hospitals charged their regular fees both for hospital care and surgical attention, the bills being presented to the Red Cross.)

4. Anti-tetanus, typhoid and small-pox serums were administered to over 1,800 people.

5. Hospital care, a general dispensary, a dental clinic, and a V. D. Clinic was equipped and put into service at the Booker T. Washington School and used there until September 1st.

In the meantime a fairly modern nine-roomed hospital has been built ready for occupancy, which was immediately pressed into service on the vacation of the school properties.

6. Over four hundred tent homes were erected with board siding and flooring with screen ventilators and screen doors, these for immediate temporary use.

Since October 1st, two hundred twenty-five of these have been converted into all wood one-room or two-room houses.

7. Over five hundred children, mostly of the lower grades, were furnished school books and many of them school clothes, at the beginning of the school year.

8. During the months of October, November, and December, an average of fifteen carpenters were kept at work on daily wages replacing

tent homes with wooden shacks. During the same months an average of fifteen women have been employed in the work room, making underwear, quilts, hospital garments, bedding and clothing equipment.

9. A total of 2480 families have been to the Red Cross office with their troubles. A thorough record of each of these has been made and individual treatment afforded according to the merits of each case. The aim in each instance has been to help the sufferers help themselves, the Red Cross giving material assistance where the needs of the case warranted. In all of these cases the Red Cross workers have acted as counselor and advisors.

Co-operation With Other Agencies

Definite cooperation of the right sort has been given by all local social agencies, the East End Relief Committee, the National Association for the Improvement of the Colored People.

Summary Medical and Surgical Relief

No. Wounded Whites Hospitalized During and After Riot at Red Cross Expense		48
No. Wounded Negroes Hospitalized during and after riot at Red Cross Expense		135
No. Negro Cases Hospitalized since Riot		98
Total Number persons receiving hospital care		233
No. patients still remaining in hospital		22
Number of persons died		18
No. persons who have from time to time been discharged		193
No. First Aid Cases during and after Riot		531
No. Colored Physicians used by Red Cross in treatment of sick since riot		11
Total No. of White Physicians whose services were paid for by the Red Cross		11
Total No. of Nurses employed by Red Cross during and and after the riot		
a. Hospital	38	
b. Field	8	46

Up to and including December 30th, the hospital has been in charge of Dr. H. S. Browne, Attending Physician and Surgeon, and under him a staff of three of the best white nurses obtainable. The white nurses, Mrs. Edmondson, Miss Sizer, and Mrs. Pendergraft, left the service December 28th, the nursing work being taken over by a staff of colored nurses. Dr. H. S. Browne is Supervising Physician and Surgeon.

A Colored Hospital Association has been organized and incorporated to take over the management of the hospital. A staff of colored physicians and surgeons has been organized by Dr. Butler, County Physician, the plan being to have the hospital entirely under the management of the colored people, the property interests for the time being to remain in the hands of the Board of Trustees—three or five white citizens yet to be selected.

1 died Dec. 30th.

Hospital Personnel

As of December 30th, 1921.

Dr. H. S. Browne and Dr. Butler, white, Supervising Physicians and Surgeons with a staff of negro physicians and surgeons.

Miss Fagg, Day Nurse
Mrs. Marshall, Night Nurse
Mrs. Ragsdale, Asst. Day Nurse
Homer Mosely, Day Orderly
John Grisson, Night Orderly
Rebecca, Nurse's Aid
Mrs. Phillips, Cook
Arthur, Asst. Cook

NOTE: Dr. H. S. Browne has consented to remain as Supervisor for a period of fifteen days or as long thereof as may be necessary to turn the patients over to the colored doctors with safety.

Patients in Hospital Dec. 30th:

1 Cal Arnley, Shot in ankle—old man—may still save leg.
2. Alex Stevenson, Shot in hand—arm and leg—Compound fractures.

Others in Hospital Since Riot:

3. Elsie Walker, 80 yrs. old—ulcers in leg—will never be well. Case for County. Homeless.
4. Frank Miller, Old man—T.B.—home burned in riot—case for county.

5. Jake Miller, Old man—suffer paralytic stroke during riot—homeless—case for county.
6. Arthur Morrison, Age 12—pelegra—homeless since riot—Mother died result injuries in riot.
7. Henry Gamble, Aneurism—may recover—old man—case for County.
8. Charles Carter, T.B.—homeless since riot—case for County Hospital.

OTHERS IN HOSPITAL

9. Charles Caldwell, Hemorrhoids
10. John Williams, Asthma—syphilitic
11. Richard Ashford, Age 12—Tumor on chest
12. Mary Stewart, Removal Fibroid tumors, appendix and ovaries
13. Harriet Pierce, Perierphium ovaries, appendix and curetment
14. Bennie Krout, Infected Jaw
15. Arthur Montgomery, Shot in abdomen
16. Arizona Robinson—Removal of ovaries and tumors.
17. Henry Oscar, Pneumonia
18. Mammie Nurse, Tonsils and throat
19. Ruth Johnson, Syphilitic—medical case
20. William Collins, Syphilitic
21. Mobeal Adams, T.B.—Case for County

(Copy)

Tulsa, Oklahoma
July 1st, 1921

Mr. Maurice Willows
Red Cross Headquarters
Tulsa, Oklahoma.

Kind Sir:

This seems to express to you the profound gratitude, not only of every negro in Tulsa, but throughout the civilized world wherever there is a negro. Words fail me in trying to express our appreciation for your noble work for us. You and the Great Red Cross are helping us as a race to shut out of our lives all that is evil, to do our "Duty," and in that way we hope to receive the pure, the beautiful, the good, the true, and when the time comes that we shall add our motto to the music of the spheres it will be full of "Joy and Thanksgiving, no harsh note to mar the full, harmonious sound."

> *"We have but faith, we cannot know;*
> *for service is of things we see,*
> *And yet we trust it comes from Thee,*
> *A beam in darkness, let it grow."*

Knowing that God will reward you for what you have striven to do for us, for what you are doing, and for what you will do; in His words we read that what is done for the least of His subjects is precious in His sight.

Is the prayer of a grateful people,

Very respectfully yours,
(Signed) Louella T. West and J. S. West, Pastor
A. M. E. Church

(Copy)

Resolutions

On the 31st night in May, 1921, the fiercest race war known to American history broke out, lasting until the next morning, June 1st, 1921. As a result of the regretable occurance, many human lives were lost and millions of dollars worth of property were stolen and burned. Hundreds of innocent negroes suffered as a result of this calamity—suffered in loss of lives, injury from gun-shot wounds, and loss of property. Many of us were left helpless and almost hopeless. We sat amid the wreck and ruin of our former homes and peered listlessly into space. It was at this time and under such conditions that the American Red Cross—that Angel of love and Mercy—came to our assistance. This great organization found us bruised and bleeding, and like the good Samaritan, she washed out wounds, and administered unto us. Constantly, in season and out, since this regrettable occurance, this great organization, headed by that high class Christian gentleman, Mr. Maurice Willows, has heard our every cry in this our dark hour and has ever extended to us practical sympathy. As best she could, with food and raimant and shelter she has furnished us. And to this great Christian organization our heartfelt gratitude is extended.

Therefore, be it resolved that we, representing the entire colored citizenship of the city of Tulsa, Oklahoma, take this means of extending to the American Red Cross, thru Mr. Willows, our heart-felt thanks for the work it has done and is continuing to do for us in this our great hour of need.

Resolved further that a copy of these resolutions be sent to the American Red Cross Headquarters, a copy mailed to Mr. Willows and his co-workers, and that a copy be spread upon the minutes of the East End Welfare Board.

Respectfully submitted,

(Signed)
B. C. Franklin, I. H. Spears, E. F. Saddler, P. A. Chappelle, J. W. Hughes, Dimple L. Bush
Committee.

OFFICE OF THE EAST END RELIEF BOARD

Tulsa, Oklahoma, December 24, 1921.

The courage with which Tulsa Negroes withstood repeated attempts of the city administration to deliver the "burned area" over to certain land grafters is the subject of most favorable comment all over the country. The rapidity with which business buildings and residences are being rebuilt, in most instances, better than before is proof in wood and brick and in stone, of the black man's ability to make progress against the most cunningly planned and powerfully organized opposition.

Without weakening the above statement and taking nothing from the Tulsa Negroes courage, fortitude and resourcefulness, gratitude forces the admission that had it not been for the helping hand of the American Red Cross Society, his morale would have broken and the splendid history he has made since June 1st, 1921, when the savings of a lifetime were reduced to ashes, would have been impossible. The Red Cross has wrought so nobly in our behalf, is due largely to the spirit of the man in charge, Mr. Maurice Willows. He is an apostle of the square deal for every man, regardless of race or color. Behind closed doors in council with bodies of influential white men he fought battles and won victories for us sufficient to merit the everlasting gratitude of our people. The Red Cross as a society, has ministered to our physical needs and Mr. Willows as a man, has stood for our civic rights at home and a fair presentation of our case abroad. When importuned by interested parties to refer to the eventualities of May 31st and June 1st, in his official report, as a "Negro uprising," he stubbornly refused and instead, called it "the Tulsa disaster" and in addition told the truth as, upon investigation, he found it.

While assembled to witness the method by which the Red Cross has elected to give Christmas Cheer to the Negro Children of Tulsa and upon the eve of Mr. Willows' departure from our midst, the undersigned thought it fitting to offer these few words of appreciation on behalf of the entire Negro population of Tulsa, for the unselfish service he has rendered us, with the added assurance that the prayers of a people whom hardship and oppression have thought how to pray will follow him and his associates wherever, in response to the call of suffering humanity and in the line of duty, they may go.

STATEMENT OF ONE OF THE NEGROES

On the night of May 31st, between nine and ten o'clock, someone told me there was a race conflict. I was asked to go down on the street, but after being told that some had gone to the Court House I refused to go, knowing that I could not use any influence with the scattered bunch. On the morning of June 1st, I arose, expecting to go to the school house. I did not have any idea that the trouble had reached such a proportion.

At five o'clock a whistle was blown, seven aeroplanes were flying over the colored district, and a Machine Gun was placed in front of my home. I was called to the door by home guards and armed citizens. I was not dressed, but was told to bring my family out. They said if we would obey they would protect us and our property. I was not allowed to go back in the house. I called my wife and son, she came out dressed only in a kimona and shoes. We were ordered to put our hands above our heads, marched up Fairview Street, then across the Stand Pipe Hill to Easton Street, where we found automobiles driven by ladies and men.

We were carried to the City Jail, the men were placed in the corridor down stairs, the women were carried up stairs. After so many were crowded into the corridor, we were carried to Convention Hall. Many people cheered and clapped their hands as we were marched four abreast with our hands above our head. A man was shot at the door of the Convention Hall while both hands were above his head. Many men who were shot out in the city were brought in the hall and we heard their cries and groans. Namely: Dr. Jackson, Johnson and Stovall. We looked out of the windows, saw our homes go up in smoke. At noon, we were fed with sandwiches and coffee.

In the late afternoon, we were allowed to leave the Convention Hall only when some white person we had worked for would come and vouch for us. Mr. Oberholtzer, City Superintendent of Public Schools, came and called for all colored teachers, and we were taken to the old City High School, where I met my wife again. All the lady teachers were taken to the homes of the city principals and cared for nicely. We were allowed to stay in the old High School all night. The next morning, I saw my wife much improved as to her dress. Miss Kimble of the Domestic Science Department of the white High School gave us our breakfast.

The next morning, without hat or shoes, I was determined to improve my personal appearance and comfort. After much solicitation I was allowed to go under the guard of a soldier down on Main Street to Renberg's Clothing Store. He gave all colored male teachers a suit of clothes and hat. In the evening of the first day after the trouble, I was allowed to go out and look over the burned area. Thirty-five blocks, including my home and eight rent houses, were in ashes.

My second night was spent in the Booker T. Washington High School, which had been placed in charge of the Red Cross. Our wives slept on one side of the house on cots and the men on the other side. I was placed temporarily in charge of conditions of the food supply. We lined the people up, many hundreds being in the line, and fed them their meals by allowing them to pass between two tables, on one was sandwiches, the other, coffee. In this way, we gave each his allowance.

In a very short while, the entire High School Plant was made into a hospital, office rooms, distributing rooms, etc., which soon brought a partial temporary relief to the many who were suffering from wounds, hunger, and the need of clothes.

The stories told by those who came for relief are so freighted with horror, I refrain from repeating them. Many of the sick were forced from home. Those on crutches were compelled to go likewise. A mother giving birth to child was no exception to the rule.

A Reconstruction Committee was appointed by the Mayor of the city. A like committee was ordered selected by his honor from the remaining negro population. We have been asked to give up the lands on which our homes, business, churches and schools were located and requested to go north and east of the city, but and rebuild. The only consideration offered us was leave our lots and when they have increased in value, they will sell them and we have the profit thereby. Thus far, we have failed to acquiesce in the recommendation of the request.

(Signed) J. W. Hughes,
Prin. City School.

To Mr. Willows

A request from a true friend,
As you must leave you do entend;
And your leaving is a regret,
As you have did for us—we can never forget.

Please take this as a token
To all whom may concern,
That you came and went as a gentleman,
And this the colored of Tulsa will confirm.

When you far away from Tulsa town,
Do not think of us with a frown,
For God only can tell
How much we appreciate you as well

Thank God for the Red Cross,
For by His hand he put you boss,
And thus He would been to blame
If you and your host had not carried out His aim.
    Amen.

A. J. Newman
Nov., 1921.

CHRISTMAS TREE

The body of the foregoing report was written prior to the one big event in the lives of the negro children of the devastated district. For the first time in their lives, these hundreds of little folks were without their former comfortable homes. The resources of their parents had been reduced to a point where Christmas could not mean much to them. The workers of the Red Cross staged for them probably the largest Christmas affair ever staged in Tulsa. A beautiful big tree was placed in front of the Red Cross Relief Headquarters. Mr. Chas. Page of Sand Springs kindly furnished the lighting and decorations. The tree was topped with a large cross.

Imagine, if you can, this huge tree brightly lighted standing on Hartford Street in the middle of a district which had once been comfortable homes, but now filled up with little one and two-room wooden shacks with here and there and everywhere large piles of brick and stone, twisted metal and debre, reminding one of the horrible fact of last June. War of the worst sort there had been. The Maurice Willows Hospital (named such by unanimous vote of the colored people of the district as a measure of their appreciation for what the Red Cross Director has meant to them) stood within a few yards of where the tree was placed. Imagine, if you can, the joy brought to the twenty-two hundred voices sang their Christmas carols and typical negro melodies. Never has the writter witnessed more spontaneous outburst of Christmas fervor than on this occasion. Whole families were there— men, women and children. "Swing Low, Sweet Chariot," "Down By The River Side," "Standing In the Need Of Prayer," coming from the throats of these people revibrated through out the night air and attracted most of the crowd gathered in the business section over on Greenwood Street. It seemed as tho the whole negro population could not resist the chance to sing. A liberal supply of candies, nuts and oranges had been tied up into half-pound packages. Twenty-seven hundred of these were distributed in orderly fashion. Individual packages had been prepared suitable to the needs of women and children. These packages had in them everything in the way of useful articles from a spool of thread to a heating stove. Bed springs, pillows, childrens underwear, quilts, cotton bats and every other sort of useful articles were brought by Santa Clause to families which needed these practical things most.

The crowning sentiment of the celebration was in a speech made by one of their leaders who said, "Let us always remember the old negro tradition, 'there is no room in our hearts for hatred." This occasion furnished what was termed as the "greatest night in the history of Tulsa negroes," and was a fitting culmination of the major relief program of the Red Cross.

APPENDIX C

TULSA CITY COMMISSION MEETING MINUTES
JUNE 14, 1921

[Selected excerpts from the original document.]

June 14, 1921   MESSAGE—MAYOR TO COMMISSIONERS

Gentleman of the Commission: In connection with the late negro uprising I desire to make some suggestions which may be helpful in arriving at a sound and correct solution of the various problems that now confront us. Since this trouble has happened, I know that you, as well as myself, have had all ordinary mortals could do to attend to the duties of the present without a thought of a permanent Policy to govern our future action as to the "Burned District" and various needs connected with the same, but we must now look to the future because of the lease of power that the people have placed in our hands and seek to do things that are best suited to the needs of our great city.

It is fitting that we first remember and thank those officers both regular and special, members of the National Guard, of the Legion, and the great number of good citizens who risked their lives to defend this city. A list of their names should be preserved that the people may in the future remember them in some fitting manner for their valiant fight to protect Tulsa and make her safe for the future. Also the Red Cross, the good work of the Churches, Salvation Army, and all other organizations and citizens who helped following this disaster should receive the thanks of the whole community.

Adjutant General Barrett won a place in the hearts of Tulsans which time will not efface. Officers, soldiers, and citizens who worked with him found him a man, a general, and a good citizen. It was a pleasure to work with him and his staff and the National Guard under his command.

The many sleepless nights put in by Police Commissioner

Adkison in directing his forces made a severe test upon the strength of any official but he is rewarded by knowing that he protected the city and did his full duty. The same may be said of Maj. T.C. Hopkins, Maj. C. F. Hopkins, Maj. Fuller, Capt. Seber, Capt. Galloway, Maj. Ballou, Lieut. Dunlap, Lieut. Bachelder, Lieut. Boushell, Lieut. Sundin, Lieut. Col. Rooney, Lieut. Col. P. J. Hurley, Maj. Alva J. Niles, Capt. Lewis Lefko, Lieut. C. A. Border, and Capt. Gerald F. OBrian, who directed the National Guards, and the boys of the American Legion.

Now, while I can't at this time cover all subjects that possibly should be covered and brought to your attention, yet a few points are suggested to mind.

First-Responsibility: Let the blame for this negro uprising lie right where it belongs—on those armed negroes and their followers who started this trouble and who instigated it and any persons who seek to put half the blame on the white people are wrong and should be told so in no uncertain terms. We are told that twice before we assumed power as city officials that armed mobs of negroes visited the white section of the city and made certain demands under threats of force. They have come only Once in this administration. We are not Prophets, but we wager that trip number two will not take place soon.

Second: No Cause for this trouble.

Even when these negroes were at the jail, there still was no reason for their making any trouble. They were assured over and over again that the prisoner held by the sheriff was safe, that no one could get him. No organized mob was in the act of getting him, nor was there any danger apparent that they would get him. The occasion brought quickly around the Court House hundreds of men, women, and children as is usually the case when any rumor of this nature gets in the air. The great, great majority of white people who ran in were wholly unarmed. There was every reason to believe that when these negroes knew their prisoner was safe that the trouble would immediately stop because usually when a cause is removed, there will be no effect. A shot fired by a fool black person, evidently without cause, set the whole affair going and set the old fires of racial war and hatred going in all their furry.

Third—Officers: For the officers in the heart of the city and in the presence of hundreds of men, women and children to have pitched a battle by shooting would have meant the lives of many men, women, and children who were in the crowd, and our list of killed and wounded might have been one or two hundred people. It is to the credit of these men who defended the city that night, being officers, National Guards, and Legion men, that they were wise enough to see this and to gradually work these disturbers back to the negro section. All this was done without a dollars loss of property by fire in the heart of Tulsa and with very minimum of loss of life or personal injury.

Fourth—Place: It is the judgement of many wise heads in Tulsa, based upon observation of a number of years, that this uprising was inevitable. If that be true and this judgement had to come upon us, then I say it was good generalship to let the destruction come to that section where the trouble was hatched up, put in motion and where it had its inception.

Fifth—Wrongs: All regret the wrongs that fell upon the innocent negroes and they should receive such help as we can give them if within our power. It, however, is true of any warfare that the fortunes of war fall upon the innocent along with the guilty. This is true of any conflict, invasion, or uprising. Think what would have happened had the Allies marched to Berlin.

Sixth—Firearms: We are told that in the colored section the negroes had guns in their homes and ammunition to use in such weapons. When, in the course of the last twenty five years or more, has that not been true and where is the law which anyone can prevent negroes having guns in their homes? We all know the law, both state and city, allows this and so far as I know, always has allowed it. In the past fourteen years I have often had occasion in dealing in lands and Farm loans in the Creek Nation particularly, to be in many negro homes. It has been much the exception to find any negro house or cabin where there was not one or two shotguns or revolvers and plenty of ammunition. I venture to say that this very day, within a radius of twenty five miles of Tulsa enough fire arms can be obtained from negro home alone, to equip five hundred men and prepare them for a pretty fair state of warfare.

Seventh: Nothing new:—These uprisings are not by any means new or novel and they are no longer confined below the Mason and Dixon line. The cities are legion who have had more or less of riot trouble. Will law-abiding citizens cease business with the City of Tulsa or refrain from coming here on account of having trouble of this kind? Have you heard of anybody staying out of Washington D.C. because there was race trouble there? Chicago killed something like two thousand negroes not long ago and I believe the trouble lasted several day there, yet does any business man stay out of Chicago or refuse to invest in property there on this account? The Court House was destroyed in a similar trouble in Omaha and the uprising was not put down there nearly so quickly as in this city, yet does anybody refrain from going to Omaha because of that affair? East St. Louis was visited by an outbreak far more serious than that in this city, yet none of us think of staying away from St. Louis. This list might be extended to cover many pages, and yet not exhaust all the illustrations. Let us immediately get to the outside the fact that everything is quiet in our city, that this menace has been fully conquered, and that we are going along in a normal condition and it will have a great influence to overcome the hundreds of wild rumors that have gone over the country. As the truth gradually reaches the outside, ninety nine per cent of the prejudices will be overcome.

Next let us look to a few general ideas pertaining to reconstruction:

(1) Let us not shirk the responsibility of doing that which is best for all, both black and white.

(2) Let every transaction pertaining to the rights of all these property owners, both black and white, be characterized by the absolute honesty and see that each gets, in the parlance of the streets, a square deal.

(3) A large portion of this district is well suited for Industrial purposes: better adapted for these purposes than for residences. Once it is assured that it will be so used there will be a decided rise in value which will give the property owners more for the naked ground than his whole property was worth before the fire. Let the negro settlement be placed farther to the north and east.

We should immediately get in touch with all the railroads with a view to establishing a Union Station on this ground. The location is ideal and all the railroads convenient. From our acquaintance with all conditions after several days for settling back to a normal state. I believe a committee of citizens can now well be selected to constitute the legally appointed committee for the city and to be known as a "Reconstruction Committee" and I recommend such action.

It is well in the selection of this committee that we fully comprehend just the nature of the locality and the people with whom they must come in contact. Many well known men in other lines could not handle this section to the best advantage. Persons who have lived here many years and helped blaze the way for greater Tulsa, who know every foot of the ground, and who are well acquainted with these colored people, and who are honest and reliable can best handle this proposition. I believe a committee consisting of the following men will be equal to the greater task of aiding and guiding us to a conclusion beneficial to all.

Vis: (1) Frank B. Long, (2) Edward Short, (3) C. G. Gump, (4) J. W. Woodford, (5) W. T. Brady, (6) A. J. Biddison, (7) S. R. Lewis, (8) J. W. Wilson

Respectfully submitted,
(Signed) T. D. Evans, Mayor.

Dated June 14, 1921.

_____ presented.

Moved by Steiner, seconded by Adkison, that said report be approved down to the section appointing the Reconstruction Committee.

Roll call:

Steiner-yea   Younkman-no
Adkison-yea   Newblock-yea.
Mayor-yea.
Yeas 4   Noes 1   Absent 0
Carried.

RECONSTRUCTION COMMITTEE

The Mayor placed in nomination the names of Frank B. Long, Edward E. Short, C. B. Gump, J. W. Woodford, W. T. Brady, A. J. Biddison, S. R. Lewis and J. W. Wilson as members of the "Reconstruction Committee."

Moved by Steiner, seconded by Younkman, that said nomination be confirmed.

Roll call:

Steiner-yea   Younkman-yea
Adkison-yea   Newblock-yea.
Mayor———
Noes 0   Absent 0   Yeas 4
Carried.

COMMISSIONER STEINER RETIRED.

APPENDIX D

EXCERPTS FROM THE NEGRO CITY DIRECTORY, TULSA, OKLAHOMA 1941

(Published by the Greenwood Chamber of Commerce)

INTRODUCTION

The Negro City Directory for Tulsa, covering a trade area of some 250 square miles, represents a combined Negro population slightly in excess of 20,000. The importance of this section of Oklahoma as a Negro center dates back to early Statehood when the great oil pools were opened in this area.

From about 1910 to the close of the World War period, Tulsa experienced its greatest era of prosperity when thousands of Negroes streamed in from every state in the Union. With this influx of colored Americans, came the Negro business man, educator, oil prospector, laborer and domestic. With each bent in a determined effort toward economic betterment, it gave rise in Tulsa to the No. 1 boom venture of the times. In mushroom-like manner homes, schools, churches, organizations and businesses sprang up over night, it seemed, to grad- ually envelop the north half of Tulsa. Meanwhile, a vast network of shops, hotels, rooming houses and stores began to spread along three principal thoroughfares, Cincinnati, Archer and Greenwood. Jobs were plentiful, wages were good, there was work for every employable, and the golden face of prosperity smiled in every home.

THE TULSA SPIRIT

Perhaps the greatest single asset of Tulsa is, after all, an intangible one—The Tulsa Spirit. With no parallel anywhere else in America, this asset in Tulsa has almost uncanny and super-human effect upon its peo- ple. There is something about the Tulsa Spirit that defies explanation. It has the peculiar power of so overwhelming one that he registers a fighting determination to carry on in the face of staggering odds. A classic illustration of this quality in Negro Tulsans is reflected in an inci- dent just after the Tulsa riot. In the wake of this racial disaster in June, 1921, the homes of the Negroes were in ruins, fire had gutted their schools and churches, their businesses had been reduced to ashes, their enterprises had been completely wrecked, life savings had been reduced to zero and the last vestige of material prosperity had been swept away—leaving a vast horde of 15,000 Negroes with no place to lay their heads. Truly a dark and gloomy picture, too black to describe.

GREENWOOD AVENUE

Perhaps nowhere else in America is there a single thoroughfare which registers such significance to local Negroes as North Greenwood Avenue in Tulsa. Today, after some twenty-five years of steady growth and development, Greenwood is something more than an avenue—it is an institution. The people of Tulsa have come to regard it as a symbol of racial prominence and progress—not only for the restricted area of the street itself, but for the Negro section of Tulsa as a whole. Domestics employed elsewhere in the city, when leaving their jobs for home in the Negro section, are referred to as 'Greenwood bound.' White managers, in discharging a Negro employee, frequently do so with the remark, 'sending him back to Greenwood.' It is not unusual for Tulsans visiting in all parts of the U. S., to be yearning for 'Dear Old Greenwood.' Ministers sometime assure their congregations that services will soon be over so that they can return to 'Greenwood.' Parents and teachers are forever concerned about keeping their children off 'Greenwood.'

Beginning at East Archer and the M-K-T tracks, this famous thoroughfare runs north to Pine Street, flanked on either side by two miles of teeming business structures. Massed along both sides of Greenwood from Archer to Pine, is unquestionable the greatest assembly of Negro shops and stores to be found anywhere in America. Like the avenue itself, merchantmen have spread their wares from one end of this two-mile long stretch to the other, in unbroken array. Into Greenwood Avenue has come the banker, the baker and the candle stick maker—all intent upon a single purpose—to make things better for himself and his community.

In this age of streamlining, neon signs and fluorescent lighting, Greenwood now presents an almost solid front of gay shops, theatres, night clubs, taverns, bars, etc, which resemble a fairyland at night. It offers business opportunity in every field.

THURSDAY NIGHT

New York has its New Year's Eve, small towns have their Saturday, Tulsa has its Thursday night. Like Greenwood, Thursday night has also become an institution for Tulsa. The day that most domestics have 'off' every week, Thursday has come to be universally recognized as a holiday for thousands of maids, butlers, cooks, chauffeurs and other domestics who make up about 50 percent of Tulsa's Negro workers. Off from their work about 10:30 a.m., they are free for the rest of the day. Their week's shopping and other personal affairs attended, the domestics stream into Greenwood that night by the hundreds. Here they are joined by admirers, friends and spectators to form a crowd somewhat like that in tumultuous Times Square. Here one gets an opportunity to see 'South Town' (those who work for rich families in the south end of Tulsa) on parade. Everywhere about can be seen cheerful groups of beautiful girls, dressed in smartly tailored suits or other street wear. Their hair done in swankiest coiffure, these young women as a whole would rival any models that have ever graced Atlantic City's Board Walk.

LOCATION

Tulsa is located along the north bank of the Arkansas River at the junction of U. S. Highways 64, 66 and 75, in Tulsa County, Oklahoma. It is a railroad center, with four principal trunk lines—the Frisco, Midland Valley, M-K-T and Sante Fe serving it form without. Tulsa is approximately 70 miles south of the Kansas southern border, about 130 miles west of the Arkansas western border, about 130 miles north of the Texas northern border and 120 miles east of the State Capitol, Oklahoma City. All highways—both state and federal—entering Tulsa are paved in all directions, thus enabling motorists to travel to and from the city in all weather with ease.

POLITICS

In a political sense, Tulsa Negroes have made tremendous progress. Constituting one-tenth of the voting strength, they easily swing elections one way or the other at will. In this respect, it has been demonstrated time after time, that no office seeker can be elected in a city-wide or county-wide political contest, where opposition is effective, without the Negro vote. Enjoying unrestricted and universal use of the ballot, Tulsa is the only city in the southwest that has ten precincts with entire Negro staffs—including judges, tellers and inspectors. This very attractive feature of political policy here, has had a most important effect upon the great exodus of Negroes into Tulsa and environs from all over the country. Many colored citizens moving into town from southern states explain how they enjoy the novelty of casting their first vote when arriving here.

SCHOOLS

Tulsa offers its Negro youth various educational opportunity with one high school, one junior high school, three grade schools and one household employee service school, employing 100 teachers and 20 other employees all supported by public taxation. Hence serving to educate the colored youth, 120 persons of their own race are employed. The public schools offer an almost unlimited number of advantages in the fields of industrial arts, household arts, commerce, national defense and general education. Outstanding features of the Tulsa schools include one of the best equipped high schools in the South, with membership in the North Central Association of Colleges and Secondary Schools; and a single salary scale for all teachers—white and colored alike—in the system.

CHURCHES

In Tulsa proper there are in all 40 Negro churches, offering a haven of worship to a combined membership of more than 5,000 Christians of all denominations. Among these churches, Tulsans have some of the best and well kept property in the State of Oklahoma. For the most part, they are pastored and shepherded by intelligent leadership, or advice.

BUSINESS

As a business opportunity, Tulsa is considered one of the nation's most favored spots. Unlike most cities of comparable size and location, Tulsa offers business advancement in more than the usual five fields—grocery, cafe, barbershop, cleaners and undertaking. On the contrary, Tulsa Negroes are very active in the fields of oil brokerage, real estate brokerage, furniture sales and service, jewelry and goldsmiths, electrical appliance sales and service, building contractors, auto tire and supply and general transportation.

APPENDIX E

NORTH TULSA HERITAGE FOUNDATION, INC. "IMAGE BUILDER" AWARD RECIPIENTS (THROUGH 1996)

Among the Image Builder Award recipients are a host of familiar names in Tulsa's African-American community and beyond:

DR. CHARLES BATE—Dr. Bate came to Tulsa from his native Tennessee in 1940. He was the first African-American doctor accepted into the Tulsa County Medical Society. In the 1960s, Dr. Bate founded "Operation Hope," a program created to help high school dropouts gain a foothold in the medical field. Dr. Bate also tirelessly promoted blood pressure screening test, setting up remote testing sites such as the Tulsa State Fair. Dr. Bate retired in 1990.

NEWTON T. BURNS—Mr. Burns was the owner/operator of N. T. Burns & Sons Grocery Store on Greenwood Avenue from 1935-1959 and charter member of the Greenwood Chamber of Commerce. Burns ultimately sold his Greenwood property to the Tulsa Urban Renewal Authority.

ELIZABETH CHAPPELLE—Ms. Chappelle was an active educator for some thirty-nine years. She devoted countless hours to the Metropolitan Tulsa Urban League, the Y.W.C.A., the Langston Alumni Association and Tulsa's Gilcrease Museum. Her civic and religious activities in the Tulsa community are legendary.

BUCK COLBERT ("B.C.") FRANKLIN—Born in 1879 in Indian Territory near Homer, Mr. Franklin attended Rogers Williams College University in Nashville, Tennessee. He later graduated from Atlanta Baptist University (now Morehouse College). He passed the Oklahoma bar in 1907 and, as a Tulsa lawyer, successfully challenged the post-Riot fire code ordinance which required that new housing in the Riot area be built with prohibitively-expensive fireproof materials. The ordinance was declared invalid. B. C. Franklin Park on Cincinnati Avenue bears his name. He served as one of the lawyers on the R. C. Foster murder trial in 1934. This would be the first case in Tulsa on which African-Americans and whites served together on a jury. Franklin later became the first African-American lawyer in Oklahoma to become a district judge.

LEROY AND ERNESTINE GIBBS—The Gibbs have a long history in

Tulsa. Mr. Gibbs opened his first business in Tulsa in 1915, Gibbs Fish and Poultry, selling everything from rabbit to chitterlings. Mr. Gibbs actively assisted young African-American men in landing jobs as delivery men in the soft drink industry. Ms. Gibbs taught school in Tulsa, and served as a volunteer for many organizations, including the Y.W.C.A., the Y.M.C.A., the N.A.A.C.P., and the Greenwood Chamber of Commerce.

EDWIN LAWRENCE ("E.L.") GOODWIN, SR.—Mr. Goodwin was the publisher of *The Oklahoma Eagle* African-American community news-paper, a lawyer, and a prominent community activist. Goodwin started *The Oklahoma Eagle* in 1936. The Chappelle-Goodwin Gallery at the Greenwood Cultural Center bears his name.

JEANNE B. GOODWIN—Ms. Goodwin graduated from Fisk University in Nashville, Tennessee. She was then chosen as a Fellow in the Atlanta School of Social Work. Noted sociologist E. Franklin Frazier recruited her and she became his teaching surrogate on those occasions when he was away. Frazier would later become a preeminent authority on the African-American family in the context of American society. Jeanne B. Goodwin and her husband, E. L., were active in civic and community affairs in the Tulsa community for decades.

AMOS T. HALL—Amos T. Hall was a lawyer and advocate who assisted Thurgood Marshall with *Ada Lois Sipuel vs. The University of Oklahoma*, the successful challenge to segregated higher education in Oklahoma. In 1970, Hall, elected Tulsa County Associate District Judge, became the first African-American elected judge in the State of Oklahoma. Hall died in 1971. Among the dignitaries attending his funeral were United States Supreme Court Justice Thurgood Marshall and Roy Wilkens, Executive Director of the N.A.A.C.P.

REV. BENJAMIN HARRISON HILL—A minister, teacher and public servant, Rev. Hill made a mark not just on the City of Tulsa, but on the State of Oklahoma. Rev. Hill, in addition to his many other endeavors, was an editorial writer for *The Oklahoma Eagle*, and a member of the Oklahoma House of Representatives. Rev. Hill was honored by The National Conference of Christians and Jews, Tulsa Region, for his humanitarian efforts. Rev. Hill was also inducted into the Tulsa Hall of Fame.

JOBIE HOLDERNESS—Ms. Holderness and her family operated the Lynn and Clark Cleaners and Banner Market in Tulsa. Banner Market came to be an area social service center, not just a grocery store. After her husband's death, Ms. Holderness continued to operate Banner Market until 1982. By then, the family had been in business for 60 years. Ms. Holderness, the librarian at Dunbar Elementary School for forty-two years, found time to be active in the Y.W.C.A., and First

Baptist Church of North Tulsa. She is a charter member of many of Tulsa's social and civic clubs. A graduate of Bishop College and a member of the Bishop College Hall of Fame, Ms. Holderness left her mark on Tulsa and Tulsans.

LEONARD C. HOLMAN—Mr. Holman founded Holman Jewelry. As a young man, he walked to Tulsa from Haskell. He got his first job at the legendary Dreamland Theatre on Greenwood Avenue. He began his career after reading and advertisement in a local paper for a porter's position at Sander-Rones Jewelry. On that job he learned the trade by observing repairmen and engravers. After passing his watchmaker's examination in Washington, D. C., Holman became the first African-American jeweler in Oklahoma. He was one of the first African-Americans to work for Douglas Aircraft, and served as deputy county treasurer for Tulsa County.

OTIS KEMP—Mr. Kemp owns and operates Tulsa Shoe Rebuilders in downtown Tulsa. He is a fixture in downtown Tulsa. Kemp the cobbler was once Kemp the teacher. Mr. Kemp taught cobbling at Langston University for several years. Mr. Kemp is known for superb craftsmanship and equally impressive character.

ED LACY—Mr. Lacy ("Coach") is a native Tulsan and a legendary athletic coach and teacher who spent years at Booker T. Washington High School, his alma mater. Lacy received his bachelor's degree from North Carolina A & T and his master's degree from Columbia (New York) University. Known community-wide for his athletic insight and community spirit, Lacy is a true community hero.

MAJOR LATIMER, SR.—Mr. Latimer taught school in South Carolina, then moved to Tulsa in the 1920s with his wife Maria, also a teacher, and their six children. Mr. Latimer worked as a custodian in May Brothers Clothing Store. He started his first business, One Stop Food Shop, in 1929. Latimer became a barbeque expert, creating a special sauce that became famous.

AUGUSTA E. MANN—Ms. Mann, together with her husband, was owner of Mann's Grocery Store, one of the African-American businesses that extended lines of credit to the victims of the Riot. The business lasted for some 40 years. Ms. Mann played active roles in a host of civic, religious, and community affairs in Tulsa throughout the years.

REVEREND G. CALVIN MCCUTCHEN—Reverend McCutchen, the longtime pastor of Mt. Zion Baptist Church, was born and raised in Kentucky. He earned two bachelor's degrees, a divinity degree, and several honorary degrees throughout the course of his life. Reverend McCutchen played an active role in ending segregation in Tulsa.

CLAUDE AND CORRINE RAMSEY—The Ramseys owned the Ramsey

Drug Store in the Corbett Building on Greenwood Avenue. Mr. Ramsey earned his pharmacy degree from Meharry Medical, Dental and Pharmaceutical College in 1922, then opened the Ramsey Drug Store in Tulsa in 1923. Mr. Ramsey, affectionately known simply as "Doc," was a strong proponent of education. In 1945, he built the Ramsey Building at Greenwood Avenue and Marshall Streets. That building housed the Ramsey Drug Store, Holman Jewelry, the T. C. Morris Barber Shop, and the Ramsey Rooms, upstairs residential lodging for single men. Mrs. Ramsey assisted in the businesses and taught at Carver Junior High School. The Ramseys were involved in all manner of community activities and affairs.

MABLE RICE—Mable Rice, a longtime Tulsa community activist, was the first African-American to operate a retail outlet in Tulsa's Williams Center Forum, a shopping mall that was located in a downtown skyscraper. She is a founding member of The Simon Estes Educational Foundation, an organization that provides substantial college scholarship assistance to a diverse group of highly-qualified high school students in the Tulsa area. Ms. Rice served as a counselor for the Morton Health Center and as associate director of the Metropolitan Tulsa Urban League. Ms. Rice also served as the executive director of the Sickle Cell Anemia Foundation of Oklahoma.

LEROY THOMAS, SR.—Founder and former chairman of Tulsa's best-known African-American financial institution, American State Bank, Mr. Thomas also played pivotal roles in the organization of a multitude of Tulsa businesses. Mr. Thomas taught at Booker T. Washington High School and served as the director of the Seminole Hills Demonstration Housing Project. A well-known and highly-regarded community volunteer, Mr. Thomas served on numerous boards of directors, including the board of the Greenwood Chamber of Commerce and the Metropolitan Tulsa Chamber of Commerce.

APPENDIX F

Table D-1 Black Business Establishments and Business Persons in Tulsa as Listed in City Directories, 1907, 1909-1914, and 1916-1923

ESTABLISHMENTS	'07	'09	'10	'11	'12	'13	'14	'16	'17	'18	'19	'20	'21	'22	'23
Bath Parlors								1							
Billiard Halls			2	1	3	3	3	6	5	4	5	6	9	4	6
Cigars and tobacco							1	2				2			
Clothing, dry goods, racket, second-hand, music, furniture, paints and oils, shoes			1	1	3	1	3		2	2	2	1	2	2	2
Confectionary, soft drinks			1	2	1	1		4	5	7	16	2	4	6	6
Feed and grain											1	1	1	1	1
Furnished rooms, boarding and rooming houses	3		2	3	2		4	3	1	6	5	9	11		3
Garages, auto repair and filling stations								1	1			1	2		3
Grocers, meat markets	3	3	2	5	8	10	9	7	18	11	21	23	41	34	31
Hotels			1	1	2	2	1	1	1	2	2	4	5	4	9
Restaurants	1	1		5	3	13	17	16	11	17	21	20	30	29	19
Theaters						1	1	1	1	1	1	1	2	1	
Undertakers' parlors									2	2	2	2	1	2	1
Total	7	4	9	18	22	31	39	42	47	52	76	72	108	83	81

PROFESSIONALS	'07	'09	'10	'11	'12	'13	'14	'16	'17	'18	'19	'20	'21	'22	'23
Dentists					1		1	1	1	1	1		2	2	2
Druggists and medicine manufacturers		1		1	1	1	1	1	4	3	3	3	4	3	3
Jewelers					1		1	1		1		1	1		
Lawyers	1	1	3	4	2	1	5	4	4	4	5	4	3	4	6
Nurses		1			1			1				2		1	

	'07	'09	'10	'11	'12	'13	'14	'16	'17	'18	'19	'20	'21	'22	'23
PROFESSIONALS															
Photographers											1	1	2	1	2
Physicians and surgeons	2	2	2	3	4	7	5	3	4	10	12	13	15	10	10
Real estate, loans, and insurance agents	2						1	2	4	4	3	6	6	4	5
Private detectives															1
Total	5	4	5	8	8	11	13	13	17	23	26	30	33	25	29
SKILLED CRAFTS PERSONS															
Bakers															
Blacksmiths		1				1	1	1	1	1	1	1		3	2
Contractors, carpenters, builders, house and sign painters								1	1	2	7	3	5	6	2
Dressmakers					1			1	1	3	4		2	1	1
Milliners															1
Plumbers										2					
Printers							1	1	1	1	1	1	1	1	
Shoemakers and shoe repairers			2	2		1	2	1	1	1	3	2	4	6	3
Tailors				1		1	2	3	2	5	6	7	10	6	9
Upholsterers													1		
Total	1		2	3	1	3	6	7	5	15	22	14	24	24	18
SERVICE WORKERS															
Barbers	1	2	2	4	3	3	5	7	6	10	11	9	12	11	13
Cleaners, hatters, dyers, and pressers				2	1	6	4	4	7	10	7	5	5	5	6
Hairdressers			2					1		3	3		3		1
Launderers							1		1			1		2	1
Shoe shiners							2	2	5	4	4	4	6	6	1
Total	1	2	4	6	4	9	12	14	19	27	27	19	26	24	22

SEMI-SKILLED WORKERS	'07	'09	'10	'11	'12	'13	'14	'16	'17	'18	'19	'20	'21	'22	'23
Expressmen and Messengers							2	1							
Housemovers					1										
News dealers											1	1		1	
Total					1		2	1			1	1		1	

Source: Scott Ellsworth, *Death In A Promised Land* (Louisiana State University Press), 1982, pp. 115-117.
[1]There is evidence in the Record of Commission Proceedings, City of Tulsa, Vol. XV, that there were a number more black plumbers in Tulsa in 1921

Table D-2 Enterprises (Service and Professional) of the Rebuilt Greenwood District as of 1942.

SERVICE	NUMBER
Auto Repair	6
Bakeries	2
Barbecue Establishments	8
Beauty Salons	28
Barber Shops	11
Cafes	34
Chili Parlors	12
Coal and Ice Dealers	5
Confectionaries	2
Drug Stores	8
Electrical Services	1
Furniture Repair Ships	3
Florists	2
Funeral Parlors	3
Furriers	8
Grocers	38
Hotels	16

SERVICE	NUMBER
Insurance Agencies	3
Jewelers	1
Laundries	7
Photographers	5
Printers	3
Radio Repair Shops	5
Realtors	6
Service Stations	7
Shoe Repair Shops	9
Stores, Clothing	6
Tailors and Cleaning Shops	15
Taxicabs	2
Theater	3
Total	242

PROFESSIONALS	NUMBER
Attorneys	5
Librarians	1
Dentists	4
Physicians	9
Pharmacists	8
Ministers	38
Social Workers	8
Nurses	12
Teachers	98
Total	183

Source: Negro City Directory—Tulsa, Oklahoma. This table was taken from a framed document that adorns a wall of the office of *The Oklahoma Eagle* newspaper in the Greenwood District.

ENDNOTES

Prologue

1. Martin Luther King, Jr., *The Strength of Love* (Harper & Row, 1963), p. 83.

2. T. P. Scott, *Negro City Directory* (The Greenwood Chamber of Commerce, 1941), pp. xiii-xiv.

The Roots

1. *Webster's New World Dictionary* (Simon and Schuster, Second College Edition, 1982), p. 1236.

2. Angie Debo, *Tulsa: from Creek Town to Oil Capital* (University of Oklahoma Press, 1943), p. 4. "The name 'Tulsa' (originally spelled Tulsey or Tulsee) is a shortened pronunciation of Tallasi, which is almost certainly a contraction of Tullahassee or Tallahassee, meaning 'Old Town' (Tulwa, 'town,' and *ahassee*, 'something old')."

3. *Tulsa Daily World*, September 5, 1920, p. A-2.

4. Walter F. White, "The Eruption of Tulsa," *The Nation*, June 29, 1921, p. 909.

5. George O. Carney, "Historic Resources of Oklahoma's All-Black Towns: A Preservation Profile," *The Chronicles of Oklahoma* (Oklahoma Historical Society, Summer 1991), vol. LXIX, num. 2, pp. 117-118.

6. Eddie Faye Gates, *They Came Searching—How Blacks Sought the Promised Land in Tulsa* (Eakin Press, 1997), pp. 113-115. (Interview with Riot survivor Wilhelmina Guess Howell.)

7. David R. Morgan, Robert E. England, George G. Humphreys,

Oklahoma Politics & Policies: Governing the Sooner State (University of Nebraska Press, 1991) (series introduction), p. xxi; p. 50.

8. *Ibid.*, foreword by Robert H. Henry.

9. Oscar Ameringer, *If You Don't Weaken: The Autobiography of Oscar Ameringer* (University of Oklahoma Press, 1983), p. 231.

10. Eddie Faye Gates, *They Came Searching*, pp. 113-115. (Interview with Riot survivor Wilhelmenia Guess Howell.)

11. Kaye M. Teall, *Black History in Oklahoma* (Oklahoma City Public Schools, 1971), p. 72.

12. *Tulsa World*, February 16, 1997, p. A-1.

13. George O. Carney, "Historic Resources of Oklahoma's All-Black Towns: A Preservation Profile," *The Chronicles of Oklahoma* (Oklahoma Historical Society, Summer 1991), vol. LXIX, num. 2, p. 118.

14. *Ibid.*, pp. 117-118.

15. *Ibid.*, pp. 119-120.

16. L. J. Abbott, "The Race Question in the Forty-sixth State," *The Independent*, n.p., July 25, 1907, pp. 209-211.

17. Jonathan Z. Larsen, "Tulsa Burning," *Civilization* (Library of Congress, February/March 1997), p. 48.

18. *Ibid.* See also Mary E. Jones Parrish, *Events of the Tulsa Disaster* (n.d., n.p.). (The self-published account of an African-American woman who survived the Riot.)

19. *Ibid.*, p. 49.

20. Scott Ellsworth, *Death in a Promised Land* (Louisiana State University Press, 1982), p. 14.

21. *Ibid.*, p. 120, n. 15.

22. Mary E. Jones Parrish, *Events of the Tulsa Disaster*, p. 7.

23. Jonathan Z. Larsen, "Tulsa Burning," p. 48.

24. Scott Ellsworth, *Death in a Promised Land*, p. 16.

25. James Haskins, *Black Music in America* (Harper Collins, 1987), pp. 56-80.

26. Archives of the North Tulsa Heritage Foundation, Inc.

27. Mary E. Jones Parrish, *Events of the Tulsa Disaster*, p. 7.

28. Archives of the North Tulsa Heritage Foundation, Inc.

29. Tulsa's Booker T. Washington High School, integrated in 1970, is now a magnet school with equal numbers of African-American and white students. It is consistently recognized as one of the premier public high schools in the nation, producing graduates of national and international renown, including historian/author Dr. John Hope Franklin, psychologist/author Dr. Julia Hare, National Basketball Asso-

ciation standout/jazz musician Wayman Tisdale, and physician/ researcher Dr. Gary R. Davis.

30. *The Oklahoma Eagle*, November 2, 1978, p. 7; Henry C. Whitlow, "The History of the Greenwood Era in Tulsa," March 29, 1973 (speech delivered at TCHS meeting).

31. Booker T. Washington High School Yearbook, 1948.

32. *Ibid.*, 1921, p. 14.

33 Eddie Faye Gates, *They Came Searching*, pp. 237-241.

34. Henry C. Whitlow, "The History of the Greenwood Era in Tulsa."

35. *Ibid.*

36. *Tulsa City Directory*, 1907.

37. Scott Ellsworth, *Death in a Promised Land*, p. 14.

38. African-Americans represent approximately 13% of Tulsa's total population currently. (1990 Census of Population, U.S. Bureau of the Census.)

39. Scott Ellsworth, *Death in a Promised Land*, pp. 2-3.

40. "Impact Raps With W. D. Williams," *Impact,* n.p., circa 1971, p. 34.

41. Ronald J. Trekell, *History of the Tulsa Police Department 1882-1990*, n.p, n.d., p. 30.

42. Scott Ellsworth, *Death in a Promised Land*, p. 15.

43. Mabel B. Little, *Fire On Mount Zion—My Life and History as a Black Woman in America* (Melvin B. Tolston Black Heritage Center, Langston University, Langston, Oklahoma, 1990), pp. 26, 32.

44. *Ibid.*, pp. 42-43, 75-76; Henry C. Whitlow, "The History of the Greenwood Era in Tulsa"; *The Oklahoma Eagle*, November 2, 1978, p. C-7.

45. Eddie Faye Gates, *They Came Searching*, pp. 181-182.

46. Mabel B. Little, *Fire On Mount Zion*, p. 76.

47. Eddie Faye Gates, *They Came Searching*, p. 203. (Interview with Jeanne B. Goodwin.)

48. Henry C. Whitlow, "The History of the Greenwood Era in Tulsa."

49. T. P. Scott, *Negro City Directory* (The Greenwood Chamber of Commerce, 1941), p. xi.

50. John Sibley Butler, *Entrepreneurship and Self-Help Among Black Americans—A Reconsideration of Race and Economics* (State University of New York Press, 1991), pp. 196-197.

51. *Ibid.*, p. 203.

52. "The Tulsa Riots," *The Crisis* (magazine of the National Association for the Advancement of Colored People) (circa June 1921), p. 114.

53. *The Oklahoma Eagle*, November 2, 1978, p. D-7 (reprinted article from the *Tulsa Star*, circa 1918).

54. *Ibid.*, p.49.

55. Tom Cowan, Ph.D., Jack Maguire, *Timelines of African-American History—500 Years of Black Achievement* (Roundtable Press, Inc., 1994), pp. 140-141.

56. "The Papers of the Ku Klux Klan," The University of Tulsa, McFarlin Library, Special Collections, box 2, folder 2.

57. Carter Blue Clark, "A History of the Ku Klux Klan in Oklahoma," 1976 (Ph.D. thesis, United States history, The University of Oklahoma—on file at The Oklahoma Historical Society).

58. *Ibid.*

59. Jimmie Lewis Franklin, *The Blacks in Oklahoma* (University of Oklahoma Press, 1980), pp. 30-31.

60. *Constitution and Laws of the Ku Klux Klan Incorporated* (Imperial Palace—Invisible Empire, Knights of the Ku Klux Klan, Atlanta, Georgia) (1934 edition), p. 4.

61. *Ibid.*, pp. 6-7.

62. *Ibid.*, p. 8.

63. "The Tulsa Riots," *The Crisis*, p. 114.

64. Walter F. White, "The Eruption of Tulsa," *The Nation*, June 29, 1921.

65. *Tulsa City Directory*, 1921. (The *Tulsa City Directory* does not list all of these establishments. It is not surprising that, for example, African-American churches, particularly small ones, did not make it on the "official" roster of churches.)

66. *The Black Dispatch*, June 10, 1921, p. 1.

67. Eddie Faye Gates, *They Came Searching*, pp. 141-144. (Interview with Clarence Love.)

The Riot

1. *Webster's New World Dictionary* (Simon and Schuster, Second College Edition, 1982), p. 1227.

2. Tom Cowan, Ph.D., Jack Maguire, *Timelines of African-American History—500 Years of Black Achievement* (Roundtable Press, Inc., 1994), pp. 156-161.

3. *Ibid.*

4. *Ibid.*

5. Jimmie Lewis Franklin, *The Blacks in Oklahoma* (University of Oklahoma Press, 1980), p. 30.

6. *Ibid.*

7. The American Red Cross initially bandied about two million dollars as a "conservative figure" of the property losses, noting: "Lawsuits covering claims of over $4,000,000.00 have been filed up to July 30th [1921]." Maurice Willows, Report—*Tulsa Race Riot Disaster Relief—American Red Cross*, June 1921.

8. *The Black Dispatch*, June 10, 1921, p. 1.

9. Ronald J. Trekell, *History of the Tulsa Police Department 1882-1990*, p. 50.

10. *Ibid.*

11. *Ibid.*

12. *Ibid.*

13. *Ibid.*

14. Scott Ellsworth, *Death in a Promised Land* (Louisiana State University Press, 1982), pp. 25-34.

15. *Ibid.*

16. *Ibid.*, pp. 20-22.

17. *Ibid.*

18. Walter F. White, "The Eruption of Tulsa," *The Nation*, June 29, 1921, p. 909.

19. *Tulsa Daily World*, August 29, 1920, p. 2.

20. *Tulsa Star*, September 4, 1920, pp. 1, 4. *Tulsa Star* editor A. J. Smitherman proclaimed: "There is no crime, however atrocious, that justifies mob violence." Foreshadowing what would become the Tulsa Race Riot of 1921, the *Tulsa Star* observed: "The lynching of Roy Belton explodes the theory that a prisoner is safe on top of the Court House from mob violence."

21. Ronald J. Trekell, *History of the Tulsa Police Department 1882-1990*, p. 50.

22. Scott Ellsworth, *Death in a Promised Land*, p. 45.

23. Jonathan Z. Larsen, "Tulsa Burning," *Civilization*, p. 49. Ms. Page was new to Tulsa, having abandoned her husband in Kansas City. Sheriff McCullough had served divorce papers on her just two months prior to the incident. Indeed, having read the divorce petition, Sheriff McCullough reportedly called into question the character of Ms. Page.

24. Ronald J. Trekell, *History of the Tulsa Police Department 1882-1990*, p. 51.

25. Lee E. Williams, Lee E. Williams, II, *Anatomy of Four Race Riots—Racial Conflict in Knoxville, Elaine (Arkansas), Tulsa and Chicago, 1919-1921* (The University and College Press of Mississippi, 1972), pp. ix-x. (Foreword by Roy Wilkens, Executive Director, National Association for the Advancement of Colored People.)

26. *Ibid.*, pp. 51-52.

27. Scott Ellsworth, *Death in a Promised Land*, p. 49.

28. Jonathan Z. Larsen, "Tulsa Burning," *Civilization*, p. 50.

29. Scott Ellsworth, *Death in a Promised Land*, p. 49.

30. *Ibid.*

31. *Ibid.*, pp. 47-48. (Author Ellsworth citing a 1946 thesis by Loren Gill.)

32. *Ibid.*, p. 48.

33. Jonathan Z. Larsen, "Tulsa Burning," *Civilization*, p. 49.

34. *Ibid.*, pp. 48-49.

35. Scott Ellsworth, *Death in a Promised Land*, pp. 50-51.

36. Ronald J. Trekell, *History of the Tulsa Police Department 1882-1990*, pp. 51-57.

37. *Ibid.*, p. 51.

38. Mary E. Jones Parrish, *Events of the Tulsa Disaster*, p. 8 (reporting 500-1,000 men); Scott Ellsworth, *Death in a Promised Land*, p. 51 (reporting 1,500-2,000 men).

39. Scott Ellsworth, *Death in a Promised Land*, pp. 51-52.

40. *Ibid.*, p. 52.

41. *Ibid.*, pp. 53-54.

42. *Ibid.*, p. 54.

43. Source uncertain—possibly *Chicago Defender*, October 14, 1921 (article entitled—"Ex-Police Officer Bares Plot of Tulsans: Officer of Law Tells Who Ordered Aeroplanes to Destroy Homes" on file at the Tulsa Historical Society).

44. "Impact Raps With W. D. Williams," *Impact*, n.p., circa 1971, p. 34. (W.D. Williams' parents owned the Williams Dreamland Theatre, one of the first movie houses in the nation built, owned, and operated by African-Americans. The Williams family also owned two other prominent businesses in the Greenwood District, Williams Confectionery and Williams One Stop Garage.)

45. *Ibid.*

46. Scott Ellsworth, *Death in a Promised Land*, p. 55.

47. *Ibid.*, p. 62.

48. Ronald J. Trekell, *History of the Tulsa Police Department 1882-1990*, p. 51.

49. *Ibid.*, pp. 56-57.

50. Mary E. Jones Parrish, *Events of the Tulsa Disaster*, pp. 36-38. (Eyewitness account of Carrie Kinlaw and A. J. Newman.)

51. Scott Ellsworth, *Death in a Promised Land*, p. 59.

52. Walter F. White, "The Eruption of Tulsa," *The Nation* (June 29, 1921).

53. Mary E. Jones Parrish, *Events of the Tulsa Disaster*, p. 41.

54. Maurice Willows, *Report—Tulsa Race Riot Disaster Relief—American Red Cross*, n.p., n.d. (circa June 1921).

55. The University of Tulsa, McFarlin Library, Special Collections.

56. Jonathan Z. Larsen, "Tulsa Burning," *Civilization*, p. 52.

57. Maurice Willows, *Report—Tulsa Race Riot Disaster Relief—American Red Cross*.

58. *Tulsa Daily World*, June 6, 1921, p. 1. It should be noted that Walter White, an official with the National Association for the Advancement of Colored People, arrived in Tulsa at the height of the Riot and told of his harrowing experience in *The Nation* magazine in June of 1921. See Jonathan Z. Larsen, "Tulsa Burning," *Civilization*, pp. 49-51.

59. *Ibid.*

60. *W.E. DuBois Speaks* (Pathfinder, 1970) (edited by Dr. Philip S. Foner), back cover.

61. *The Daily Oklahoman*, June 2, 1921, p. 2.

62. Maurice Willows, *Report—Tulsa Race Riot Disaster Relief—American Red Cross*.

63. Mary E. Jones Parrish, *Events of the Tulsa Disaster*, p. 19.

64. *Ibid.*, p. 23.

65. *Ibid.*, pp. 34-35.

66. Scott Ellsworth, *Death in the Promised Land*, p. 59.

67. *The Black Dispatch, June 10, 1921, p. 1.*

68. Ronald J. Trekell, *History of the Tulsa Police Department 1882-1990*, p. 57.

69. Maurice Willows, *Report—Tulsa Race Riot Disaster Relief—American Red Cross*.

70. Scott Ellsworth, *Death in a Promised Land*, p. 69.

71. *Ibid.*

72. *Ibid.*

73. *Ibid.*, pp. 80-81.

74. *The Oklahoma Eagle*, September 14, 1978, Sec. A, p. 10.

75. Maurie Willows, *Report—Tulsa Race Riot Disaster Relief—American Red Cross*, June 1921.

76. *Ibid.*

77. *Ibid.* (Excerpt from the "Miscellaneous" section of the Report. The excerpt is entitled "Statement of one of the Negroes.")

78. *Tulsa Daily World*, July 8, 1921, p. 9.

79 Scott Ellsworth, *Death in a Promised Land*, p. 71.

80. *Tulsa Daily World*, June 2, 1921, p. 14.

81. Scott Ellsworth, *Death in a Promised Land*, p. 99.

82. "The Papers of the Ku Klux Klan," The University of Tulsa, McFarlin Library, Special Collections, box 2, folder 2.

83. Scott Ellsworth, *Death in a Promised Land*, p. 101-102; Ronald J. Trekell, *History of the Tulsa Police Department 1882-1990*, p. 57.

84. Carter Blue Clark, "A History of the Ku Klux Klan in Oklahoma," 1976 (Ph.D. thesis, United States history, The University of Oklahoma—on file at The Oklahoma Historical Society).

85. Eddie Faye Gates, *They Came Searching—How Blacks Sought the Promised Land in Tulsa* (Eakin Press, 1997), pp. 62-64.

86. *Ibid.*, pp. 39-43.

87. Scott Ellsworth, *Death in a Promised Land*, p. 94.

88 *State of Oklahoma vs. Dick Rowland*, Case No. 2239, Tulsa County District Court, filed June 18, 1921.

89. *Ibid.*

90. "The Papers of the Ku Klux Klan," The University of Tulsa, McFarlin Library, Special Collections, box 2, folder 2.

91. *State of Oklahoma vs. Dick Rowland*, Case No. 2239, Tulsa County District Court, filed June 18, 1921.

92. Scott Ellsworth, *Death in a Promised Land*, p. 95.

93. *Ibid.*, p. 96.

94. *Ibid.*, p. 97.

95. *Ibid.*

96. *Ibid.*

97. *The Oklahoma Eagle*, November 2, 1978, p. D-9 (reprinted article from the *Tulsa Star*, circa 1918).

98. Mary E. Jones Parrish, *Events of the Tulsa Disaster*, p. 76-79.

99. Letter from Judge Cornelius E. Toole to Mayor M. Susan Savage, Mayor of the City of Tulsa, et al., June 25, 1996.

100. *Tulsa Daily World*, June 12, 1921; *Tulsa Daily World*, June 16, 1921, p. 1.

101. Eddie Faye Gates, *They Came Searching*, pp. 279-280.

102. *State of Oklahoma vs. J. B. Stradford*, Case Number 2227, Tulsa County District Court, October 16, 1996.

103. Letter from Judge Cornelius E. Toole to Mayor M. Susan Savage, Mayor of the City of Tulsa, et al., June 25, 1996.

104. Scott Ellsworth, *Death in a Promised Land*, p. 97.

105. Ronald J. Trekell, *History of the Tulsa Police Department 1882-1990*, p. 57.

106. Robert N. Hower, *Angels of Mercy—The American Red Cross and the 1921 Tulsa Race Riot*, n.p., 1993, pp. 71-77. (Interview of Damie Rowland Ford, Dick Rowland's mother, by Ruth Sigler Avery, July 22, 1972, Tulsa, Oklahoma.)

107. Ronald J. Trekell, *History of the Tulsa Police Department 1882-1990*, p. 57.

108. *Ibid.*, p. 58.

109. Jonathan Z. Larsen, "Tulsa Burning," *Civilization*, p. 53.

110. *The Oklahoma Eagle*, August 30, 1930.

111. *Tulsa World*, May 25, 1997, p. G-6.

112. Robert N. Hower, *Angels of Mercy—The American Red Cross and the 1921 Tulsa Race Riot*, n.p., 1993, p. 90.

113. Mary E. Jones Parrrish, *Events of the Tulsa Disaster*, pp. 94-95.

114. Scott Ellsworth, *Death in a Promised Land*, pp. 84-85.

115. Mary E. Jones Parrish, *Events of the Tulsa Disaster*, p. 51-52; *The Oklahoma Eagle*, November 2, 1978, Sec. E, p. 5. The actual case was *Joe Lockard v. the City of Tulsa*. Joe Lockard, owner of a barbecue establishment on Cameron Street in the Greenwood District, was the plaintiff in this "test case." Lockard, represented by the African-American law firm of P.A. Chappelle, I.H. Spears, and B.C. Franklin, persuaded judges that the fire ordinance as enacted amounted to an unconstitutional taking of property. The judges voided the ordinance.

116. *The Oklahoma Eagle*, November 2, 1978, p. E-5.

117. *Ibid.*

118. Scott Ellsworth, *Death in a Promised Land*, p. 93.

119. Tulsa City Commission, Minutes of June 14, 1921, Tulsa City Commission meeting, 1921.

120. *Ibid.*

121. Handwritten notes of unidentified Riot survivor, n.p., n.d.

122. *Tulsa Daily World*, July 10, 1921, p. 1.

123. Mary E. Jones Parrish, *Events of the Tulsa Disaster*, pp. 94-95.

124. *Ibid.*, pp. 80-84.

125. *Tulsa World (Your Community World—Central Tulsa)*, January 29, 1997, p. 1; *Tulsa World*, March 9, 1997, p. G-2 ("Point of View" editorial by Eddie Faye Gates).

126. *Ibid.*

127. *Ibid.*, March 14, 1997, p. A-1.

128. *The Oklahoma Eagle*, July 10, 1997, p. 1.

129. *Ibid.*

130. *Ibid.*

131. *Ibid.*, February 13, 1997 (editorial), p. 14.

132. Remarks of Dr. John Hope Franklin, Rogers University, Tulsa, Oklahoma, June 9, 1997 (world premiere, "First Person Singular," a Public Broadcast Service documentary on the life of Dr. John Hope Franklin).

133. Tulsa City Commission, Minutes of June 14, 1921, Tulsa City Commission Meeting, 1921.

134. Maurice Willows, *Report—Tulsa Race Riot Disaster Relief—American Red Cross*, June 1921.

135. Jonathan Z. Larsen, "Tulsa Burning," *Civilization*, p. 53.

136. Scott Ellsworth, *Death in a Promised Land*, p. 91.

137. *Ibid.*

138. Restitution for World War II Internment of Japanese-Americans and Aleuts, P.L. 100-383, 50 U.S.C.S. app. sec. 1989 *et seq.* (1988).

139. Rosewood Family Scholarship Program, 11A Fla. Stat. Ann sec. 240.4126 (West 1997).

140. Restitution for World War II Intenment of Japanese-Americans and Aleuts, P.L. 100-383, 50 U.S.C.S. app. sec. 1989 *et seq.* (1988).

141. Rosewood Family Scholarship Program, 11A Fla. Stat. Ann sec. 240.4126 (West 1997).

142. John Sibley Butler, *Entrepreneurship and Self-Help Among Black Americans—A Reconsideration of Race and Economics* (State University of New York Press, 1991), p. 217.

143. Mary E. Jones Parrish, *Events of the Tulsa Disaster*, pp. 37-52. (Riot survivors consistently contend that the disaster could have been prevented if law enforcement had reacted properly and if positive race relations had been previously established.)

144. Maya Angelou, *On the Pulse of Morning* (poem delivered on the occasion of the inauguration of President William Jefferson Clinton, January 20, 1993).

The Regeneration

1. *Webster's New World Dictionary* (Simon and Schuster, Second College Edition, 1982), p. 1195.

2. Mabel B. Little, *Fire On Mount Zion—My Life and History as a Black Woman in America* (Melvin B. Tolston Black Heritage Center, Langston University, Langston, Oklahoma, 1990), pp. 32-44.

3. Henry C. Whitlow, "The History of the Greenwood Era in Tulsa," March 29, 1973 (speech delivered at TCHS meeting).

4. *The Tulsa Tribune*, June 4, 1921, p. 8.

5. Jimmie Lewis Franklin, *The Blacks in Oklahoma* (University of Oklahoma Press, 1980), pp. 39-40.

6. *Tulsa City Directory*, 1921.

7. *The Bible*, Psalms 48, verses 1-3.

8. Rev. R. H. Brewster, *I Will Move On Up A Little Higher*, November 23, 1954 (as arranged and recorded by Mahalia Jackson on Columbia Records).

9. *A Story of Renaissance*, n.p., n.d. (from the archives of Mt. Zion Baptist Church, circa 1994).

10. Archives of Vernon Chapel A. M. E.

11. Archives of the First Baptist Church of North Tulsa.

12. *Ibid.*

13. Scott Ellsworth, *Death in a Promised Land*, pp. 87-88.

14. Mary E. Jones Parrish, *Events of the Tulsa Disaster*, pp. 88-89.

15. Eddie Faye Gates, *They Came Searching—How Blacks Sought the Promised Land in Tulsa* (Eakin Press, 1997), pp. 113-115.

16. *Ibid.*, pp. 110-113.

17. Scott Ellsworth, *Death in a Promised Land* (Louisiana State University Press, 1982), p. 75.

18. Mary E. Jones Parrish, *Events of the Tulsa Disaster*, pp. 93-94 (quoting from the *St. Louis Argus,* April 21, 1922).

19. Maurice Willows, *Report—Tulsa Race Riot Disaster Relief—American Red Cross*, June 1921.

20. *The Oklahoma Eagle,* July 28, 1988 (story by Jeanne B. Goodwin based on her personal recollections).

21. Archives of the Greenwood Chamber of Commerce.

22. Eddie Faye Gates, *They Came Searching*, pp. 110-113.

23. James Baldwin, *The Fire Next Time* (The Dial Press, 1963), pp. 68-69.

24. James O. Goodwin, "Action for Better Employment," June 1961 (senior essay submitted to the undergraduate school of the University of Notre Dame in partial fulfillment of the requirements for the degree of bachelor of arts), pp. 40-41.

25. Telephone interview with Nancy Feldman, Tulsa, Oklahoma, June 7, 1997.

26. Interview with Rev. G. Calvin McCutchen, April 16, 1997.

27 Hannibal B. Johnson, *Legacy of Leadership—Reminiscences of the Tulsa Urban League on the Occasion of its Fortieth Anniversary*, n.p., 1993.

28. *Guinn vs. United States*, 59 L. Ed. 1340 (1915).

29. *Lane vs. Wilson*, 83 L. Ed. 1281 (1939).

30. *Sipuel vs. Board of Regents of the University of Oklahoma*, 92 L. Ed. 247 (1948).

31. Jimmie Lewis Franklin, *The Blacks in Oklahoma* (University of Oklahoma Press, 1980), pp. 35-37.

32. Eddie Faye Gates, *They Came Searching*, p. 161-165.

33. Dana Sterling, *Tulsa Metropolitan Ministry 1937 - 1997—a sixty year Ecumenical and Interfaith journey*, n.p., 1997.

34. Interview with Jeanne B. Goodwin, Tulsa, Oklahoma, June 7, 1997; telephone interview with Nancy Feldman, Tulsa, Oklahoma, June 7, 1997.

35. Interview with Rev. G. Calvin McCutchen, April 16, 1997.

36. James O. Goodwin, "Action For Better Employment," June 1961, p. 8.

37. *Ibid.*

38. "The Glory of Greenwood," —*Tulsa100 Business* (*Tulsa World* supplement), March 10, 1997, p. 22.

39. James O. Goodwin, "Action For Better Employment," June 1961, pp. 4-5.

40. John Sibley Butler, *Entrepreneurship and Self-Help Among Black Americans—A Reconsideration of Race and Economics* (State University of New York Press, 1991), p. 224.

41. Letter from Barbara Baer Capitman to Jeanne, Ed, and Jim Goodwin (June 4, 1983).

42. "The Glory of Greenwood," —*Tulsa100 Business* (*Tulsa World* supplement), March 10, 1997, p. 22.

43. Eddie Faye Gates, *They Came Searching*, pp. 107-109.

44. *The Oklahoma Eagle*, November 6, 1978, Sec. A, p. 1.

45. "The Glory of Greenwood," —*Tulsa100 Business* (*Tulsa World* supplement), March 10, 1997, p. 17.

46. *A Proposal For: An Economic Development Plan for North Tulsa (Administered By: The Tulsa Urban League, Inc.)*, Submitted By: Don Ross & Associates, Inc./Wendell Campbell Associates, Inc. (November 10, 1980).

The Renaissance

1. *Webster's New World Dictionary* (Simon and Schuster, Second College Edition, 1982), p. 1203.

2. *Tulsa World*, July 23, 1972, p. H-6.

3. James Haskins, *Black Music in America* (Harper Collins, 1987), p. 56.

4. *Ibid.*, pp. 57-58.

5. *Ibid.*, p. 64.

6. *Ibid.*, p. 69.

7. Max DePree, *Leadership Jazz* (Dell Publishing, 1992), pp. 8-9.

8. *Tulsa World*, February 9, 1997, p. A-1.

9. See Appendix A for a listing of Oklahoma Jazz Hall of Fame honorees.

10. Eddie Faye Gates, *They Came Searching—How Blacks Sought the Promised Land in Tulsa* (Eakin Press, 1997), pp. 191-195.

11. *Ibid.*

Epilogue

1. Verse on Greenwood Cultural Center, Inc. invitation, quoted in Jonathan Z. Larsen, "Tulsa Burning," *Civilization* (Library of Congress February/March 1997), p. 55.

INDEX

Escoe, 100
Eunice, 100
Little Willie, 162
Mahalia, 83, 152, 172, 173, 175-176
Sam, 16, 100
Jackson Funeral Home, 100
James, G. F., 193
Harry, 177
Japanese internees, 76-77
Jarrett family, 101
jazz, 9, 26, 149-182
Jefferson, Blind Lemon, 151, 155, 172
Jett, William, 180
Jim Crow laws, 17, 51, 108, 139
Joash Chest, 87
Joe Lockard vs. The City of Tulsa, 95
John Hope Franklin Boulevard, 120
Johnson, Dr., 56, 234
Ben, 169
Dr. C. D. [D. C.], 190, 191
Dr. J. W., 94
Ella Bell, 83
H. T. S., 68
J. Homer, 117, 120
J. J., 159
James Weldon, 28
Jane, 11
Lizzie, 25
Rev. John Henry, 156
Roy, 100
Ruth, 230
Shirley, 121
Willie, 174
Jones, Jim, 123
Joplin, Scott, 154
Jordan, Louis, 176, 181
Rev. Leroy K., 94
Jubilee Singers, 129
Julian, Percy, 18
Juneteenth on Greenwood Heritage Festival, 130, 153, 160, 165
Junior League of Tulsa Tea Room, 120
jury service, 109

Kates, —, 194, 195

Keating, Frank, 66, 73
Kemp, Otis, 249
Kessel, Barney, 129, 157, 169, 170
Kilgore, Kenneth E., 161-162
Kimble, Miss, 56, 234
Kimbro, George Jr., 21
King, B. B., 151, 153, 173, 178
Dr. Martin Luther, Jr., 111, 139, 172
Kirk, Andy, 152, 159, 179
Kirkpatrick, Bryan, 189
Kirsh, Rev. J. F., 92
"Klan Kreed," 22
Klan "Objects and Purposes," 23-24
"Kleagles," 21
"Knights of Liberty," 34
Krout, Bennie, 230
Krupa, Gene, 163
Ku Klux Klan, 7, 20-24, 28, 34, 38, 57, 61
Kyle's Drugstore, 100

Lacy, Ed, 249
Lafontant-Mankarious, Jewel, 65-67
LaFortune, Robert, 117
William D., 66
Lane, Lee, 164
Lane v. Wilson, 109-110
Langston Herald, 5
Langston, John M., 5
Langston, Oklahoma, 5, 6
Langston University, 120
Lansing Street, 16
Lark, James, 128, 180
Latimer, J. C., 86
Major, 179, 249
Maria, 179
W. S., 86
Latimer School of Music, 179
Latimer-Warren, Julia, 179
Lee, George, 154
Lefko, Louis, 185, 205, 239
Lehman, Dr. Lowell, 170
Leonard, Rev. T. L., 84
Leslie, Mildred, 185
Levaggi's, 180
Lewis, Ramsey, 130
S. R., 242

FINAL REPORT OF THE
TULSA RACE RIOT COMMISSION
FEBRUARY 28, 2001

The 1921 Tulsa Race Riot Commission originated in 1997 with House Joint Resolution No.1035. The act twice since has been amended, first in 1998, again two years later. The final rewriting passed each legislative chamber in March and became law with Governor Frank Keating's signature on April 6, 2000.

In that form, the State of Oklahoma extended the commission's authority beyond that originally scheduled, to February 28, 2001. The statute also charged the commission to produce, on that date, "a final report of its findings and recommendations" and to submit that report "in writing to the Governor, the Speaker of the House of Representatives, the President Pro Tempore of the Senate, and the Mayor and each member of the City Council of the City of Tulsa, Oklahoma."

This is that report. It accounts for and completes the work of the 1921 Tulsa Race Riot Commission.

A series of papers accompanies the report. Some are written by scholars of national stature, others by experts of international acclaim. Each addresses at length and in depth issues of expressed legislative interest and matters of enormous public consequence. As a group, they comprise a uniquely special and a uniquely significant contribution that must be attached to this report and must be studied carefully along with it.

Nonetheless, the supporting documents are not the report,

itself. The scholars' essays have their purposes; this commission's report has another. Its purpose is contained in the statutes that first created this commission, that later extended its life, and that each time gave it the same set of mandates. That is why this report is an accounting, presented officially and offered publicly, of how Oklahoma's 1921 Tulsa Race Riot Commission has conducted its business and addressed its statutory obligations.

Its duties were many, and each presented imposing challenges. Not least was the challenge of preparing this report. Lawmakers scheduled its deadline and defined its purpose, and this report meets their requirements. At the same time, four years of intense study and personal sacrifice surely entitle commission members to add their own expectations. Completely reasonable and entirely appropriate, their desires deserve a place in their report as well.

Together, then, both the law's requirements and the commissioners' resolves guide this report. Designed to be both concise and complete, this is the report that law requires the 1921 Tulsa Race Riot to submit to those who represent the people. Designed to be both compelling and convincing, this also is the report that the 1921 Tulsa Race Riot Commission chooses to offer the people whom both lawmakers and the commissioners serve.

. . .

The Commission shall consist of eleven (11) members....

The legislative formula for commission membership assured it appropriate if unusual composition. As an official state inquiry, the state's interest was represented through the executive, legislative, and administrative branches. The governor was to appoint six members, three from names submitted by the Speaker of the House, three from nominees provided by the Senate President Pro Tempore. Two state officials—the directors of the Oklahoma Human Rights Commission (OHRC) and of the Oklahoma Historical Society (OHS)—also were to serve as ex officio members, either personally or through their designees.

Reflecting Tulsa's obvious interest, the resolution directed the city's mayor to select the commission's final three members. Similar to the gubernatorial appointments, they were to come from names proposed by Tulsa's City Commission. One of the mayor's appointees had to be "a survivor of the 1921 Tulsa Race Riot incident;" two had to be current residents of the historic Greenwood community, the area once devastated by the "incident."

The commission began with two ex officio members and ended with two others. After Gracie Monson resigned in March 2000, Kenneth Kendricks replaced her as OHRC's interim director and its representative to the commission. Blake Wade directed the historical society until Dr. Bob Blackburn succeeded him in 1999. Blackburn had been Wade's designated representative to the commission anyway. In fact, the commission had made him its chairman, a position he would hold until June 2000.

Governor Frank Keating's six appointees included two legislators, each from a different chamber, each from an opposite party, each a former history teacher. Democrat Abe Deutschendorf's participation in the debate over the original house resolution echoed his lingering interest in history and foretold his future devotion to this inquiry. As a history teacher, Robert Milacek had included Tulsa's race riot in his classes. Little did he know that he, himself, would contribute to that history as a Republican legislator, but he has.

Governor Keating turned to metropolitan Tulsa for two appointees. T. D. "Pete" Churchwell's father serviced African-American businesses in the Greenwood district, and Churchwell has maintained concern for that community and with the 1921 riot that nearly destroyed it. He was Blackburn's replacement as chairman during the commission's closing months. Although born in Oklahoma City, Jim Lloyd and his family moved to Turley (the community just north of Greenwood) when he was three. Raised in Tulsa, he graduated from Nathan Hale and the University of Tulsa's College of Law. He now practices law in Sand Springs and lives in Tulsa.

The governor's other appointees entered the inquiry less with geographical than with professional connections to Tulsa and its history. Currie Ballard lives in Coyle and serves neighboring Langston University as historian-in-residence. Holding a graduate degree in history, Jirnmie White teaches it and heads the social science division for Connors State College.

Tulsa Mayor Susan Savage appointed the commission's final three members. If only five in 1921, Joe Burns met the law's requirement that one mayoral appointee be a survivor of the 1921 "incident." He brought the commission not faint childhood memories but seasoned wisdom rooted in eight decades of life in the Greenwood community and with Greenwood's people.

As the resolution specified, Mayor Savage's other two appointees live in contemporary Greenwood, but neither took a direct route to get there. Eddie Faye Gates's path began in Preston, Oklahoma, passed through Alabama's Tuskegee Institute, and crisscrossed two continents before it reached Tulsa in 1968. She spent the next twenty-four years teaching its youngsters and has devoted years since researching and writing her own memoirs and her community's history. Vivian Clark-Adams's route took nearly as many twists and turns, passing through one military base after another until her father retired and the family came to Oklahoma in 1961. Trained at the University of Tulsa, Dr. Vivian Clark-Adams serves Tulsa Community College as chair of the liberal arts division for its southeast campus.

In the November 1997 organizing meeting, commissioners voted to hire clerical assistants and expert consultants through the OHS. (The legislature had added $50,000 to the agency's base appropriations for just such purposes.) They then scheduled their second meeting for December 5 to accommodate the most appropriate and most eminent of all possible authorities.

John Hope Franklin is the son of Greenwood attorney B. C. Franklin, a graduate of Tulsa's Booker T. Washington High School (Fisk and Harvard, too), and James B. Duke Professor of History Emeritus at Duke University. Recipient of scores of academic and literary awards, not to mention more than a hundred honorary doctorates, Franklin came back for another honor. He received the Peggy V. Helmerich Distinguished Author Award on December 4 and stayed to meet and help the commission on the fifth.

Commissioners were delighted to learn that Franklin was anxious to serve, even if he confessed the contributions limited by age (he was eighty-two at the time) and other obligations. They enthusiastically made John Hope Franklin their first consultant, and they instantly took his advice for another. Dr. Scott Ellsworth, a native Tulsan now living in Oregon, was a Duke graduate who already had written a highly regarded study of the riot. Ellsworth became the second consultant chosen; he thereafter emerged first in importance.

As its work grew steadily more exacting and steadily more specialized, the commission turned to more experts. Legal scholars, archeologists, anthropologists, forensic specialists, geophysicists—all of these and more blessed this commission with technical expertise impossible to match and unimaginable otherwise. As a research group, they brought a breadth of vision and a depth of training that made Oklahoma's commission a model of state inquiry.

Ten consultants eventually provided them expert advice, but the commissioners always expected to depend mostly on their own resources, maybe with just a little help from just a few of their friends. Interested OHS employees were a likely source. Sure enough, a half-dozen or so pitched in to search the agency's library and archives for riot-related materials.

That was help appreciated, if not entirely unexpected. What was surprising—stunning, really—was something else that happened in Oklahoma City. As the commission's work attracted interest and gathered momentum, Bob Blackburn noticed something odd: an unusual number of people were volunteering to work at the historical society. Plain, ordinary citizens, maybe forty or fifty of them, had asked to help the commission as unpaid researchers in the OHS collections.

At about that time, Dick Warner decided that he had better start making notes on the phone calls he was fielding for the Tulsa County Historical Society. People were calling in, wanting to contribute to the inquiry, and they just kept calling. After two months, his log listed entries for 148 local calls. Meanwhile, Scott Ellsworth was back in Oregon, writing down information volunteered by some of the three hundred callers who had reached him by long distance.

Most commission meetings were in Tulsa, each open to any and all. Oklahoma's Open Meetings Law required no less, but this commission's special nature yielded much more. It seemed that every time the commissioners met at least one person (usually several) greeted them with at least something (usually a lot) that the commission needed.

Included were records and papers long presumed lost, if their existence had been known at all. Some were official documents, pulled together and packed away years earlier. Uncovered and examined, they took the commission back in time, back to the years just before and just after 1921. Some were musty legal records saved from the shredders. Briefs filed, dockets set, law suits decided—each opened an avenue into another corner of history. Pages after pages laid open the city commission's deliberations and decisions as they affected the Greenwood area. Overlooked records from the National Guard offered overlooked perspectives and illuminated them with misplaced correspondence, lost after-action reports, obscure field manuals, and self-typed accounts from men who were on duty at the riot. Maybe there was a family's treasured collection of yellowed newspaper clippings; an envelope of faded photographs; a few carefully folded letters, all handwritten, each dated 1921.

One meaning of all of this is obvious, so obvious that this report pauses to affirm it.

Many have questioned why or even if anyone would be interested now in events that happened in one city one time one day long ago. What business did today's state lawmakers have in something so old, so local, and so deservedly forgotten? Surely no one cares, not anymore.

An answer comes from hundreds and hundreds of voices. They tell us that what happened in 1921 in Tulsa is as alive today as it was back then. What happened in Tulsa stays as important and remains as unresolved today as in 1921. What happened there still exerts its power over people who never lived in Tulsa at all.

How else can one explain the thousands of hours volunteered by hundreds of people, all to get this story told and get it told right? How else can one explain the regional, national, even international attention that has been concentrated on a few short hours of a mid-sized city's history?

As the introductory paper by Drs. Franklin and Ellsworth recounts, the Tulsa disaster went largely unacknowledged for a half-century or more. After a while, it was largely forgotten.

Eventually it became largely unknown. So hushed was mention of the subject that many pronounced it the final victim of a conspiracy, this a conspiracy of silence.

That silence is shattered, utterly and permanently shattered. Whatever else this commission has achieved or will achieve, it already has made that possible. Regional, national, and international media made it certain. The *Dallas Morning News*, the *Los Angeles Times*, the *New York Times*, National Public Radio (NPR), every American broadcast television network, cable outlets delivering Cinemax and the History Channel to North America, the British Broadcasting Corporation—this merely begins the attention that the media focused upon this commission and its inquiry. Many approached it in depth (NPR twice has made it the featured daily broadcast). Most returned to it repeatedly (the *New York Times* had carried at least ten articles as of February 2000). All considered it vital public information.

Some—including some commission members—thought at least some of the coverage was at least somewhat unbalanced. They may have had a point, but that is not the point.

Here is the point: The 1921 Tulsa Race Riot Commission is pleased to report that this past tragedy has been extensively aired, that it is now remembered, and that it will never again be unknown.

. . .

The Commission shall undertake a study to (include) the identification of persons....

No one is certain how many participated in the 1921 riot. No one is certain how many suffered how much for how long. Certainty is reserved for a single quantifiable fact. Every year there remain fewer and fewer who experienced it personally.

Legislation authorizing this commission directed that it seek and locate those survivors. Specifically, it was to identify any person able to "provide adequate proof to the Commission" that he or she was an "actual resident" of "the 'Greenwood' area or community" at the time of the riot. The commission was also to identify any person who otherwise "sustained an identifiable loss...resulting from the...1921 Tulsa Race Riot."

Some considered this the commission's most difficult assign-
ment, some its most important duty, some its most compelling
purpose. They all were right, and had Eddie Faye Gates not
assumed personal and experienced responsibility for that mandate, this commission might have little to report. Because she did,
however, it principally reports what she and those who worked
with her were able to accomplish in the commission's name.

Commissioner Gates's presence gave this commission a
considerable and welcomed head start. She already had included several riot victims early pioneers whom she had interviewed
for *They Came Searching: How Blacks Sought the Promised Land in
Tulsa*. The book finished, she had an informal list of survivors,
but the list kept changing. Death erased one name after another. Others appeared. Many were of old people who had left
Oklahoma years, even decades, ago; but she heard about them
and patiently tracked them down. As lawmakers were authorizing this inquiry, the count stood at thirteen, nineteen if all the
leads eventually panned out. No one presumed that even nineteen was close to final, but no one knew what the accurate total
might be either.

At its very first organizing meeting on November 14, 1997,
this commission established a "subcommittee on survivors,"
headed by Commissioner Gates and including Commissioner
Burns and Dr. Clark-Adams. From that moment onward, that
subcommittee has aggressively and creatively pursued every possible avenue to identify every possible survivor.

Letters sent over Dr. Ellsworth's signature to *Jet* and *Ebony*
magazines urged readers to contact the commission if they knew
of any possibilities. From *Gale's Directory of Publications*,
Commissioner Gates targeted the nation's leading African-
American newspapers (papers like the *Chicago Defender* and the
Pittsburgh Courier), appealing publicly for survivors or to anyone
who might know of one. The commission's website, created and
maintained by the Oklahoma Historical Society, prominently
declared a determination to identify and register every survivor,
everywhere. For affirmation, it posted the official forms used as
the subcommittee's records, including instructions for their
completion and submission.

An old-fashioned, intensely personal web turned out to be

more productive than the thoroughly modern, entirely electronic Internet. Like historical communities everywhere, modern Greenwood maintains a rich, if informal, social network. Sometimes directly, sometimes distantly, it connects Greenwood's people, sometimes young, sometimes old. Anchoring its interstices are the community's longest residents, its most active citizens, and its most prominent leaders.

One quality or another would describe some members of this commission. After all, these are the very qualifications that lawmakers required for their appointments. Others share those same qualities and a passion for their community's history as well. Curtis Lawson, Robert Littlejohn, Hannibal Johnson, Dr. Charles Christopher, Mable Rice, Keith Jemison, Robert and Blanchie Mayes—all are active in the North Tulsa Historical Society, all are some of the community's most respected citizens, and all are among this commission's most valuable assets.

The initial published notices had early results. Slowly they began to compound upon themselves. The first stories in the national and international media introduced a multiplying factor. Thereafter, each burst of press attention seemed to increase what was happening geometrically. People were contacting commissioners, some coming forward as survivors, more suggesting where or how they might be found. Names came in, first a light sprinkle, next a shower, then a downpour, finally a flood.

Old city directories, census reports, and other records verified some claims, but they could confirm only so much. After all, these people had been children, some of them infants, back in 1921. After eighty years, could anyone remember the kind of details—addresses, telephone numbers, property descriptions, rental agreements, business locations—someone else could verify with official documents? Not likely. In fact, these were exactly the kind of people most likely to have been ignored or lost in every public record. Officially, they might have never existed.

Except that they did, and one who looked long enough and hard enough and patiently enough could confirm it—that is, if one knew where to look and whom to ask.

That is what happened. Name-by-name, someone found somebody who actually knew each person. In fact, that is how many names surfaced: a credible figure in the community knew how to find older relatives, former neighbors, or departed friends. Others could be confirmed with equal authority. Maybe someone knew the claimant's family or knew someone that did. If a person claimed to be kin to someone or offered some small detail, surely someone else knew that relative or remembered the same detail as well. Some of those details might even be verified through official documents.

It was a necessary process but slow and delicate, too. As of June 1998, twenty-nine survivors had been identified, contacted, and registered. (The number did not include sixteen identified as descendants of riot victims.) It took another fourteen months for the total to reach sixty-one. It would have been higher, except that three of the first twenty-nine had died in those months. This deadline had an ominous and compelling meaning.

Work immediately shifted through higher gears. In March 2000, the identification process finished for forty-one survivors then living in or near Tulsa. Just a few more still needed to be contacted. The real work remaining, however, involved a remarkable number of survivors who had turned up outside of Oklahoma. Following a recent flurry of media attention, more than sixty out-of-state survivors had been located. They lived everywhere from California to Florida, one in Paris, France!

All of that work is complete. As the commission submits its report, 118 persons have been identified, contacted, and registered as living survivors of the 1921 Tulsa Race Riot. (Another 176 persons also have been registered as descendants of riot victims.)

The 1921 Tulsa Race Riot Commission thereby has discharged the mandate regarding the identification of persons.

. . .

The Commission shall... gather information, identify and interview witnesses..., preserve testimony and records obtained, [and] examine and copy documents... having historical significance.

Whatever else this commission already has achieved or soon will inspire, one accomplishment will remain indefinitely. Until recently, the Tulsa race riot has been the most important least known event in the state's entire history. Even the most resourceful of scholars stumbled as they neared it for it was dimly lit by evidence and the evidentiary record faded more with every passing year.

That is not now and never will be true again. These few hours—from start to finish, the actual riot consumed less than sixteen hours—may now comprise the most thoroughly documented moments ever to have occurred in Oklahoma. This commission's work and the documentary record it leaves behind shines upon them a light too bright to ignore.

The Oklahoma Historical Society was searching its existing materials and aggressively pursuing more before this commission ever assembled. By the November 1997, organizing meeting, Bob Blackburn was ready to announce that the society already had ordered prints from every known source of every known photograph taken of the riot. He was contacting every major archival depository and research library in the country to request copies of any riot-related materials they might hold themselves. Experienced OHS professionals were set to research important but heretofore neglected court and municipal records.

This was news welcomed by commission members. It assured early momentum for the job ahead, and it complemented work that some of them were already doing. Eddie Faye Gates, for one, had pulled out every transcript of every interview that she had made with a riot witness, and she was anxious to make more. Jim Lloyd was another. Lloyd already had found and copied transcripts from earlier interviews, including some with Tulsa police officers present at the riot. He also had a hunch that a fellow who knew his way around a courthouse just might turn up all sorts of information.

That is how it began, but that was just the beginning. In the months ahead, Larry O'Dell and other OHS employees patiently excavated mountains of information, one pebble at a time, as it were. They then pieced together tiny bits of fact, carefully fitting one to another. One by one, completed puzzles emerged. Arranged in different dimensions, they made magic: a vision of Greenwood long since vanished.

Master maps, both of the community on the eve of the riot and of the post-riot residue, identified every single piece of property. For each parcel, a map displayed any structure present, its owner and its use. If commercial, what firms were there, who owned them, what businesses they were in. If residential, whether it was rented or owned. If the former, the landlord's name. If the latter, whether it was mortgaged (if so, to whom and encumbered by what debt). For both, lists identified each of its occupants by name.

It was not magic; it was more. Larry O'Dell had rebuilt Greenwood from records he and other researchers had examined and collected for the commission. Every building permit granted, every warranty deed recorded, every property appraisal ordered, every damage claim filed, every death certificate issued, every burial record maintained—the commission had copies of every single record related to Greenwood at the time of the riot.

Some it had only because Jim Lloyd was right. Able to navigate a courthouse, he ran across complete records for some 150 civil suits filed after the race riot. No one remembered that they even existed; they had been misplaced for thirty-five years. When Jim Lloyd uncovered and saved them, they were scheduled for routine shredding.

The commission gathered the most private of documents as well. Every form registering every survivor bears notes recording information taken from every one of 118 persons. With Kavin Ross operating the camera, Eddie Faye Gates videotaped interviews with about half of the survivors. Each is available on one of nine cassettes preserved by the commission; full transcripts are being completed for all. Sympathetic collectors turned over transcripts of another fifty or more. Some had been packed away for twenty, even thirty years.

Others, including several resourceful amateur historians, reproduced and gave the commission what amounted to complete documentary collections. There were sets of municipal records, files from state agencies, reports kept by social services, press clippings carefully bound, privately owned photographs never publicly seen.

People who had devoted years to the study of one or more aspects of the riot supplied evidence they had found and presented conclusions they had reached. Beryl Ford followed the commission's work as a Tulsan legendary for his devotion to his

city and its history. William O'Brien attended nearly every commission meeting, sometimes to ask questions, sometimes to
answer them, once to deliver his own full report on the riot.
Robert Norris prepared smaller, occasional reports on military
topics. He also dug up and turned over files from National Guard
records. Others located affidavits filed with the State Supreme
Court. The military reports usually had been presumed lost; the
legal papers always had been assumed unimportant.

Commissioners were surprised to receive so much new evidence and pleased to see that it contributed so much. They were
delighted to'note that so much came from black sources, that it
documented recorded black observations.

It had not always been that way. Too many early journalists
and historians had dismissed black sources as unreliable. Too
few early librarians and archivists had preserved black sources as
important. Both thereby condemned later writers and scholars
to a never ending game of hide-and-go-seek, the rules rigged so
no one could win.

This commission's work changes the game forever. Every
future scholar will have access to everything everyone ever had
when the original source was white. In fact, they will have a lot
more of it. They also will have more from sources few had before
when the original source was black.

Because they will, the community future scholars will
behold and the property they will describe was a community of
black people, occupied by black people. The public records they
will examine involved black people and affected black people.
Objects they will touch came from black people. Interviews they
will hear and transcripts they will read were recorded from black
people. The evidence they will explore reveals experiences of
black people.

Consider what so much new information and what so many
new sources can mean for future historians. Consider what it
already has meant for one.

Read closely Scott Ellsworth's accompanying essay, "The
Tulsa Riot," a rather simple title, as titles go. Much more sophis-
ticated is the title he gave the book he wrote in 1982, *Death in a
Promised Land: The Tulsa Race Riot of 1921*.

It is fair that they have different titles. They tell somewhat different stories in somewhat different ways. The chief difference is that the one titled so simply tells a tale much more sophisticated.

For one thing, it is longer. The report attached here filled 115 typed pages in the telling; the comparable portion of the book prints entirely in 25 pages. The report has to be longer because it has more to report, stories not told in the first telling. It offers more because it draws upon more evidence. The report packs 205 footnotes with citations for "its story; 50 did the job for the first one.

Within that last difference is the difference that causes every other difference. To write this report, Scott Ellsworth used evidence he did not have—no one had it—as recently as 1982. He cites that new evidence at least 148 times. He had information from black sources accessible now because of this commission. That knowledge contributed to Scott Ellsworth's citations from black newspapers, black interviews, or black writings. He cites black sources at least 272 times.

No wonder the two are different. From now on, everything can be different. They almost have to be.

Before there was this commission, much was known about the Tulsa race riot. More was unknown. It was buried somewhere, lost somewhere, or somewhere undiscovered. No longer. Old records have been reopened, missing files have been recovered, new sources have been found. Still being assembled and processed by the Oklahoma Historical Society, their total volume passed ten thousand pages some time ago and well may reach twenty thousand by the time everything is done.

The dimensions of twenty thousand pages can be measured physically. Placed side-by-side, they would reach across at least ten yards of library shelving, filling every inch with new information. The significance of these twenty thousand pages has to be gauged vertically and metaphorically though. Stacked high, they amount to a tower of new knowledge. Rising to reach a new perspective, they offer visions never seen before.

The 1921 Tulsa Race Riot Commission thereby has discharged the mandate to gather and preserve a record of historical significance.

. . .

The Commission shall...develop a historical record of the 1921 Tulsa Race Riot....

The commission's first substantive decision was to greet this obligation with a series of questions, and there was compelling reason why. Eighty years after the fact, almost as many unresolved questions surround the race riot as did in 1921—maybe even more. Commissioners knew that no "historical record" would be complete unless it answered the most enduring of those questions—or explain why not. That was reason enough for a second decision: Commissioners agreed to seek consultants, respected scholars, and other experts to investigate those questions and offer answers.

Their findings follow immediately, all without change or comment, each just as the commission received it. Accompanying papers present what scholars and others consider the best answers to hard questions. The reports define their questions, either directly or implicitly, and usually explain why they need answers. The authors give answers, but they present them with only the confidence and exactly the precision they can justify. Most retrace the route they followed to reach their positions. All advance their positions openly. If they sense themselves in hostile territory, some stake their ground and defend it.

The commissioners harbor no illusion that every reader will accept their every answer to every question. They know better. Why should everyone else? None of them do. All eleven have reservations, some here, some there. Some dispute this point; some deny that one. Some suggest other possibilities. Some insist upon positions squarely opposite the scholars'.

None of that matters. However they divide over specifics, they also are united on principles. Should any be in need, they endorse and recommend the route they took to reach their own consensus. The way around an enraged showdown and the shortest path to a responsible solution is the line that passes through points ahead. Each point marks a big question and an important answer. Study them carefully.

What was the total value of property destroyed in the Tulsa race riot, both in 1921's dollars and in today's? Larry O'Dell has the numbers. Anyone of them could be a little off, probably none by very much. Could a lawyer argue, and might a judge decree, that citizens living now had a duty to make that good, had to repay those losses, all because of something that happened eighty years ago? Alfred Brophy can make the case, and he does.

Over eight decades, some Tulsans (mostly black Tulsans) have insisted that whites attacked Greenwood from the air, even bombed it from military airplanes. Other Tulsans (mostly white Tulsans) have denied those claims; many have never even heard them. In a sense, it is a black-or-white question, but Richard S. Warner demonstrates that it has no black-or-white answer.

He proves it absolutely false that military planes could have employed military weapons on Greenwood. He also proves it absolutely true that civilian aircraft did fly over the riot area. Some were there for police reconnaissance, some for photography, some for other legitimate purposes. He also thinks it reasonable to believe that others had less innocent use. It is probable that shots were fired and that incendiary devices were dropped, and these would have contributed to riot-related deaths or destruction. How much? No one will ever know: History permits no black-or-white answer.

Can modern science bring light to old, dark rumors about a mass grave, at least one, probably more, somewhere in Tulsa? Could those rumors be true? If true, where is one? Robert L. Brooks and Alan H. Witten have answers. Yes, science can address those rumors. Yes, there are many reasons to believe that mass graves exist. Where? They can point precisely to the single most likely spot. They can explain why scientists settle on that one—explain it clearly enough and completely enough to convince non-scientists, too. Without making a scratch on the ground, they can measure how deep it has to be, how thick, how wide, how long. Were the site to be exhumed and were it to yield human remains, what would anyone learn? Quite a bit if Lesley Rankin-Hill and Phoebe Stubblefield were to examine them.

How many people were killed, anyway? At the time, careful calculations varied almost as much as did pure guesses—forty, fifty, one hundred, two hundred, three hundred, maybe more. After a while, it became hard to distinguish the calculations from the guesses. By now, the record has become so muddied that even the most careful and thorough scientific investigation can offer no more than a preliminary possible answer.

Clyde Collins Snow's inquiry is just as careful and just as thorough as one might expect from this forensic anthropologist of international reputation, and preliminary is the word that he insists upon for his findings. By the most conservative of all possible methods, he can identify thirty-eight riot victims, and he provides the cause of death and the burial site for each of them. He even gives us the names of all but the four burned beyond recognition.

That last fact is their defining element. Thirty-eight is only the number of dead that Snow can identify individually. It says nothing of those who lost their lives in the vicious riot and lost their personal identities in records never kept or later destroyed. An accurate death count would just begin at thirty-eight; it might end well into the hundreds. Snow explains why as many as 150 might have to be added for one reason, 18 more for another reason. What neither he nor anyone can ever know is how many to add for how many reasons. That is why there will never be a better answer to the question of how many died than this: How many? Too many.

For some questions there will never be answers even that precise. Open for eighty years and open now, they will remain open forever because they are too large to be filled by the evidence at hand.

Some of the hardest questions surround the evidence, itself. Evidence amounting to personal statements—things said to have been seen, heard, or otherwise observed—raises an entire set of questions in itself. Surely some statements are more credible than others, but how credible is that? Most evidence is incomplete; it may be suggestive but is it dispositive? Evidence often inspires inference, but is the inference reasonable or even possible? Evidence is usually ambiguous, does it mean this or does it mean that? Almost every piece of evidence requires an interpretation, but is only one interpretation possible? Responsibilities will be assigned, decisions will be evaluated, judgments will be offered—on what basis?

These are not idle academic musings. On the contrary: This small set of questions explains why so many specific questions remain open. They explain how people—reasonable, fair-minded, well-intended people—can disagree so often about so much.

Consider a question as old as the riot itself. At the time, many said that this was no spontaneous eruption of the rabble; it was planned and executed by the elite. Quite a few people—including some members of this commission—have since studied the question and are persuaded that this is so, that the Tulsa race riot was the result of a conspiracy. This is a serious position and a provable position—if one looks at certain evidence in certain ways.

Others—again, including members of this commission—have studied the same question and examined the same evidence, but they have looked at it in different ways. They see there no proof of conspiracy. Selfish desires surely. Awful effects certainly. But not a conspiracy. Both sides have evidence that they consider convincing, but neither side can convince the other.

Another nagging question involves the role of the Ku Klux Klan. Everyone who has studied the riot agrees that the Klan was present in Tulsa at the time of the riot and that it had been for some time. Everyone agrees that within months of the riot Tulsa's Klan chapter had become one of the nation's largest and most powerful, able to dictate its will with the ballot as well as the whip. Everyone agrees that many of the city's most prominent men were Klansmen in the early 1920s and that some remained Klansmen throughout the decade. Everyone agrees that Tulsa's atmosphere reeked with a Klan-like stench that oozed through the robes of the Hooded Order.

Does this mean that the Klan helped plan the riot? Does it mean that the Klan helped execute it? Does it mean that the Klan, as an organization, had any role at all?

Or does it mean that any time thousands of whites assembled—especially if they assembled to assault blacks—that odds were there would be quite a few Klansmen in the mix? Does the presence of those individuals mean that the institution may have been an instigator or the agent of a plot? Maybe both? Maybe neither? Maybe nothing at all? Not everyone agrees on that.

Nor will they ever. Both the conspiracy and the Klan questions remain what they always have been and probably what they always will be. Both are examples of nearly every problem inherent to historical evidence. How reliable is this oral tradition? What conclusions does that evidence permit? Are these inferences reasonable? How many ways can this be interpreted?

And so it must go on. Some questions will always be disputed because other questions block the path to their answers. That does not mean there will be no answers, just that there will not be one answer per one question. Many questions will have two, quite a few even more. Some answers will never be proven. Some will never be disproved. Accept it: Some things can never be known.

That is why the complete record of what began in the late evening of May 31 and continued through the morning of June 1 will never quite escape those hours, themselves. They forever are darkened by night or enshrouded by day.

But history has a record of things certain for the hours between one day's twilight and the next day's afternoon. These things:

- Black Tulsans had every reason to believe that Dick Rowland would be lynched after his arrest on charges later dismissed and highly suspect from the start.
- They had cause to believe that his personal safety, like the defense of themselves and their community, depended on them alone.
- As hostile groups gathered and their confrontation worsened, municipal and county authorities failed to take actions to calm or contain the situation.
- At the eruption of violence, civil officials selected many men, all of them white and some of them participants in that violence, and made those men their agents as deputies.
- In that capacity, deputies did not stem the violence but added to it, often through overt acts themselves illegal.
- Public officials provided firearms and ammunition to individuals, again all of them white.
- Units of the Oklahoma National Guard participated in the mass arrests of all or nearly all of Greenwood's residents, removed them to other parts of the city, and detained them in holding centers.

- Entering the Greenwood district, people stole, damaged or destroyed personal property left behind in homes and businesses.
- People, some of them agents of government, also deliberately burned or otherwise destroyed homes credibly estimated to have numbered 1,256, along with virtually every other structure—including churches, schools, businesses, even a hospital and library—in the Greenwood district.
- Despite duties to preserve order and to protect property, no government at any level offered adequate resistance, if any at all, to what amounted to the destruction of the neighborhood referred to commonly as "Little Africa" and politely as the "Negro quarter."
- Although the exact total can never be determined, credible evidence makes it probable that many people, likely numbering between one and three hundred, were killed during the riot.
- Not one of these criminal acts was then or ever has been prosecuted or punished by government at any level, municipal, county, state, or federal.
- Even after the restoration of order it was official policy to release a black detainee only upon the application of a white person, and then only if that white person agreed to accept responsibility for that detainee's subsequent behavior.
- As private citizens, many whites in Tulsa and neighboring communities did extend invaluable assistance to the riot's victims, and the relief efforts of the American Red Cross in particular provided a model of human behavior at its best.
- Although city and county government bore much of the cost for Red Cross relief, neither contributed substantially to Greenwood's rebuilding; in fact, municipal authorities acted initially to impede rebuilding.
- In the end, the restoration of Greenwood after its systematic destruction was left to the victims of that destruction.

These things are not myths, not rumors, not speculations, not questioned. They are the historical record.

The 1921 Tulsa Race Riot Commission thereby has discharged the mandate to develop a historical record of the 1921 Tulsa Race Riot.

. . .

The final report of the Commission's findings and recommendations . . . may contain specific recommendations about whether or not reparations can or should be made and the appropriate methods. . . .

Unlike those quoted before, these words give this commission not an obligation but an opportunity. Nearly every commissioner intends to seize it.

A short letter sent Governor Frank Keating as a preliminary report in February 2000 declared the majority's view that reparations could and should be made. "Good public policy," that letter said, required no less. This report maintains the same, and this report makes the case.

Case, reparations—the words, themselves, seem to summon images of lawyers and courtrooms, along with other words, words like culpability, damages, remedies, restitution. Each is a term used in law, with strict legal meaning. Sometimes commissioners use those words, too, and several agree—firmly agree— that those words describe accurately what happened in 1921 and fit exactly what should happen now.

Those, however, are their personal opinions, and the commissioners who hold them do so as private citizens. Even the most resolute of its members recognizes that this commission has a very different role. This commission is neither court nor judge, and its members are not a jury. The commission has no binding legal authority to assign culpability, to determine damages, to establish a remedy, or to order either restitution or reparations. In fact, it has no judicial authority whatsoever.

It also has no reason or need for such authority. Any judgments that it might offer would be without effect and meaning. Its words would as well be cast to the winds. Any recommendations that it might offer neither have nor need judicial status at all. Statutes grant this commission its authority to make recommendations and the choice of how—or even if—to exercise that authority.

The commission's majority is determined to exercise its discretion and to declare boldly and directly their purpose: to recommend, independent of what law allows, what these commissioners believe is the right thing to do. They propose to do that in a dimension equal to their purpose. Courts have other purposes, and law operates in a different dimension. Mistake one for the other—let this commission assume what rightly belongs to law—does worse than miss the point. It ruins it.

Think of the difference this way. We will never know exactly how many were killed during the Tulsa race riot, but take at random any twenty-five from that unknown total. What we say of those we might say for every one of the others, too.

Considering the twenty-five to be homicides, the law would approach those as twenty-five acts performed by twenty-five people (or thereabouts) who, with twenty-five motives, committed twenty-five crimes against twenty-five persons. That they occurred within hours and within a few blocks of each other is irrelevant. It would not matter even if the same person committed two, three, ten of the murders on the same spot, moments apart. Each was a separate act, and each (were the law to do its duty) merits a separate consequence. Law can apprehend it no other way.

Is there no other way to understand that? Of course there is. There is a far better way.

Were these twenty-five crimes or one? Did each have a separate motive, or was there a single intent? Were twenty-five individuals responsible, those and no one else? The burning of 1,256 homes—if we understand these as 1,256 acts of arson committed by 1,256 criminals driven by 1,256 desires, if we understand it that way, do we understand anything at all?

These were not any number of multiple acts of homicide; this was one act of horror. If we must name the fires, call it outrage, for it was one. For both, the motive was not to injure hundreds of people, nearly all unseen, almost all unknown. The intent was to intimidate one coImmunity, to let it be known and let it be seen. Those who pulled the triggers, those who struck the matches—they alone were lawbreakers. Those who shouted encouragement and those who stood silently by—they were responsible.

These are the qualities that place what happened in Tulsa outside the realm of law—and not just in Tulsa, either. Lexington, Sapulpa, Norman, and Shawnee; Lawton and Claremore; Perry; Waurika, Dewey, and Marshall—earlier purges in every one already had targeted entire black communities, marking every child, woman, and man for exile.

There is no count of how many those people numbered, but there is no need to know that. Know that there, too, something more than a bad guy had coImnitted something more than a crime against something more than a person. Not someone made mad by lust, not a person gripped by rage, not a heartbroken party of romance gone sour, not one or any number of individuals but a collective body—acting as one body—had coldly and deliberately and systematically assaulted one victim, a whole community, intending to eliminate it as a Community. If other black communities heard about it and learned their lessons, too, so much the better; a little intimidation went a long way. All of this happened years before, most fifteen or twenty years before Dick Rowland landed in jail, but they remained vivid in the recent memories of Greenwood's younger adults.

This, or something quite like it, was almost always what happened when the subject was race. Here was nothing as amorphous as racism. Here were discrete acts—one act, one town— each consciously calculated to have a collective effect not against a person but against a people.

And is that not also the way of Oklahoma's voting laws at the time? The state had amended its constitution and crafted its laws not to keep this person or that person or a whole list of persons from voting. Lengthen that list to the indefinite, write down names to the infinite—one still will not reach the point. For that, one line, one word is enough. The point was to keep a race, as a race, away from the polls.

Jim Crow laws—the segregation commands of Oklahoma's statutes and of its constitution—worked that way, too. Their object was not to keep some exhausted mother and her two young children out of a "white car" on a train headed somewhere like Checotah and send them walking six miles home. (Even if John Hope Franklin could recall that about his own mother and sister and himself as he accepted the Helmerich

Award some three-quarters of a century afterwards.) No, the one purpose was to keep one race "in its place."

When Laura Nelson was lynched years earlier in Okemah, it was not to punish her by death. It was to terrify the living. Why else would the lynchers have taken (and printed and copied and posted and distributed) that photograph of her hanging from the bridge, her little boy dangling beside her?

The lynchers knew the purpose; the photographer just helped it along. The purpose had not changed much by 1921, when another photographer snapped another picture, a long shot showing Greenwood's ruin, smoke rising from fires blazing in the background. "RUNING THE NEGRO OUT OF TULSA" someone wrote across it, candor atoning for misspelling. No doubt there. No shame either.

Another photograph probably was snapped the same day but from closer range. It showed what just days before must have been a human being, maybe one who had spent a warm day in late May working and talking and laughing. On this day, though, it was only a grotesque, blackened form, a thing, really, its only sign of humanity the charred remains of arms and hands forever raised, as if in useless supplication.

Shot horizontally, that particular photo still turns up from time to time in the form of an early use: as a postcard. People must have thought it a nice way to send a message. It still sends a message, too big to be jotted down in a few lines; but, then, this message is not especially nice either. The message is that here is an image of more than a single victim of a single episode in a single city. This image preserves the symbol of a story, preserves it in the same way that the story was told: in black-and-white.

See those two photos and understand that the Tulsa race riot was the worst event in that city's history—an event without equal and without excuse. Understand, too, that it was the worst explosion of violence in this state's history—an episode late to be acknowledged and still to be repaired. But understand also that it was part of a message usually announced not violently at all, but calmly and quietly and deliberately.

Who sent the message? Not one person but many acting as one. Not a "mob;" it took forms too calculated and rational for that word. Not "society;" that word is only a mask to conceal responsibility within a fog of imprecision. Not "whites," because this never spoke for all whites; sometimes it spoke for only a few. Not "America," because the federal government was, at best, indifferent to its black citizens and, at worse, oblivious of them. Fifty years or so after the Civil War, Uncle Sam was too complacent to crusade for black rights and too callous to care. Let the states handle that—states like Oklahoma.

Except that it really was not "Oklahoma" either. At least, it was not all of Oklahoma. It was just one Oklahoma, one Oklahoma that is distinguishable from another Oklahoma partly by purpose. This Oklahoma had the purpose of keeping the other Oklahoma in its place, and that place was subordinate. That, after all, was the object of suffrage requirements and segregation laws. No less was it the intent behind riots and lynchings, too. One Oklahoma was putting the other Oklahoma in its place.

One Oklahoma also had the power to effect its purpose, and that power had no need to rely on occasional explosions of rage. Simple violence is, after all, the weapon of simple people, people with access to no other instruments of power at all. This Oklahoma had access to power more subtle, more regular, and more formal than that. Indeed, its ready access to such forms of power partially defined that Oklahoma.

No, that Oklahoma is not the same as government, used here as a rhetorical trick to make one accountable for the acts of the other. Government was never the essence of that Oklahoma. Government was, however, always its potential instrument. Having access to government, however employed, if employed at all—just having it—defined this Oklahoma and was the essence of its power.

The acts recounted here reveal that power in one form or another, often several. The Tulsa race riot is one example, but only an example and only one. Put alongside it earlier, less publicized pogroms—for that is what they were—in at least ten other Oklahoma towns. Include the systematic disfranchisement of the black electorate through constitutional amendment in 1910, reaffirmed through state statute in 1916. Add to that the constitution's segregation of Oklahoma's public schools, the First Legislature's segregation of its public transportation, local segregation of Oklahoma neighborhoods through municipal ordinances in Tulsa and elsewhere, even the statewide segregation of public telephones by order of the corporation commission. Do not forget to include the lynchings of twenty-three African-Arnericans in twelve Oklahoma towns during the ten years leading to 1921. Stand back and look at those deeds now.

In some government participated in the deed.

In some government performed the deed.

In none did government prevent the deed.

In none did government punish the deed.

And that, in the end, is what this inquiry and what these recommendations are all about. Make no mistake about it: There are members of this commission who are convinced that there is a compelling argument in law to order that present governments make monetary payment for past governments' unlawful acts. Professor Alfred Brophy presses one form of that argument; there doubtless are others.

This is not that legal argument but another one altogether. This is a moral argument. It holds that there are moral responsibilities here and that those moral responsibilities require moral responses now.

It gets down to this: The 1921 riot is, at once, a representative historical example and a unique historical event. It has many parallels in the pattern of past events, but it has no equal for its violence and its completeness. It symbolizes so much endured by so many for so long. It does it, however, in one way that no other can: in the living flesh and blood of some who did endure it.

These paradoxes hold answers to questions often asked: Why does the state of Oklahoma or the city of Tulsa owe anything to anybody? Why should any individual tolerate now spending one cent of one tax dollar over what happened so long ago?

The answer is that these are not even the questions. This is not about individuals at all—not any more than the race riot or anything like it was about individuals.

This is about Oklahoma—or, rather, it is about two Oklahomas. It must be about that because that is what the Tulsa race riot was all about, too. That riot proclaimed that there were two Oklahomas; that one claimed the right to push down, push out, and push under the other; and that it had the power to do that.

That is what the Tulsa race riot has been all about for so long afterwards, why it has lingered not as a past event but lived as a present entity. It kept on saying that there remained two Oklahomas; that one claimed the right to be dismissive of, ignorant of, and oblivious to the other; and that it had the power to do that.

That is why the Tulsa race riot can be about something else. It can be about making two Oklahomas one—but only if we this is what reparation is all about. Because the riot is both symbolic and singular, reparations become both singular and symbolic, too. Compelled not legally by courts but extended freely by choice, they say that individual acts of reparation will stand as symbols that fully acknowledge and finally discharge a collective responsibility.

Because we must face it: There is no way but by government to represent the collective, and there is no way but by reparations to make real the responsibility.

Does this commission have specific recommendations about whether or not reparations can or should be made and the appropriate methods? Yes, it surely does.

When commissioners went looking to do the right thing, that is what nearly all of them found and what they recommended in last year's preliminary report. To be sure they had found the right thing, they have used this formal report to explore once more the distant terrain of the Tulsa race riot and the forbidding territory in which it lies. Now, they are certain. Reparations are the right thing to do.

What else is there to do? What else is there to find?

CPSIA information can be obtained at www.ICGtesting.com
Printed in the USA
LVOW12s0539300615

444311LV00002B/3/P